Sea Room

Sea Room

AN
ISLAND LIFE

ADAM NICOLSON

HarperCollins*Publishers*

HarperCollins*Publishers*
77–85 Fulham Palace Road,
Hammersmith, London w6 8jb

www.**fire**and**water**.com

Published by HarperCollins*Publishers* 2001
1 3 5 7 9 8 6 4 2

Copyright © Adam Nicolson 2001

Adam Nicolson asserts the moral right to
be identified as the author of this work

A catalogue record for this book is
available from the British Library

isbn 0 00 257164 1

Bird illustrations by Rex Nicholls
Maps by John Gilkes

Set in PostScript Linotype Minion by
Rowland Phototypesetting Ltd,
Bury St Edmunds, Suffolk

Printed and bound in Great Britain by
Clays Ltd, St Ives plc

For my father

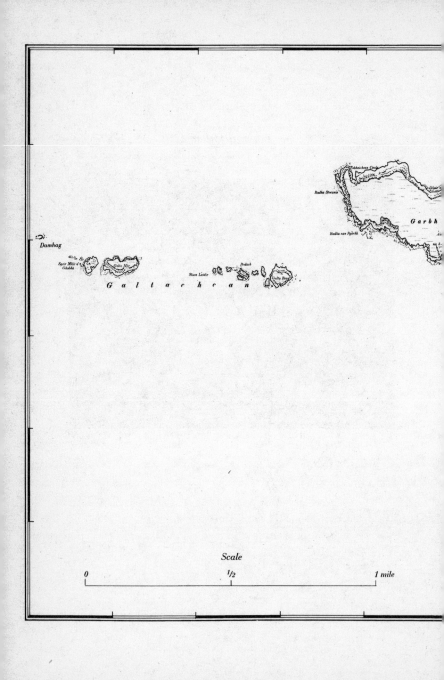

Damhag

Tabbachean Croig

Rudha Stocania

Glaic

Garbh

Rudha nan Sgarbh

Sgeir Mhic a'
Ghobha

Galta Mor

Bodach

Sluca Laidir

Galta Beag

Galtachean

Scale

0   1/2   1 mile

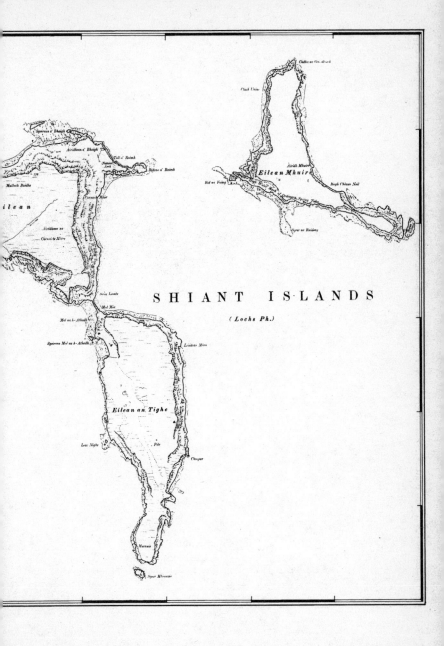

S H I A N T   I S L A N D S

(*Lochs Ph.*)

Eilean Mhuire

Eilean an Tighe

1

FOR THE LAST TWENTY YEARS I have owned some islands. They are called the Shiants: one definite, softened syllable, 'the Shant Isles', like a sea shanty but with the 'y' trimmed away. The rest of the world thinks there is nothing much to them. Even on a map of the Hebrides the tip of your little finger would blot them out, and if their five hundred and fifty acres of grass and rock were buried deep in the mainland of Scotland as some unconsidered slice of moor on which a few sheep grazed, no one would ever have noticed them. But the Shiants are not like that. They are not modest. They stand out high and undoubtable, four miles or so off the coast of Lewis, surrounded by tide-rips in the Minch, with black cliffs five hundred feet tall dropping into a cold, dark, peppermint sea, with seals lounging at their feet, the lobsters picking their way between the boulders and the kelp and thousands upon thousands of sea birds wheeling above the rocks.

In summer, the grass on the cliff-tops is thick with flowers: bog asphodel and bog pimpernel; branched orchids, the stars of tormentil and milkwort. 'Under such skies can be expected no great exuberance of vegetation,' Dr Johnson wrote, but this miniature spangle of Hebridean flora, never protruding its yellows and deep purples more than an inch or two above the turf, is a great and scarcely regarded treasure. I think of it when in England I walk on expensive Persian rugs; the same points of dense, discreet colour, the same proportion of ground to decoration; a sudden flash of the Hebrides in a rich man's rooms. It is a private signal to me, a bleeping underfoot, winking through the burr of conversation and offered drinks: *Remember me.*

At times in the last two decades, these islands have been the most important thing in my life. They are a kind of heartland for me, a core place. My father bought them over sixty years ago for £1,400, he gave them to me when I was twenty-one, and I shall give them to my son Tom when he is twenty-one in four years' time. This is not, as cynics have sometimes said, for tax reasons. The Shiants seem scarcely to do with money and, anyway, they have been a catastrophic investment. For the same amount, at the same time, my father could have bought a Jacobean manor house in Sussex or a two hundred-acre farm of prime arable in Cambridgeshire. Each would be worth a million or more by now. As it is, if I sold the Shiants, I could perhaps buy a two-bedroom flat in Fulham.

This was never a question of financial riches. My father bought the islands and gave them to me because as a very young man he had felt enlarged and excited by the ownership of a place like this, by the experience of being there alone or with friends, by an engagement with a nature so unadorned and with a sea- and landscape so huge that it allowed an escape into what felt like another dimension. It was a way of leaving home, a step into a different world. He described this, fitfully, in a letter to his brother Ben on first going there in 1937: 'I would wake up the next morning to find the sun in a sky as pure as a Bavarian virgin,' the twenty-year-old Balliol undergraduate half-joked.

I would lie all morning with no clothes on, on a rock overlooking the sea, reading and annotating Hegel. In the afternoons I used to run bare-footed across the mile of heather to the edge of the northern cliff, there flinging myself down, to read, or write, or gaze out to sea thinking about life, and what Heaven this was. The view from the top is such that only Greece could parallel.

And then he torpedoed it, embarrassed: 'One becomes very *Golden Bough* in these conditions, I'm afraid.'

For all the camouflage, the experience was real, and forty years later he wanted, I think, to give that same enlargement to me: that wonderful sea room, the surge of freedom which a moated island provides. The gift was this: the sensation I can now summon, anywhere and at any time, of standing in the pure air streaming in off the Atlantic, alone on these islands which the last inhabitants left a hundred years ago. I have peered at them in every cranny: I have hauled lobsters and velvet crabs from the sea; picked the edible dulse from the walls of the sea caves and of the great Gothic natural arch which perforates a narrow horn of one of the islands; scrambled among the hissing shags and looked down the dark slum tunnels where the puffins live and croak their curious, endearing note, like a heavy door opening on a rusted hinge; and I have lain down in the long grass while the ravens honked and flicked above me and the skuas cruised in a milk-blue sky. I have felt at times, and perhaps this is a kind of delirium, no gap between me and the place. I have absorbed it and been absorbed by it, as if I have had no existence apart from it. I have been shaped by those island times, and find it difficult now to achieve any kind of distance from them. The place has entered me. It has coloured my life like a stain. Almost everything else feels less dense and less intense than those moments of exposure. The social world, the political world, the world of getting on with work and a career – all those have been cast in shadow by the scale and seriousness of my brief moments of island life.

There was a time when I thought that to give the islands away, even to Tom, would be an unbearably difficult thing. Sometimes, away from them, late at night in strange hotels, I would listen to the shipping forecast – 'Hebrides, Minches, Storm Force Ten, backing southwesterly, sleet, visibility two hundred yards'. I would think of them then, wet, battered and impossible, the rain slinging itself in handfuls of rice against the windows of the bothy, the churning of the sea, when, as it says in a famous Gaelic poem, 'The whorled dun whelk that was down on the floor of the ocean,/ Will snag on the boat's gunwales and give a crack on her floor,' when the cowering birds would be tucked in behind the boulders, and the sheep would be enduring the storm with the patience of saints and the dignity of martyrs. Those were the moments, not in their presence, when I felt most deeply attached to them. The Shiants are the most powerful absence I know. On every flight across the Atlantic, I would peer out for them, looking for an opening in the clouds to see them there, still and map-like below me, with the sea sheened and glittery around them, while the stewardess handed out headsets and warm towels. That too would be a moment of dreaded loss.

That has changed now. I have changed and I do not, I think, need them as much as I once did. The gift I received is the gift I want to make. They are a young man's place and always have been. Tom will have his time there too, with his own friends and his own discoveries. He will know the Shiants in ways different from his father's and grandfather's. A place evolves in the minds of the people who possess it and it is Tom's turn now.

This book is my final immersion in them. I have tried to get to know them as I have scarcely done before. No one previously has written at any length about the Shiants and this is both an opening and, for me anyway, a closing of their account. It is an attempt to tell the whole story, as I now understand it, of a tiny place in as many dimensions as possible: geologically, spiritually, botanically, historically, culturally, aesthetically, ornithologically, etymologically, emotionally, politically, socially, archaeologically and personally. It is a description of what my father gave to me and of what, in the spring of 2005, I shall give to my son.

A year or so ago, the *West Highland Free Press*, the radical(ish) anti-lairdist paper produced in Broadford in Skye, heard that I was planning to write a book about the islands and produced this cartoon:

I am the English toff. I am drowning in everything the guillemots can throw at me and I am burped at by sea monsters. I might crouch on the slippery rock ledges but I don't belong there. I might dream of the Shiants, but I should by rights be back in my natural environment, the club in St James's, brushing up my bowler, sprucing up my moustache, talking to other members about the state of the market or the loss of empire. My presence on the Shiants is about as easy or convincing as a basking shark ordering *Sole Véronique* in the dining room at the Ritz.

In the Hebrides, that is a widely shared, if rarely stated, attitude.

The English landowner is an alien, part joke, part irritant, a tourist who thinks he has some claim on the place. Once in the midday dark of Macleod's Bar next to the quayside in Tarbert, I was having a drink with Uisdean MacSween. Hughie MacSween, as I know him, the shepherd from Scaladale on Loch Seaforth, is one of the great sheep men on Harris. For many years of my boyhood and young adulthood he had the flock on the Shiants. He became, technically, my tenant. He paid me fifty pounds a year for the grass. But the reality was different: he was the master and I the pupil. I always felt embraced by his presence. He whispered his stories through lips that clung doggedly to the crushed stub-end of a roll-up, his eyebrows, like sprigs of long-grown lichen, leaping at the punch lines. The movement of his mouth was so quiet, like the fluttering of a flame, that you would always be creeping closer to hear him, to put your ear to his lips. And while he spoke, his eyes would move from you to the horizon and back: you, the listener, the target of the words, the horizon somehow their source. As he plied me with another pint and another chaser, long, growling laughs would come sloping out of his chest, breaking off into bronchial chaos, and then he would suddenly grasp my arm at some urgent point, some critical fact, some hilarious aspect – a long, deep drag on the last of the cigarette – of human folly.

For years, Hughie MacSween was the Shiants for me. He told me once, long after ill health had forced him to give up the islands, that he never went to sleep at night without his mind roving across them from one end to the other: up the steep climb from the landing beach, along the sheep paths there, over the shoulder and on to the broad back of Garbh Eilean, skirting the edge of the big peat-filled hollow, down to the valley at Glaic na Crotha, on towards the far end of Stocanish, where the lambs used to jump one by one down the steps of the north cliffs to the grass growing ever greener nearer the sea, until they found

themselves stranded, and he would have to rescue them, bringing them back tucked under his arm one at a time like a job lot of bagpipes. 'I know those islands inch by inch,' he said, and then added the words I have treasured ever since: 'And I know it is the same with you.'

A man came up to us, a little drunk, his cap on his head, his skin white. He ignored Hughie. 'Are you the man who says he owns the Shiants?' he said to me, standing over me.

'Yes,' I said, smiling charm, the English defence, 'I am actually.'

'Well you're a sackful a shite.'

I laughed.

'You can no more say that those islands belong to you than I can say that I'm the landlord of the moon.'

Hughie rolled his head and smiled at the man, there-thereing, calming the situation, murmuring to both of us that quietening growl he uses to his dogs. 'Sit down, sit down,' he said, patting the bench beside him.

The man sat down and went on. He took Hughie by the arm. 'This is the man who owns the Shiants. They're yours, aren't they, Uisdean?'

Hughie looked down, his turn for bashfulness. 'Oh, I wouldn't quite say that, Murdo.'

'Well, this is the man who should say he owns the Shiants anyway. He's got the sheep on the place. He does the work there. And he looks after it. And what have you got to say about it? What do you do to say that the Shiants are yours?'

The answer, if I had given it, would have ended in a fight. The Shiant Isles are mine; I can say that they are my five hundred acres of rock, grass, cliff and wildness, stuck out in the middle of the Minch between Skye and Lewis, besieged by the seas around them, because my father gave them to me. He had bought them after his grandmother had died and left him some money. The advertisement had been seen by his mother in the *Daily Telegraph*. Colonel Macdonald from Tote in Skye, who had bought the islands the year before, had imagined they might be ideal as a stud where he could breed racehorses. He had been sweet-talked into the ridiculous purchase by Compton Mackenzie, the novelist, who owned the islands at the time and was, as ever, strapped for cash. Mackenzie had acquired them in 1925 from the executors of Lord Leverhulme, and Leverhulme had bought them in 1917, along with the whole of Lewis and Harris, from the Mathesons. The Mathesons, in their turn, afloat on opium millions from trade between Hong Kong and mainland China, had in 1844 bought Lewis from the Mackenzies, the ancient family of the Earls of Seaforth, who withdrew to their territories on the mainland. The Mackenzies, in a chaotic period of unparalleled violence and treachery at the beginning of the seventeenth century known, in one document, as 'The Ewill Trowbles of the Lewes,' in which 'the Macleoid of the Lewes was with his whol Trybe destroyed and put from the possession of the Lewes', had bought the property from some gentlemen of Fife, who had been granted it by the Crown to set up a colony, even though the hereditary owners, the Macleods of Lewis, were still, at least partly, in possession. Only 'after great trouble and much blood' did the Mackenzies get hold of the islands. For their part, the Macleods – 'the stoutest and prettiest men, but a wicked bloody crew whom neither law nor reason could guid or moddell, perpetuallie destroying one another' – had stolen it in the twelfth century from the Nicolsons, who had arrived as Vikings perhaps three hundred years earlier. Presumably they – we – had done dreadful things to the previous inhabitants.

Nicolson, Macleod, Mackenzie, Matheson, Leverhulme, Mackenzie, Macdonald, Nicolson: twelve hundred years, eight sets of landlords claiming the Shiants as theirs. I was their heir and that's why I could claim to be their owner and Hughie MacSween couldn't. But I didn't say any of that. Hughie bought the man a drink and – the blood of the Vikings running a little thin – I hid behind him.

In 1894, the Reverend Donald MacCallum, the highly emotional Minister of the Parish of Lochs in Lewis, of which the Shiants have been a part since the 1720s, made a long and passionate statement to a Royal Commission that was hearing evidence on the state of crofters in the island. Rolling in its Biblical allusions, wildly overstated, dependent more on a rhetoric that goes back to the subversive roots of Christianity itself than to any modern understanding of rights and responsibilities, it is one of the grandest attacks ever made on the idea of the landlord. 'Great evils,' MacCallum began largely,

> have necessarily resulted from the fact that land, lake, river, and estuary are appropriated to the sole use, and regulated by the will of a few irresponsible individuals styled by themselves and others as lords. Every man has a right, natural, and God-given, to the earth and its fullness – its fullness of light, air and water, of vegetation and fruit, of beast, bird and fishes, of metals and minerals. The lords who first sold the land had no right to do so, and therefore the lords who bought the land are not the owners thereof. That which a man has no right to sell cannot become the property of the man who buys it.

My apostolic succession from the Nicolson Vikings a millennium ago means nothing. The idea of ownership is itself illegitimate. MacCallum went on:

> Lordism impoverishes the land. The wealth that is on sea and land, instead of being used in rearing the families of those who earn it, is spent in providing luxuries for idle lords. The destitution and the plague which follow in the wake of this usurper lift up their voices against it and condemn it. Lordism devastates the land. On the face of the deserted villages, once the happy homes of the free and the brave, now lying in silent desolation, we read: 'The scourge of lordism has passed over us.' I never heard of any creature having a swallowing capacity equal to that of lordism. The cattle and the ears of corn which Pharaoh saw in his dream come nearest to it.

There are many ruins and signs of abandonment on the Shiants and in Pairc, the big block of Lewis nearest to the islands, and that emptiness now is a symptom of the very landlordism of which I am the current beneficiary.

Under cross-examination from the Commission, MacCallum was taken apart. He clearly knew very little indeed about the issue over which his pulpit language had taken such magnificent flight. He had no idea of the acreage of his parish, the number of its inhabitants, the amount of fertile arable ground available to them or the productivity of the lands which he claimed they were denied. He was humiliated by the lawyers. But his words, which I first read twenty years ago in the enormous volume the Commission produced, continue to resonate with me. Perhaps what MacCallum has to say is true of all property, but the outlines are especially clear in this stark and naked landscape. My claim on the Shiants, not to put it too finely, is dependent on a succession of acts of violence, quite literally of murder, rape and expulsion. Money may have passed hands recently – my father paid £1400,

Macdonald £1500, Compton Mackenzie £500 – but what the Rev. MacCallum said is true: 'The lords who first sold the land had no right to do so, and therefore the lords who bought the land are not the owners thereof.'

My islands are not a place from which to exclude others. I have derived more richness from the Shiants than from anywhere else on earth. I have felt utterly sustained for years at a time by this wild and magnificent place. Is it for me, given this, to shut anyone else out? There are several good landlords on Lewis and Harris, who allow free, universal and weekly access on a Saturday to their salmon rivers; who encourage those who might want to poach the deer to come and shoot the hinds, again for free, in the season. These are recent developments and not all Lewis landlords have subscribed to them. There are one or two who still operate estate policies of rigid and at times harsh exclusivity, who do their best to prevent people walking on their hill, at least during the stalking season, who send out their gamekeepers and water bailiffs to search through the fishing boats in the coastal townships, looking for the nets used by salmon poachers, who have even sent helicopters out to look for nets in the sea, who in the last few years have attempted to have a stretch of public road privatised. There are some estate owners, in other words, who continue to behave as if their ownership of these pleasure zones bears few or even no responsibilities to neighbouring communities.

That, I think, is wrong and this book is in part a response to it. I may be in possession of the deeds of the Shiants, I may love them more than anywhere else on earth, but I do not feel that I have anything resembling an exclusive right to them, or that any landlord could. For all MacCallum's afflatus – you can see his face reddening as he makes his statement, his rhetoric inflating and wobbling like the proboscis of an elephant seal in front of the Commissioners, and then its collapse as their scepticism exacts its price, his deflation afterwards, his running over it in his mind back at the manse: the passages where it had sounded good; those where, as even he suspected, it hadn't – despite all of that, he was right about this. Land – particularly land that is out on the edge of things, and particularly land that is a rich concentration of the marvels of the natural world – is to be shared. This book is an attempt to share the Shiants.

They are not really a lonely place. That is a modern illusion. For the Shiants, the question of solitude figures only twice: once in the flowering of Columban monasticism between the seventh and tenth centuries, and once in the twentieth century. For most of their history, the Shiants were not, like some piece of Wagnerian stage scenery, lumps of rock in a hostile sea, beside which the solitary hero could exquisitely expire. They were profoundly related to the world in which they were set. Until 1901 they were almost continuously inhabited, perhaps for five thousand years. Our modern view of such places as orphans or widows, drenched

in a kind of Dickensian poignancy of abandonment, is, on the whole, wrong. The Shiants are rich: in the kind of island beauty to which, it is clear, men have been drawn over many thousands of years; in soils and natural fertility; in the seas around them thick with plankton, and with the layers of predatory fish and sea birds stacked four or five tiers above that. These islands in their season are the hub for millions of bird and animal lives, as dynamic as any trading floor, a theatre of competition and enrichment. They are the centre of their own universe, the organising node in a web of connections, both human and natural, which extends first to the surrounding seas, then to the shores on all sides and beyond that, along the seaways that stretch for thousands of miles along the margins of the Atlantic and on into the heartlands of Europe.

For all the illusion of remoteness, the Shiants have never been parochial. They are part of the whole world and are a profoundly human landscape, the subject of stories, songs and poems. They have been the scene of attempted murder, witchcraft and terrible accidents. They have witnessed all kinds of happiness and cruelty. They have known great riches and devastating poverty. They can be as sweet as Eden and as malevolent as Hell. They can envelop you and reject you, seduce you into thinking nowhere on earth is as perfect and then make you long to be anywhere but this. I have never known a place where life is so thick, experience so immediate or the barriers between self and the world so tissue-thin. I love the Shiants for all their ragged, harsh and delicate glory and this book is a love letter to them.

2

EARLY APRIL AND A COLD WIND was cutting up from the south-west. *Freyja* was anchored in the little rocky inlet at the head of Flodabay on the east coast of Harris. A seal watched from the dark water. Acid streams were draining off the moorland into the sea. The boat swung a little and the reflected sun glinted up at the strakes of her bilges. I was shivering, not because of the cold, but because I was frightened at the idea of sailing out alone in this small boat to the Shiants. The halyard was slapping against the mast and the tiny waves clucked as they were caught against the underside of the hull. The shores of Flodabay were sallow and tussocky with the dead winter grasses and the boat was washed in late-winter sun. *Freyja* is sixteen feet from stem to stern and looks from the shore as slight as a balsawood toy. She and the Minch are not to the same scale.

It was the first time I was going to sail to the Shiants on my own. Always before, I had allowed myself to be carried out by fishermen from Scalpay or boatmen from Lewis, travelling as I now see it like a man in a sedan chair, gracefully picked up, carefully taken over and gently set down. That could never be enough. That was not being engaged with the place. An island can only be known and understood if the sea around it is known and understood.

Six months previously, I had read a history of the *birlinn*, the sailing galley descended from Viking boats that was used in these waters by the highland chiefs, at least until the seventeenth century. They raided and traded with them. Their lives were as much bound up with them as with any land-based habitation. The book described the carving of a *birlinn* surviving on the tomb of Alasdair Crotach, Hunchback Alasdair, the Macleod chieftain in Harris in the mid-sixteenth century. He was a violent man, the mass murderer of a cave-full of Macdonalds on Eigg, men, women and children, three hundred and ninety-five of whom he suffocated with the smoke of a fire lit at its narrow mouth.

This killer's *birlinn* is an image of extraordinary beauty.

The form and curve of each strake, the fixings of the rudder, even the lay of the rope in the rigging: everything is carved with exactness, clarity and what can only be called love. Around it are the relative crudities of angels, apostles and biblical stories. Their forms never escaped the stone but the carved ship shows the panels of cloth in the bellied-out sail. It even shows the way a sail can be creased against a forestay that is faintly visible through it. Above all, though, it lovingly described the form of the hull, the depth of its keel and the fullness of the bilges. All of this was carved in millimetre detail, testament of something that mattered. The *birlinn* was shown at full stretch and fully rigged, but out of the water, so that the swept beauty of the hull could be seen. Only a shipwright or a sailor could have carved such a thing: it is the mental, not the actual image of a ship at sea, a depiction of what you can imagine of a boat at its most perfect moment, made by a man who knew it. The author of the *birlinn* history had set a Gaelic proverb at the head of his central chapter:

'S beag 'tha fios aig fear a bhaile,
Cia'mar 'tha fear na mara beò.

The landlubber [literally the man of the village] has no idea
How the sailor [the man of the sea] exists.

That was the gap I wanted to cross; to acquire the habits of
mind which the carver of the *birlinn* had so easily conveyed. I
rang the author, John MacAulay. He lived in Flodabay in South
Harris. Did he know of anyone who might be able to build me
a boat that would take on something of that Norse tradition?
That I could sail single-handed? Which would be safe and strong
enough to survive in the Minch, even on a bad day, and which
might be hauled up a beach, at least with the help of a winch?

'Ah yes,' John said, a light, slight voice. Definite, polite, cour-
teous, withdrawn, sharp, sprung.

'In Harris, would that be?' I asked him.

'Yes, I think it would.'

Wonderful news. And who was the shipwright?

'Well, I think you are speaking to him now.'

John MacAulay was not only a historian of the Viking inheritance, but a boat builder of thirty-five years' experience. He had
made and repaired fishing boats in the Shetland island of Unst,
and at Oban and Kyle. He had been a fisherman and was an
experienced yacht sailor. He was one of the leading experts on
both the history of the sea kayak and the traditional working
boats of the Hebrides. He was an elder of his church in Leverburgh
and author of a book on the church at Rodel in which the *birlinn*
carving was to be found. For two months or so John and I
corresponded by letter and occasionally by phone. I said I thought
I could do what I needed to do with a twelve-foot boat. He said
it would have to be at least sixteen foot. 'I'm not sending you
out there in something twelve foot long.' I wanted something
'double-ended', coming to a point at bow and stern. John said,

'That would be a waste of wood. You'll want a transom on it.'
A sixteen-footer with a transom – the stern cut off square – was
the equivalent of a twenty-footer that came to a point at the
stern. Timber in the treeless Hebrides was always at a premium.
'It would be a waste of wood. And time. And money,' he said.

He posted me drawings of the boat he proposed. Unpractised
at reading such things, and unable to guess performance or quality
from buttock lines or the sheer of the gunwale, I took him at his
word. I had yet to meet him but even at a distance he exuded
an authority and conviction which it was not easy to deny. I
would turn repeatedly to a passage in his book about the *birlinn*:

> A close relationship, like a spiritual bonding, develops
> between the shipwright and the finished vessel, which con-
> tinues throughout its entire material life. It has been known
> for certain boatbuilders to refuse to build for a particular
> client, if they did not feel an affinity towards one another.
> A reputable shipwright might not want to see some work
> of devotion fall into the wrong hands, and would rather
> find some obscure reason for refusing to build, than later
> be in the position of accusing an untrustworthy client of
> incompetence . . .

Austerity lay like an acid on the page. The Nicolsons might
claim to be descended from the ancient chiefs of Lewis. Their
birlinn might have been run down by the Macleods in the Minch,
somewhere off the Shiants. Norse blood might have been running
in me, but it was scarcely the purest of streams. John MacAulay,
though, was the real thing. 'MacAulay,' he said to me one day,
'is only the Gaelic for Olafson.' The world of the sagas, a thousand
years away, came reeking down the telephone.

The severity was a guarantee of his seriousness. I met him for
the first time when the boat was almost finished. His workshop
is a Nissen hut on the shores of Flodabay. A curling strip of

tarmac makes its tortuous way across rocks and around inlets down to the settlement. Nowhere in the British Isles that has been long inhabited can be bleaker than this. The ice-scraped gneiss shelters little more than dark peat hollows and sour grass. The houses of the people who live here are scattered along the road. There is no visible sign of community. It looks like a barren world.

That is certainly how outsiders have always seen such places: as an environment and a people in need of improvement and enrichment, a place of material poverty and actual sterility. But come a little closer and the picture turns on its head. A richness flowers among the rocks. John met me in front of the boat he had made. He stood four square, legs apart and shoulders back, resting a hand on the gunwale. His long, grey hair was brushed back from his temples. He wore a small grey moustache and looked me straight in the eye: a straight, calm, evaluating look. 'Are you up to the boat I have made?' it said. Could the shipwright trust the client? But instead, he said, 'Welcome, welcome.'

We went over it together for two hours, inch by inch. Although I had paid for it, and I was to use it, I was to trust my life to it, there was no doubt whose boat this was. John was describing his world. The boat to my eye was extraordinarily deep and wide for its length: sixteen feet long but six feet, two inches in the beam, and drawing at least two feet below the water line at the stern. 'Take me through it,' I said. Little spits of rain were coming in through the open doors of the workshop. 'This boat is for the Minch,' he said. 'She is not off the shelf. She knows the conditions in which she'll have to work. And she's within your capabilities for handling. Twelve feet would be too small and anything bigger would be too big for you.'

John enlarged on the difference between this and 'most boats'. 'Most boats are a tub' – he outlined the body of a pig in the air – 'and a keel. A tub for buoyancy, a keel for lateral stability. Easy

to make, cheap to build. This boat is different. It's the hull planking itself which makes the keel. It is a highly complex and inte-
grated form, and that integral keel running the whole length of
the boat gives you directional stability as well as lateral stability.'
The form he was describing clearly derived from the deep-
draughted *birlinn*. There was 'more boat in the water' built like
this. You might see her afloat and think, just from the shore, that
she was a slip of a thing. She wouldn't show a great deal. The
meat of the boat was unseen, in the water, and it was that which
made her a good sea boat and a good sailing boat. She had a
better grip in the water that way and you wouldn't get anything
like the rolling effect you would with 'most boats'.

Everything was precision here. The language John was using
was scientific in its exactness. The saws, drawknives, hand-drills,
chisels, disc-grinders and hammers were hung cleanly and neatly,
ranged by size, along the corrugated metal walls of the workshop.

A mallet and a measuring tape lay on the work bench. Timber was stacked on shelving in the roof and one of John's padded checked shirts hung from the end of the baulks. The wind coming in from the large open garage doors was the only thing unregulated here. 'Where did you learn to be so neat, John?' I asked him.

'I can't bear untidiness of any kind,' he said.

I felt a little fat in his presence, mentally fat, from the world beyond here, the world of cheap options and short cuts, the world of 'most boats', where the rigour of this man and his workshop was not applied. I slowly came to understand something: this was not a very large dinghy. It was a very small ship. This was the *birlinn* translated for me. All the principles of sea-kindliness, of robustness of construction and yet lightness of form, of a craft designed to protect its crew and save their lives, miraculously transmitted to this man and his meticulous workshop, had been poured into the boat which he would allow me to call mine. John himself, and the boat he had made, were a transmission from the world of the Shiants' past.

But there was more to it. 'The entry is fine' – it comes to a sharp and narrow point at the bow – 'which makes her easy to row. And the underwater lines are clean: a clean fine exit.' Underwater, the stern sweeps to as narrow and subtle a point as the bow. Seen from astern, the boat's form is a wineglass. I – the crew – would inhabit the bowl, but the sea would come into contact only with the stem of the glass. As far as the sea knew, the boat gradually slipped away to nothing. Smooth, laminar flow along the hull would allow her to slide along, no eddies, no drag. Only 'amidships' – John's word, all the implications of this tradition buried in it – does she fill out. But again the middle path must be chosen. She is not so fine that she will roll too quickly, but not so full that the drag is too great. The mast and yardarm, cut and planed from lengths of Scottish larch, the oars (larch) and rudder (oak, bound and tipped with galvanised iron) had all been made by John without compromise or trimming. Everything was as full and robust as it needed to be, but not more than that. This was no butcher of a thing. It had a slightness for all its strength. He had forged the iron for the mooring rings, the eyebolts and hooks for the halyard, the upright pins for the rowlocks and the gudgeons and pintles for the rudder. Everything was fully itself, designed not only for appearance but to last and to work in difficult and harsh conditions. Nothing was too heavy or too massive. Accommodation was all.

'A boat for the Shiants then?' I said. John nodded silently. 'I think she's beautiful,' I said. He said nothing, but shrugged.

'How long will she last?' I asked him.

'It'll last longer than you,' he said, and then turning away, 'There are boats at Geocrab, the next bay up, that are more than a hundred years old and they're still sailing.'

'And do you think I'll make a good sailor of her?'

'If you had another life,' John said.

'Ah yes,' I said, reeling a little, 'I suppose one needs to know these things instinctively.'

'No,' he said. 'You need to be entirely conscious of what you are doing and why you are doing it.'

Sharp, educative, exact: the mind was as clear and as precisely arranged as the tools on the workshop wall. John uses words like 'declivity', 'counteraction', 'silicon bronze' as if they were chisels. One of his saws was stamped with its date of manufacture: 1948. It hung on its hook in as clean a condition as the day it was made.

It was not hostility. Far from it. He had done his extraordinary best for me. He had wetted the keel, as one should, with a glass of whisky when it was first laid. He had buried deep in the woodwork at the stern a threepenny bit from the year of his birth, 1941. He had given the stern his own signature, a little 'tumblehome', a slight curving of the hull in towards the gunwale 'because it looked right.' He had poured himself into this beautiful thing for me. But this is not a sentimental tradition. This was a man who had grown up with boats. He had been sailing his first small boat like this when he was a teenager. His grandfather and great-grandfather had big herring drifters, fifty, sixty, seventy feet long, built in Stornoway, with which they had followed the herring on its seasonal migration around Cape Wrath, through the Pentland Firth, down the east coast of Scotland and on as far as Yarmouth. The herring have long since gone now and that is not an option.

'Is there much fishing in this loch now?' a Lewis crofter was asked by one of the investigating Commissioners in 1894.

'There used to be when herring came into it,' he said. 'There is very little fishing except when there are herring.'

'Do you know the reason why the herring are not coming now?'

'Providence,' the crofter said, 'the administration of the Creator.'

The herring are gone but John had been at sea all his life and he had completed a five-year apprenticeship in shipbuilding. Who was I to ask if I might be a sailor like them?

Looking back on it now, I can see that I was asking him for too much, too quickly. Again and again I asked him, 'Show me how to do this, tell me about the tides, tell me how to cope when the wind and tide run into each other. Where are the places not to be? Take me out in the boat and show me how to do it.' And again and again, with the mixture of sharpness and distance, he said no.

I was up for a week early in the year with a friend of mine, a writer, Charlie Boxer. Each of us was as green as the other, each as hurried and muddled in our dealing with the rig or our attempts to tack. He left us to it. Day after day, Charlie and I hacked along the Harris shore, seeing how close we could bring her to the wind, frightening ourselves in the tide rip off Stocanish, suddenly finding the boat going backwards in the tide while sailing at full speed with the wind, and once, like tourists, landing in the little loch at Scadabay to buy some tweed.

John came out with us once, a gentle afternoon in Flodabay, and the boat flew under his hands. Niftily, he threaded her through a maze of unseen rocks out to the headland on which a Norse seamark stood and then back to the jetty. He stood at the stern with the tiller between his knees, the nonchalant man against the sky behind him. He showed me, in other words, the condition I hoped to reach. It was not his business to provide any waymarks towards it.

And for all this I am grateful. I loved the boat. I felt that in the boat, and in this teaching by not teaching, I was learning more about the world of the islands than I had ever grasped. Here with John MacAulay I was seeing beyond their holiday face. The tradition in which he believed was too valuable to be tarted about.

When on that April morning, I finally left Flodabay in the boat, John helped me load her up with all my odds and ends in waterproof bags. It was, or so I felt anyway, an emotional moment. The tide that would carry me north would only start to run in the early afternoon and so most of the morning I was getting things ready. A seal dawdled in the weedy shadows. The oystercatchers peeped from one rock to the next. I had the mast up and the sail unfurled. Already there was some wear on the boat where Charlie and I had sailed her up and down the coast of Harris, the sheer presence of a friend in the boat giving me the confidence to do things I wouldn't have dreamed of doing on

my own. The cleats were now worn where the sheets had tightened against them. The knots in the oak thwarts had opened in a spell of dryish weather. I said goodbye to John, a hard handshake. He was off to the General Assembly of the Church of Scotland. Clause 28, and all the larger questions of homosexuality which clustered around it, was the issue of the day. 'Oh, you would be surprised. Even in the Church of Scotland there's a big gay lobby,' he said. He wasn't in favour himself. I didn't tell him that most of my family was gay, but I'm sure he guessed it anyway. I thanked him for everything he had done.

The inflatable dinghy in and deflated, the oars stowed, the charts in the stern sheets, the laminated folder of the pilot tucked in under the stern thwart, the compass, the VHF and GPS, the mobile phone and binoculars, the bread rolls I had bought outside Tarbert, the lump of cheese; my drysuit, life-jacket, harness, life-line, the little knowledge I had acquired with Charlie of how the Minch might be, how it threatens you even on the gentlest of days: with all of this, and the trust in the boat, I was equipped. I raised the anchor, washed off the black mud that clung to it, stowed it away and hoisted the sail.

The wind, coming down off the hills in South Harris, snatching at the foot of the sail, pulled the bow around. The still bay water rippled against the strakes of the hull. The sunshine flicked up at me from each small wave. As the boat moved out towards the open sea, past Bogha Creag na Leum, the underwater rock which guards Flodabay against the unwary incomer, and as the surface of the water started to lift with the swelling of the Minch outside, there on the headland by the Norse seamark, a tall, lichened stone pillar, stood a man. He was waving to me. I couldn't see for a moment who it was. I waved back, and then I realised: it was John MacAulay. He must have run half a mile to get there in time. He had made no mention of it, but this was his farewell, the shipwright saying goodbye to his boat. As the sea began to take up its longer, bigger rhythm, and the stem bit and rose in the swells, with the bow wave running and rippling the length of the hull beside me, and the wake starting to gurgle behind, I waved back to him.

'Good luck!' he shouted.

'Thank you!' I shouted back, 'Thank you, thank you!'

*   *   *

The air has closed in and the north is now a featureless absence. Between me and the mist-wall, a gannet cruises above the Minch. It must be in from St Kilda, sixty miles away to the west, low over the water, quartering it, looking for the flash of silver there, cutting sickle curves across the grain of the swell. It is a frightening sea. I see a big tanker coming south down the Minch. The spray bursts around its bow as it slaps into each of the swells. No contact with its crew or master, but I feel them looking at me from the bridge and wondering what that tiny boat must be about. Not that the swells are particularly big; they lift *Freyja* five or six feet in a long, rolling motion. It is just that the boat seems small, the sea wide and the land in all directions a long way off.

Like a climber on his ledge, I have to suppress the awareness of all that room beneath me. Concentrate on the boat. Look to the sail. Check you are on course. Do not consider the hugeness of the sea.

The muscles across my chest have tightened and my whole body is tensed, waiting for some relief. I am not at home here. I don't have the sailor's ease. I look at each coming sea as a possible enemy. The sea surface is streaked white as if the fat in meat has been dragged downwind. Why did I think this would be a thing to do, to push myself out here on a slightly difficult day, with the wind rising and the passage untried? It was not wise, but I am committed now. It would be just as bad turning back as going on. The sea extends like a hostile crowd around me. I want to arrive. I want to be out of uncertainty. At least on the island, however much the sea might batter it, there is no fear of the ground beneath your feet breaking or of it somehow abandoning you. An island is loyal in the way that a boat can never be. A boat can go wrong, the gear can fail. The sheer solid stillness of the islands is not like that. An island is a presence, not a motion, and there is faithfulness in rocks.

I look for the Shiants but they have yet to appear. I am shut in the world of the boat and the compass. At sea, something sixteen feet long does not feel large.

I wanted to call her *Maighdean nan Eileanan Mora*, the Gaelic for 'Shiant Girl' until John MacAulay pointed out that saying that to the Coastguard over the VHF was not going to sound quite right. Besides, the name wouldn't fit on the boat. So I have called her *Freyja*, after the Norse goddess of love and fertility, who could turn herself into a falcon and fly for a day and a night over the sea; who could shepherd the fish into the nets of fishermen; who could happily sleep with an entire family of elves, each one of which would present her with a link in an amber necklace after the night she had given them. One shape *Freyja* would never adopt was the chaste and abstinent virgin. She was always fully engaged with life, ripe in body and desire.

I love *Freyja*'s beautiful fatness around her middle. (I had said this to John. 'Not fat,' he said. 'Full.') She is uncompromisingly robust and strongly nailed for all the travails she will have to go through; nothing fey but nothing brutish. The Norse used to have both their houses and their graves made in the shape of boats, smoothly narrowing to the ends. It is the most accommodating form man has ever devised. I focus on that, on the coherence of what John has made compared with all the incipient anarchy of the sea.

A gannet suddenly slaps into the sea beside me. No warning. I start at it and remember this, the story of one of the stewards of St Kilda. At some time in the seventeenth century, (no date, because dates are rarely certain here), the steward, sailing out from Harris to his island responsibilities forty miles away across the Atlantic, found his boat passing through a shoal of herring so thick that the bodies of the fish lay like a pavement on the surface of the water. There was a silver skin to the sea and any man could have walked across it. A south wind was blowing and the boat was skimming through the bodies of the herring as if skating across them. All around them the gannets were diving, again and again, no hesitation necessary, no accuracy needed. It was the atmosphere of a tobogganing party. If the gannets had been children they would have been shrieking at the pleasure. The steward and his companions were gliding to St Kilda as if to Heaven.

A gannet, mistaking his moment, plunging for fish but ignoring the people, dived for his prey but missed his mark, his narrowed, darting body slicing down past mast, sail and shrouds, past the crew at the sheets, into the body of the open boat where its beak and head were impaled in the bottom strakes of the hull. The bird was dead on impact. Its enormous wings stretched across the frames and thwarts of the boat almost from one gunwale to another. Its perfect white body, six feet across from black wing-tip to black wing-tip, and a yard long, took up as much room as a man. The bubble of perfection had been pierced. The plank was splintered through. Twenty miles of the Atlantic separated the steward and his party from Harris and twenty from St Kilda. Could they mend the punctured hull? Would they drown here? Was water coming in faster than they could keep it out? Searching for the damage down in the bilges, the steward and his crew, scrabbling the ropes and creels out of the way, looked for signs of water bubbling in. There was none. Miraculously, the bilges were dry. The gannet's head had plugged the hole its dive had made and its body was left there for the rest of the voyage, four hours to the bay on Hirta, with the enormous corpse beside them performing its role as feathered bung.

I was first told that story when I was a ten-year-old boy. I stood up with shock as the crisis hit and, of course, I have never forgotten it. I have learned since how prone to accident the gannet is. Every year in each of the great rocky gannetries around the Scottish coast, on Ailsa Craig and Bass Rock, in the stupendous avian city of St Kilda, hundred of gannets crash on arrival, breaking a wing or a neck, either dying then or over many weeks as their thick reservoirs of subcutaneous fat slowly wither in the breast, a pitiable death. Evolution does not create the perfect creature, only the creature that is perfect enough.

It is the one bird I wish would come to live on the Shiants. For a few years in the 1980s, the islands were the smallest gannetry in the world. Like a corporal among dukes, the Shiants made their glorious appearance in the ranks of the great: starting with St Kilda 100,100 gannets and Grassholm 60,000, the list ends with:

Shiants: 1.

He was to be seen for a few years perched solemnly on one of the north-facing rock buttresses of the islands, looking out woefully to the Lewis shore, hoping, I always imagined, that a lovely gannet girl might think this a suitable place to make her life. Around him, the guillemots stared and squabbled. Above them, the fulmars spat and cackled. No other gannet came to join him and by 1987, the Shiants, still listed in the wildly prestigious catalogue of British gannetries, now had an even more woeful entry:

Shiants: 0

The mind is distracted for a moment and then returns to the foolishness of what you have done. It was not exactly the vision of the drowning man but I found myself thinking of the people I love and have loved. Do men drown regretting what they have done with their lives, all the stupidities and meannesses, the self-delusions and deceits? I was driving blind and it was not comfortable. I had been in the boat nearly three hours and even through all the layers of clothes I was getting cold. I had a hand-held GPS with me and it put my position at just about six degrees, twenty-seven minutes west, fifty-seven degrees, fifty-four minutes north. I should have been almost on the islands now but I could not see into the mist-bank to the north and east of me. I needed to come round to the north side of the Shiants to bring the boat into the bay between them, protected there from the south-westerlies. I had to overrun them and then turn for shelter. I hadn't been here for a year and by now I was in a state of high anxiety.

This approach is larded with danger. Lying off the islands to the west is a chain of rocks and small steeply banked islets called the Galtachan or Galtas. No one knows what their name means but it may perhaps come from the Old Norse word, *Gaflt*, meaning the gable-end of a house. That, at least, is John MacAulay's suggestion. It is a derivation which even now makes me smile. So much for these savage seas! So much for the tides that rip through the narrow channels between the Galtas! When the

Ordnance Survey first came here on 27 October 1851, the surveyor wrote a hurried and unpunctuated description in his notebook:

> Received Name: Galltachan
> Object: Islands
> Description: This is a range of Several [?] High and Low water Rocks extending from east to west three of which has a little of their top covered with rough pasture and surrounded by small but steep rocky Cliffs. there is a channel between each and every one of the High Water Rocks. at a distance they appear low but are no way inviting as at all times especially at Spring tides there is a rapid current about them the tide flows exceedingly strong flowing the same as a large River.

That is the modern voice; the survey officer, Thomas O'Farrell, measuring, estimating, a little fearful, unable to disassociate his description of the place from his apprehension over it. It could easily have been my voice, frightened now of being swept by the tide into the channels between the Galtas through which the deep-drawing *Freyja* might not have passed. Perhaps John MacAulay would have felt relaxed here, but neither I nor O'Farrell were Vikings. Would either of us so calmly have named these rocks 'the gable-ends'? Would we have wanted to or been able to domesticate them so casually? The Gables? It is a joke, a place with a double garage and stuck-on timbers outside Beaconsfield. To know them as the Gables is evidence of an attitude of heroic calm; a sudden jump into the Viking world. To call them that is as cool as the gannet, as easy in the sea as by the hearth, almost literally at home there. Or maybe something else: the roofs of buried houses, mansions drowning in the Minch.

Freyja does at least belong to that world. I hold her tiller and she is my link to a chain that stretches over five hundred miles and a thousand years to the coast of Norway. Because there is no timber on the Outer Hebrides, the commercial connection with the Baltic has remained alive. Until no more than a generation ago, Baltic traders brought Finnish tar, timber and pitch direct to Stornoway and Tarbert in Harris. Although *Freyja*'s own timber comes from the mainland of Scotland, her waterproofing below the water-line is known as 'Stockholm tar': a wood tar, distilled from pine and imported from the Baltic at least since the Middle Ages. Until well into the nineteenth century, kit boats in marked parts came imported from Norway to the Hebrides, travelling in the hold of merchant ships, and assembled by boat builders in any notch or loch along the Harris or Lewis coast. In 1828, Lord Teignmouth, the ex-Governor-General of India, friend of Wilberforce, came out to the Shiants in the company of Alexander Stewart, the farmer at Valamus on Pairc, who had the tenancy of the islands. They

> launched forth in this gentleman's boat, a small skiff or yawl built in Norway, long, narrow, peaked at both ends, extremely light, floating like a feather upon the water, and when properly managed, with the buoyancy and almost the security of a sea-bird on its native wave.

The British Imperialist, the liberal evangelical, member of the Clapham Sect, travels in a Viking boat on a Viking sea. I nearly called *Freyja* 'Fulmar' because of that phrase of Teignmouth's. No bird is more different on the wing than on the nest and in flight the fulmar is the most effortless of all sea birds. It was that untroubled buoyancy in wind and water that I was after. But *Freyja*'s fatness was what settled it.

Almost everything in her and the world now around her, if described in modern Gaelic, would be understood by a Viking. The words used here for boats and the sea all come from Old Norse and the same descriptions have been on people's lips for a millennium. If I say, in Gaelic, 'windward of the sunken rock', 'the seaweed in the narrow creek', 'fasten the buoy', 'steer with the helm towards the shingle beach', 'prop the boat on an even keel', 'put the cod, the ling, the saithe and the coaley in the wicker basket', 'use the oar as a roller to launch the boat', 'put a wedge in the joint between the planking in the stern', 'set the sea chest on the frames amidships', 'the tide is running around the skerry', 'the cormorant and the gannet are above the surf', 'haul in the sheet', 'tighten the back stay', 'use the oar as a steerboard', or say of a man, 'that man is a hero, a stout man, the man who belongs at the stem of a boat', every single one of those terms has been transmitted directly from the language which the Norse spoke into modern Gaelic. It is a kind of linguistic DNA, persistent across thirty or forty generations.

Sometimes the words have survived unchanged. Oatmeal mixed with cold water, ocean food, is *stappa* in Norse, *stapag* in Gaelic, although *stapag* now is made with sugar and cream. With many, there has been a little rubbing down of the forms in the millennium that they have been used. A tear in a sail is *riab* in Gaelic, *rifa* in Old Norse. The smock worn by fishermen is *sguird* in Gaelic, *skirta* in Old Norse. *Sgaireag* is the Gaelic for 'seaman', *skari* the Norse word. And occasionally, there is a strange and suggestive transformation. The Gaelic for a hen roost is the Norse word for a hammock. Norse for 'strong' becomes Gaelic for 'fat'. The Norse word for rough ground becomes 'peat moss' in Gaelic. A hook or a barb turns into an antler. To creep – that mobile, subtle movement – translates into Gaelic as 'to crouch': more still, more rooted to the place. A water meadow in Norway, *fit*, becomes *fidean*: grass covered at high tide. 'To drip' becomes 'to melt'. A Norse framework, whether of a house, a boat or a basket, becomes a Gaelic creel.

But it is the human qualities for which Gaelic borrowed the Viking words that are most intriguingly and intimately suggestive of the life lived around these seas a thousand years ago. There is a cluster of borrowings around the ideas of oddity and suspicion. Gaelic itself, if it had not taken from the invaders, would have no word for a quirk (for which it borrowed the Old Norse word meaning 'a trap'), nor for 'strife', nor 'a faint resemblance' – the word it took was *svip*, the Norse for 'glimpse'. The Gaelic for 'lullaby' is *taladh*, from the Norse *tal*, meaning 'allurement', 'seduction'.

The vocabulary for contempt and wariness suddenly vivifies that ancient moment. Gaelic borrowed Norse revulsion wholesale. Noisy boasting, to blether, a coward, cowardice, surliness, an insult, mockery, a servant, disgust, anything shrivelled or shrunken (*sgrogag* from the Old Norse *skrukka*, an old shrimp,) a bald head, a slouch, a good-for-nothing, a dandy, a fop, a short, fat, stumpy woman (*staga* from *stakka*, the stump of a tree), a sneak (*stig/stygg*), a wanderer – all this was something new, and had arrived with the longships. Fear and ridicule, the uncomfortable presence of the distrusted other, the ugly cross-currents of two worlds, the broken and disturbing sea where those tides met: all this could only be expressed in the odd new language the strangers brought with them.

I was steering west of the Galtas but I had to make sure it was a long way west. The water had turned, as it does sometimes with the tide, into strange, long slicks, each slab of water as smooth as a hank of brushed hair. It is a horrible sensation in the mist, a strangeness at sea, when all you want is normality and predictability. Was this the effect of a rock ahead of me which I couldn't see? About five hundred yards off the westernmost Galta was the most dangerous rock in the Shiants: Damhag, perhaps meaning 'ox-rock' in Gaelic (no one knows why) or more likely 'a rock awash'. It is pronounced 'Davag'. O'Farrell had heard of its terrors:

Received name: Damhag
Object: Rock
Description: This is a Small low water Rock seen only at Spring tides which makes it very dangerous to mariners, lying about 15 Chains west a Group of high and low water ones, the tide flows so Strong and rapid here that unless Mariners were aware of its Situation it would often become fatal. there has been not long ago a large vessel wrecked on it the vessel and crew were all lost. at neap tides if the wind is high there is always Breakers seen on it.

That ship was in fact the Norwegian schooner, *Zarna*, of Christiansund, which was wrecked here on 13 February 1847, en route to Norway from Liverpool with a cargo of salt.

None of this is pleasant in a small boat in a rising sea. If the GPS could be relied on, I was well clear but I didn't want to overrun too far. The long slicks of water were giving way to a broken, pitted surface like the skin of an orange.

North-west of the islands is the Sound of Shiant, separating them from the bulk of Lewis five or so miles to the west. The Sound is a place of deep discomfort. I have never been in there in a small boat and the fishermen in Scalpay have warned me away from it. Donald MacSween (another Viking name, Sveinson), whom I have known since I was a boy, and who, for a few years after his cousin Hugh MacSween gave up, was the tenant of the Shiants, told me only that I had to respect the Minch. 'Pick your day and pick where you go and you will be all right.' After supper in Rosebank, his house in Scalpay, in the sitting room, with the coal fire burbling beside us and Rachel, his wife, looking through the packets of seeds she was to plant that spring, from time to time telling me that I was a disgrace, 'walking around the way you do with holes in your socks the like of which I have never seen in my life', Donald and I sat over a chart together.

He is a strict churchman, a man of immense propriety and overwhelming charm. 'What do you talk about all the time on the radio to each other when you are out at sea?' I asked him once. Channel 6 on the VHF is solid with Gaelic chat, day and night, between the fishermen. 'Local talent,' he said, with a face like a gravestone. Rachel told me that in three decades of marriage she has never once seen him angry. 'He must be a saint then,' I said.

'Well, he's a saint to me.'

Donald knows all there is to know about the Minch. Without a second thought I would trust my life to him. He has fished it since he was a boy and he knows every one of its 'dirty corners'. 'Oh yes,' Mary Ann Matheson, the mother of John Murdo, the present shepherd on the Shiants, said to me once, 'you need to listen to Donald. He knows all the crooks and crannies of the wind.'

With his glasses on and his enormous, scarred hands feeling their way across the figures and the submarine contours, he went through the chart with me. Off the mouths of Lochs Seaforth, Bhrollúm and Cleidh there are big riffles on the ebb as the lochs drain out. There is a bar across the mouths of each of them so that the draining water has to rise from something like sixty to twenty fathoms as it emerges. That does not make for an easy sea and in my boat I should avoid them.

But the real danger was in a triangle of sea between the Shiants, Rubha Bhrollúm, which is the nearest point of Pairc on Lewis, and the mouth of Loch Sealg, five miles or so to the north. I was not to enter it. The sea there was not, Donald said, 'very pleasant'. Heavy, fast tides ebbing down from Cape Wrath or flooding up from the southern Hebrides are squeezed by the islands here into a narrower channel. At the same time, the water is forced to run over a knotted and fractured sea-bed.

A huge ridge of rock, three miles long and more than three hundred and fifty feet high, coming within seventy or eighty feet of the surface, stretches most of the way across the Sound, a sharp-edged submarine peninsula reaching out from the Shiants

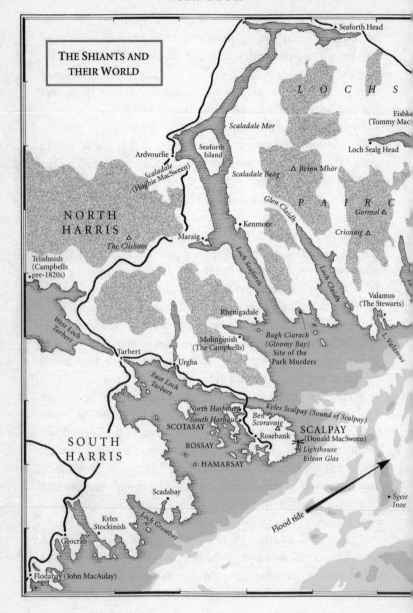

THE SHIANTS AND
THEIR WORLD

L O C H S

Seaforth Head

Eishk
(Tommy Mac

Scaladale Mor

Loch Sealg Head

Ardvourlie

Seaforth
Island

Scaladale
(Hughie MacSween)

△ *Beinn Mhór*

Scaladale Beag

P A I R C

Gormol △

Glen Claidh

NORTH
HARRIS

The Clisham △

Maraig

Kenmore

Crionaig △

Loch Claidh

Loch Seaforth

Valamus
(The Stewarts)

Telishnish
(Campbells
pre-1820s)

Rhenigadale

L. Valamus

West Loch
Tarbert

Molinginish
(The Campbells)

Bagh Ciarach
(Gloomy Bay)
Site of the
Park Murders

Tarbert

Urgha

East Loch
Tarbert

North Harbour
South Harbour
SCOTASAY

Kyles Scalpay (Sound of Scalpay)

Ben
Scoravaig

SCALPAY
(Donald MacSween)

SOUTH
HARRIS

ROSSAY

Rosebank

Lighthouse
Eilean Glas

HAMARSAY

Scadabay

Loch Grosebay

Kyles
Stockinish

Sgeir
Inoe

Geocrab

Flood tide

Flodabay (John MacAulay)

Gravir (John Murdo Matheson)
Loch Odhairn
Kebock Head

Orinsay
emreway
Lemreway (Dan Macleod)

Loch Sealg
Srianach
EILEAN IUBHAIRD
Ailtenish

Mulhagery (Kate Morrison)

Mol Truisg

Camas Thomascro
Rubh' Uisenis
The cave of the eviscerated mother

S O U N D   O F   S H I A N T
(The Stream of the Blue Men)

Ebb tide

T H E   M I N C H

Galtachan
SHIANT ISLANDS
(na h-Eileanan Mora)

Land above 200m
Sea level
50m
100m
Below 100m

0   1   2   3
Nautical miles

W   E
N   S

towards Rubh' Uisenis on Lewis. It makes that short passage on which the Admiralty chart-markers print an innocuous-looking set of wrinkly lines, meaning 'tidal overfalls', the equivalent of a set of rapids in a river. But the river coming up to them is five miles wide and four hundred and fifty feet deep, that enormous mass of water running at the height of spring tides at almost three knots, the speed of a fast walk. Any idea of a river is of the wrong scale. This is the equivalent in tonnage and in volume of an entire range of hills on the move. At certain states of high wind against spring tide, the sea here can turn into a white and broken mass of water, a frothing muddle of energies stretching across the whole width of the Sound, a chaos in which there are not only steep-faced seas coming at you from all directions, but, terrifyingly, holes, pits in the surface of the sea, into which the boat can plunge nose-first and find it difficult to return.

The Sound of Shiant is also known as *Sruth na Fear Gorm*, the Stream of the Blue Men, or more exactly the Blue-Green Men. The adjective in Gaelic describes that dark half-colour which is the colour of deep sea water at the foot of a black cliff. These Blue-Green Men are strange, dripping, semi-human creatures who come aboard and sit alongside you in the sternsheets, sing a verse or two of a complex song and, if you are unable to continue in the same metre and with the same rhyme, sink your boat and drown your crew.

The Reverend John Gregorson Campbell, Minister of Tiree from 1861 to 1891, and a renowned collector of folklore in the Hebrides, claimed to have met a fisherman who had seen one. It was, Campbell reported, 'a blue-coloured man, with a long, grey face and floating from the waist out of the water, following the boat in which he was for a long time, and was occasionally so near that the observer might have put his hand upon him.'

Something about the Blue Men has attracted one folklorist after another. Donald A Mackenzie, author of *Scottish Folk Lore and Folk Life*, published in 1936, even claimed to have preserved a fragment of verse dialogue between skipper and Blue Man tossing beside him in the billows. Both had, it seems, been studying the verses of Edward Lear and the rhythms of Coromandel and the Hills of the Chankly Bore were still ringing in their ears:

> Blue Chief: Man of the black cap, what do you say
>   As your proud ship cleaves the brine?
> Skipper: My speedy ship takes the shortest way
>   And I'll follow line by line.
> Blue Chief: My men are eager, my men are ready
>   To drag you below the waves.
> Skipper: My ship is speedy, my ship is steady.
>   If it sank it would wreck your caves.

'Never before,' Mackenzie wrote, 'had the chief of the blue men been answered so aptly, so unanswerably. And so he and his kelpie brethren retired to their caverns beneath the waves of the Minch.'

Mackenzie went on to describe how 'Once upon a time,' – a giveaway phrase, if ever there was one, for non-first hand information – 'a ship passing through the Stream of the Blue Men came upon a blue coloured man asleep on its waters. The sleeper for all his nimbleness was captured and taken aboard.' The crew bound him hand and foot but were appalled to see two of his friends following. Mackenzie then reports the conversation between the pair of Blue Men: 'One said to the other: "Duncan will be one man." The other replied: "Farquhar will be two."'

This was clearly a threat to the crew but luckily, before disaster could strike, the Blue Man they had captured 'broke his ropes and over he went.'

Is there anything more serious one can say about this? TC Lethbridge, sailor, archaeologist, savant, Keeper of Anglo-Saxon Antiquities at the University Museum of Archaeology and

Ethnology in Cambridge for much of the twentieth century, who believed that Druidism and Brahmanism were the same, had an intriguing theory about the Blue Men. In *The Power of the Pendulum*, his final, eccentric and free-spirited book, published in 1976, he touched briefly on the survival of beliefs such as these. Making connections which more strait-laced archaeologists are wary of, he identified the Blue Men with Manannan, the Celtic sea-god remembered in the place-name of Clackmannan, meaning 'Manannan's stone', and Manannan with Poseidon. The seaways around the shores of Europe bring stories, and ways of looking at the world, as well as goods. He plunged on into dangerous territory. A ditty had been recorded in the early twentieth century that was still being said or muttered among the fishermen of Mallaig:

Ickle Ockle, Blue Bockle	*Little youthful Blue God*
Fishes in the Sea. or	*Of the fishes of the sea*
If you're looking for a lover	*If you're looking for devotion*
Please choose me.	*Please choose me.*

It is a charm-cum-game-cum-riddle for Poseidon, of whom the Blue Men in the Minch were the last, rubbed-down remnants. 'How would you describe a god of this kind?' Lethbridge asked. 'As a cloud of past memories, to some extent animated by the minds of those who retained it.'

John MacAulay as a fifteen-year-old boy forty-five years ago, spending a season 'at the fishing' on the Monachs, to the west of Uist, heard stories from fishermen who had been out in the Sound of Shiant. On a wild day, they had hauled something or other very strange from the sea. They had no idea what it was. Other creatures of the same sort seemed to be visible in the surf around them and they didn't like it. Nothing is easier than being spooked at sea in a small boat, and the Sound of Shiant seemed to be turning into that horrible continuity of white and broken water. All sense of one's own fragility; the thumping of the hull against each new wave, the distance from shore, one's own pitiable progress to windward, the sheer size of the cold, hateful sea, the knowledge of all the others that have been drowned here before you: your throat constricts, you feel it in your chest and the stories start to turn real.

The fishermen, rather than carry their mysterious catch back home in triumph or as a curiosity, threw it back into the thrashing water among its companions, and it was lost to sight. Surely not a Blue-Green Man? John MacAulay guesses that it might have been a walrus, of which one or two occasionally wander south from their Arctic breeding grounds, appearing here as enormous mustachioed aliens to Hebridean eyes. Donald MacSween is scepticism itself: 'How have you got on with your investigations into the mermaids?' he asks from time to time.

I wasn't interested now. I was straining for the sight either of a Galta, a blessed gable-end, or of Damhag in front of me. Some of the swells were just breaking under their own weight. Behind me, the little grinning teeth of the breaking seas were scattered across the whole visible width of the Minch. Downwind I couldn't see them. If I looked ahead of me, it was like a crowd from behind, a sea of wind-coiffed heads. The slick black-grey backs of the waves moved on in front of me. Scarcely any whiteness was apparent. It was like two different seas.

The wind was coming and going around me. I called the Coastguard on the VHF, Channel 16. 'Stornoway Coastguard, Stornoway Coastguard, this is *Freyja*, *Freyja*, *Freyja*.' My eyes were on the sea ahead for the white on Damhag, the appearance of a Galta, the radio in its waterproof case in one hand, the tiller in the other communicating the quiver of the sea to my hand. Out of the radio a voice:

'*Freyja*, *Freyja*, *Freyja*, this is Stornoway Coastguard, Stornoway Coastguard.' A young woman in a calm, warm office twenty miles away, grey carpet on the floor, magnetic charts of the Sea Area

Hebrides covering half of one wall, men and women in their blue uniforms at the desks, coffee there on plastic coasters, a normal call on a normal day.

She gave me the forecast but we exchanged no names. She was the Coastguard, I was *Freyja*. She was providing a service. I was on my own. The weather would stay as steady as it was for the next twenty-four hours, south, southwesterly, four to five, with the wind dropping away after that. There would be something like calm for a day or two.

I was cold. I reached down into the bag at my feet for my own coffee in the thermos. My hands fumbled with it. Sandwiches in the plastic bag. I checked my position on the GPS again. It all feels a little absurd, to think that I might ever reach the condition in which it would be natural to call those rocks 'The Gables'. I am in my own world of bags from the Stornoway Co-op, the VHF in its 'Aquapac', the GPS locating me through the American military satellites orbiting above. They tell me that I have passed Damhag and the Galtas. It is time to turn east.

It's a relief. I must be nearly there. Simply taking the stern of the boat through the wind and gybing, moving the sail over to the other side, it feels better. That is a sign of arrival, or at least of near-arrival. I have got that amount of sea under my belt. All that strange width of sea has now, oddly, changed in my mind. Uncrossed, it felt terrifying. Having crossed it, I feel as if I could cross it any number of times. I sense John MacAulay at my shoulder. Is this all right John? 'Yes,' he says, 'you're not doing too badly.'

Now, though, I was moving into the shadow of the known, the sea around the Shiants. Because the Shiants are themselves such a disturbance to the flow of the tide, for others this would seem like the most hazardous and hostile section of the passage. But I'm familiar with the sea here. It is like knowing an old ill-tempered dog. I know how to get round him. Moving across the swell, a different pattern, *Freyja* was making a rolling barrel

along the crests and then slewing into the troughs behind them. Looking up, back in the stern, with the boat underway, I saw that things would be all right. The sky was lifting. From a satellite, I would have seen the shifting of an eddy, the slight revolution of some huge cloud crozier turning on the scale of Europe, the planetary mixing of Arctic and tropical air. This was the south-eastern limb of a giant depression rolling in out of the Atlantic and on to Scandinavia. It had blown me here. I felt a little sick but I could see where I was and it was where I had hoped to be. The seas breaking on Damhag were a mile to the south-east, that silent flinging of spray into the air above the rock, like a hand repeatedly flicking out its fingers, signalling 'Keep away, keep away!' I was well clear of it. The broken line of the Galtas extended for a mile beyond the rock, black and bitter, the knobbled spine of a half-submerged creature: one like an old woman with a bonnet, called Bodach, or Old Man; others blocky, fretted.

Beyond them, arrival, emergence, home. Coming out of the mist, draped with cloud ribbons like feather boas across their shoulders, were the islands, my islands, my destination. The Shiants are the familiar country, the place around whose shores I feel safe. Even in all its masculine severity, I know where the tide rips and bubbles, exactly where the rocks are, and the known, however harsh, is the safe and the good. Even though the sea now was more uncomfortable than anywhere on the journey, I started to feel easy. A small wave slopped aboard and I pumped it out. A shearwater cut past me and the birds were hanging around the Galtas like bees. But the relief, as ever, was ambivalent.

It's always like this. I never quite feel the comfort of arrival that I expect. It is enigmatic. This is the longed-for place, but it is so indifferent to my presence, so careless of my existence, that I might as well not have been here.

A remembered room is never as big as you think, but the Shiants always emerge much larger than I have remembered them. They are called *na h-Eileanan Mora* in Gaelic, which perhaps means 'the Big Islands', and here, now, they slowly billowed above me, a new world. They expand into reality, growing out of the mist, and their big, green, wrinkled forms drifted at me like half-inflated balloons. I let out the breath I had been holding in for hours. A home-coming to a place that provides no welcome. They come at you one by one. First Garbh Eilean, the Rough Island (*garbh* is the adjective you would use to describe someone who was strong, stocky, 'a big lad'), the most masculine and the westernmost. *Freyja* pushed steadily eastwards, along its northern cliffs, a mile-long wall of black columned rock, slightly higher in the centre, dropping at each side, each of the columns eight or ten feet wide, bending slightly as they rise from the sea, like a stand of bamboos swayed in a breeze. The sea sucks and draws in the caves and hollows and the birds are spattered across them like paint flicked from a brush. *Freyja* keeps to her line without my hand on the tiller. In the lee of the cliffs, their ribbed surfaces are like the ripples of an enormous curtain, gathered in its folds; or a vast black shell.

A scallop boat skipper waves to me as my sail snaps from one side to another in the gusts off the islands. The Shiants are stretching their arms around me. Around the corner comes Eilean Mhuire, Mary Island, the sweetest, the softest, the lowest, the most feminine and the most fertile. It is early in the year and the grass has yet to grow. The islands' skin is pale, a musty green. The sea is a little quieter here, protected by the islands from the swell. I am still a little dazed from the journey, as if I have emerged into the quiet from a room filled with noise. I slide along and remember the past.

At last, I turn into the bay which the three islands encircle. Eilean an Tighe, House Island appears, enclosing it to the south, the third of the three. Together they have always seemed to me like a family: Garbh the father, Mhuire the mother and this most domestic of the islands as their child, taking some of its character from each. The wind is less here but fluky. I let go of the tiller and the boat sails wherever it will as I tidy things away. I have crossed a sea which I have spent my life looking at: sixteen miles in three and a half hours, about four and a half miles an hour. I look back at it. There is no way I would set out on it now. Long, grey-faced waves come on at me from the south-west. For a moment I have a companion. A kittiwake, one of the smallest of the gulls, hangs buoyed above me. The way is still on the boat, making its easy last strides into the ring of islands. There is calm water in their shelter, and as if suspended above us the kittiwake comes to a point just beyond the stern, bobbing above me, curious, its arched wings like the curve of the sail, peering down from mast height into the boat, looking at me and all my possessions in their waterproof bags. Kittiwakes often hang after fishing boats, waiting for the offal as the fish are gutted. That is all it was, a hungry bird in pursuit of food, and it was only for a moment or two, but I took it as a sign of arrival.

The boat ran on into the bay. If the word 'here' has any meaning beyond simply the label of a place where you happen to be; if 'here' can be the name for the place to which you belong for more than just a moment, then this was my here. I let the anchor go and the chain ran out through the fairlead and down into the patch of sand, just off the Garbh Eilean screes where men have always anchored in a southwesterly. I unstepped the mast and folded the sail into its bag. I had arrived. I could hear the wind on the far side of the island beating without thought on the shore.

3

'THE SEA WANTS TO BE VISITED', a Gaelic proverb says and, as scarcely needs to be added, the host will murder its guests. Nothing can be understood about these islands, about the life that has been lived on them, and about the tensions under which people have existed here, without grasping that dual fact. The sea invites and the sea destroys. It is often said that the Hebrideans are not as natural seamen as the islanders in Orkney or Shetland, and that the northerners were fishermen who occasionally farmed and the Hebrideans farmers who occasionally fished. That isn't entirely true, particularly in Lochs. In 1796, there were three hundred and sixty-six families. The ability of the ground itself to sustain the people was minimal. They were lucky if for every oat or grain of barley sown, they could harvest three or four.

Before the nineteenth-century Clearances, when the inhabitants of twenty-seven townships in Pairc were evicted, about three hundred of those Lochs families, distributed like limpets around the shore in their tiny hamlets, were dependent on fishing, mostly of cod and ling which were at their best between February and May. There were seventy fishing boats in Lochs, each with a crew of three or four. The Shiants would probably have had a single boat, or at most two, shared between the five families that lived here. The boats were, essentially, the same as my *Freyja*, although a little longer, twenty rather than sixteen feet, undecked, with six or eight oars, a heavy dipping lug rig and a hull made of pine (or larch for the better quality) on oak frames. The timber would have been imported, as it was for *Freyja*, from the mainland.

They can be horribly dangerous in a rising sea, when large volumes of water can land inboard without warning, and I know what would happen if a sea ever came into *Freyja*. Beside me in the stern I have a large bucket and I would start baling with that. I have watched myself in these situations: a kind of cold panic grips me, a terse rejection of terror. Of course it wouldn't be enough. With the boat half full, *Freyja* would be riding lower than before. Almost certainly the next wave or the one after that would come in too. There would be no chance of keeping it out. The stern which John MacAulay had made for me, with that little sprung lift to its line, would not have the buoyancy. Within a minute or two the boat would be awash and there's no baling then. That's why the fishermen on Scalpay always ask me if I am going alone, why I am not taking anyone with me. Donald MacSween asks me every time: he smiles with the question, but not with his eyes. They say, 'You don't know what it will be like out there if something goes wrong. You would be safer with two.' I know he thinks that, but he has never once said it.

I have seen one of these boats sunk before, in the warm, still conditions of a quiet bay in the Hebrides. It had been out of the water for a while, the wood had shrunk and when it was launched, the sea poured in like miniature Niagaras between the strakes on either side, rippling down step by step into a widening pool in the bilges. In half an hour she was down to her gunwales. I watched entranced as she went under. It was a blessing, not a catastrophe. I could feel the wood absorbing the water and it was like giving a thirsty animal a drink, a gulping at the longed-for element. The boat looked buried in the sea that morning. She no longer had an existence independent of the water, but sat there still and submerged as if in jelly, an embalming of her life, neither sinking nor floating but absorbed by the water from which she was usually so distinct.

That is a picture you see all around the Hebrides in the early spring, as men who have kept their boats ashore in the winter sink them for a week or so before the summer fishing. Each is tethered to its mooring in the loch like a cow in her paddock. She is happy there ingesting the goodness around her. The season of fatness is to hand and her belly is filling. It is an image of contentment but it is also a prefiguring of something worse: what happens to these small open boats when caught out in the wrong weather. They do not sink but they fill. The sea invades them. All weight in the boat must be thrown out if it is not to pull the hull down. I kept a knife beside me in the stern, ready to cut the rope which was holding down my belongings amidships so that once the hull filled I too could throw everything away. The sea, Donald MacSween told me, would soon turn the boat over and your only chance of survival was to hold onto that upturned hull. It is not easy. The little ledges formed by one strake overlapping the next do provide the thinnest of rock climbers' footholds but the underwater profile is coated in the deliberately slimy Stockholm tar. As the weather worsens and the cold loosens your grip, the next big wave will wash you off into the sea. Then you are lost.

Records of boat losses are thin before 1800 but the nineteenth century in Lewis and Harris records again and again the loss of these boats and the drowning of their men. In February 1836, two boats from Point were caught out in a sudden gale. They were forced south before the wind, running for the Lochs coast at Cromore, just north of the Shiants. The crew of one boat survived. In the other, the four young men, inexperienced and perhaps underdressed, died of cold. Township after township lost their men. Year after year, boats went down from Barvas, Skigersta, in the district of Ness. In 1875 an oar was all that was found of a boat from Borve, coming ashore at Bragar. Two years later, a Bernera boat was lost with all its crew off the Flannans. Between 1862 and 1889, seventy fishermen from the district of Ness were drowned, in 1895, nineteen men from Back. Almost three hundred Lewis men were drowned in the second half of the nineteenth century, all of them within a few miles of their home shores, some of them watched by their families and friends as the small boats struggled to get home through the surf.

If the bodies came ashore, which they often didn't, they, like the boats, were smashed into pieces or rotted beyond recognition. It was the pattern all down the western seaboard of the British Isles. Poor soils drive men to boats in which they drown.

At the Shiants themselves, in the spring of 1881 four young fishermen from the village of Lemreway in Lochs came out to the islands to catch a few puffins. None of them was more than twenty years old: Murdo Macmillan, Norman's son; John Macinnes, Donald's son; Angus Ferguson, Murdo's son, and Donald Macdonald, Kenneth's son. That's how Dan Macleod, a retired merchant seaman, weaver, story-teller and the carrier of memories and traditions in Lemreway, described them to me. He tells the story in the way Hughie MacSween does, twisting his roll-up between his fingers, looking away to draw on the memory, looking at you to communicate it. Dan also gave me their addresses: the Macmillans lived at 1 Lemreway, the Fergusons at 3 Lemreway, the Macinneses at 5, the Macdonalds at 7. None of the boys was married. 'They were young boys,' Dan says. 'And they wouldn't be salting the puffins. They'd be giving them away.'

For several decades, probably since the beginning of the nine-teenth century, the Lemreway men had come out to the Shiants

in May and June to catch the puffins. In the 1850s, Osgood
Mackenzie, then still a boy, but in time the creator of the sub-
tropical gardens on his inherited estate at Inverewe, near Gairloch,
on the mainland, came out to the Shiants and witnessed the
Lemreway men catching the puffins: 'They brought back boat-
loads of them because they valued the feathers,' he wrote in his
autobiography.

> They also enjoyed big pots of boiled puffins for their dinners
> as a welcome change from the usual fish diet. They told us
> how they slaughter the puffins. They choose a day when
> there is a strong breeze blowing against the steep braes
> where the puffin breed, and the lads then lie on their backs
> on these nearly perpendicular slopes holding the butt-ends
> of their fishing rods. These stiff rods would be about nine
> or ten feet long [and almost certainly at this time made of
> bamboo]. Holding them with both hands, they whack at
> the puffins as they fly past them quite low in their tens of
> thousands, and whether the puffin is killed outright or only

stunned he rolls down the hill and tumbles on the shore
or into the sea, where the rest of the crew are kept busily
employed, gathering them into the boat.

It is possible to reconstruct something of the conditions in
May 1881. The steep braes to which Mackenzie refers are on the
north face of Garbh Eilean, a big, green, grassy bank, the grass
itself thickly enriched by the generations of puffin droppings that
have fallen on it. You cannot spend five minutes there without
being spattered yourself. The puffin bank faces the small rocky inlet
called simply Bagh, the Bay, and beyond it the Stream of the Blue
Men and the square outline of Kebock Head in Lewis. A strong
breeze blowing on to them, creating the conditions the fowlers pre-
ferred, would have been a northerly. That would also be the wind
that would carry the boys easily down southwards from Lemreway
to the Shiants. With an ebb tide under them, it would scarcely take
more than an hour to run down the six miles or so.

You can imagine the dream of the day. The colours which
drain out of the Hebrides in the winter, leaving the black rock
and grey turf as a monochrome ghost of the summer life, have
now begun to return. The lichen glows yellow on the rocks. The
off-lying skerries are pink with the thrift in flower. Fat red and
white campions make cushions in the nicks of the cliffs. The sea
is silk, patterned in the Stream of the Blue Men with the twisted
curls and table-top bubbles of the upwelling sea.

It would have been the same in the 1850s and the 1880s as it
is today: that glowing light, the notched outline of the mainland
to the east hazed by the rising sun, the hills of Skye still wrapped
in the morning clouds, the long broken back of the Hebrides
running down to south Harris, the Uists and to Barra, and the
Shiants hanging in the middle distance, a secret world, asking to
be visited.

The Lemreway boys in 1881 planned to stay overnight on the

islands. There was a shepherd and his family living there at the time. Donald Campbell, better known as Domhnall nan Eilean, or Donald of the Islands, had come over from Molinginish, a small township on the coast of Harris near the mouth of Loch Seaforth, twenty years before. He had his wife and children with him and together they lived in a good house of two rooms on the island, which had previously been called Eilean na Cille, the Island of the Church, but which they called Eilean an Tighe, House Island, the name it has today.

Summer was the time for visiting. Winters for the Campbells would have been lonely, but come April and May, with the stilling of the sea, the network of connections that have always bound the summer Shiants to the neighbouring islands, would re-emerge. Campbell's employer, the farmer and Stornoway merchant, Roderick Martin of Orinsay, would bring out to him the meal and other supplies he needed. The socks which the Campbell girls had knitted over the winter would be sold or even given to anyone visiting. Gentlemen in yachts might arrive to investigate the geology or the birds. There were plenty of diversions.

The fowlers, as a courtesy as much as anything else, would

have taken their boat to the anchorage just in front of the shepherd's house on the west side of Eilean an Tighe. Courtesy and hospitality remain the norm here. Even nowadays, when a stranger arrives and the shepherds happen to be there, the greetings are warm, welcoming and generous, far more than among English people in the same situation. 'Hallo, hallo, hallo, hallo, hallo, hallo,' I heard Donald 'Nona' Smith, one of the modern shepherds, say to a man landing on the beach here one day, a rising chorus of delighted welcome.

'Do you know him well?' I asked Nona later.

'No, I've never met him before,' he said. 'But you've got to be diplomatic.' There is no sense of anyone's isolation being invaded. Sociability has always included the Shiants. But it can only be presumed on to a certain extent. The Lemreway boys brought their own provisions with them, some oatmeal and perhaps some of the cod or ling they might have caught on the way down.

There is a patch of sandy grey mud on the sea-bed a hundred yards or so offshore in front of the house, and in a northerly it is protected from the worst of the sea. A cairn high on the hill may well be a mark of this anchorage. Its stones are hairy with a long-bearded lichen, and because lichen takes a long time to grow, that alone is a mark of its age. Although people are always ready to attribute seamarks in the Hebrides to the Norse, there is no real way of dating them. The boys would have dropped anchor, unstepped the mast, furled the sail and would have come ashore in their dinghy to the beach next to the Campbells' house.

The time of birds is the time of abundance, the season of summer-time adventure but the expedition to the Shiants of the Lemreway boys ended in disaster. Their boat, 'an Orkney-type boat, a double ender, a stout boat', Dan Macleod calls it, eighteen feet in the keel, a little longer than *Freyja*, had been safe enough overnight, protected from the northerlies by the bulk of Garbh

Eilean. It can be quite still in there even on a wild day. While you hear the groaning of the breakers on the other side a mile away, plunging their long tongues into the caves at the cliff foot and exploding inside them – a heavy, quarryman's boom reverberating through the island, at your feet, in the lee of the vast, whale body of Garbh Eilean, the water laps on the rocks and the eiders paddle from one inlet to another as if asking for bread in St James's Park.

The boys spent the night with the Campbells and were due to return home the following day – it was a Wednesday – but they never arrived. That evening, as Dan Macleod has written,

> their families, neighbours and friends gathered around scattered vantage points anxiously scanning the surface of the water to see if they could detect any sign of their loved ones' boat coming home. Alas, there was none and the young men's fathers resolved to sail out to the Shiants at first light the following day.

The party of fathers arrived at the shepherd's cottage, and Domhnall nan Eilean told them that the boys had stayed with him on the Tuesday night but when the wind changed direction on Wednesday morning, they had decided to move the boat to a more sheltered spot.

The wind had gone round to the south-west and stiffened. In that wind the anchorage off the house was the most exposed place on the Shiants and there was no way they could leave it there. In a southwesterly, the only usable place is in the shadow of the giant boulder screes that run along the eastern side of Garbh Eilean. Looking down from the cliff-top there on a sunny day, at low tide, with the light driving down through the twenty feet or so of water, in which the puffins and the other auks dive and dart for food, you can see the pale turquoise patch of sand into which boats can drop their anchor. All around are boulders, in which an anchor would get caught and could never be retrieved; or cobbles, through which the anchor would slither in a wind. That sandy patch is well tucked in, sheltered from the west by the block of land above it, and sheltered from the north by a narrow arm of the island which stretches out eastwards towards Eilean Mhuire.

It would have been tricky work, getting the dinghy away from the beach, with the sea coming straight on to them, then sailing the boat away from the now aggressive and surf-lined shore. These long-keeled, broad-beamed boats do not point high into the wind. You are lucky if you can bring the boat to within sixty degrees. The wind that day had become a gale. The seas as they arrived at the Shiant shore were kicking up into long, whitened combers, driving into the notches and crannies of the coastline where they burst into plumes reaching fifty or sixty feet on to the grass. But the boys knew what they were doing. Keeping just out from the shore, with the boat on a broad reach, they could make their way to the far corner of Garbh Eilean. Donald Campbell told their fathers that he had watched them get away, pulling with the oars to begin with and then hoisting the sail, covering the mile or so westwards at a fair pace, reaching the far point of Garbh Eilean, the headland called Stocanish, before disappearing around the corner.

No one can know what happened next. Out there, beyond Stocanish, in a southwesterly gale, with the tide ebbing southwards, can be as good a version of hell as the Hebrides can offer. I have taken *Freyja* in there on a bad day; not a gale but blowing perhaps Force 5 or 6 with the ebb coming down from Cape Wrath. The sea picks up. When you are in among it, there seems to be no pattern. It stands in little peaks all around you, like the points into which the whipped whites of egg can be made to stand. Or more like that miniature thorny landscape which is left behind if you pick one recently glued plank away from another.

As the two separate, the glue is pulled up into little pinnacles with sharp, cup-shaped valleys between them. There is no structure to this form, no readable order, just a little world of mobile chaos, a dancing three-dimensional spiky surface through which you can only hope to make your way. It is disconcerting even in a slight wind, the randomness of it, the unpredictability of those mobile pin-ranges, the lurching and jumping of the boat from one side to another, the steep little walls of sea that the wind makes against the tide, the picture of anarchy and its primordial threat. If you increase the energy in that system, if you turn a gale on to it, if you make these water pinnacles eight rather than four feet high, this stretch of sea would be unsailable.

After an hour or so the Campbells started to get worried. The Lemreway boys had not come back to the house. Donald sent his son John, a blond giant who was deaf and dumb, down to the beach connecting Garbh Eilean and Eilean an Tighe to see if he could make out what was happening in the bay. John returned, highly agitated, somehow communicating to his father the fact that the boat was not to be seen. It had vanished. The Lemreway boys had left their provisions in the Campbells' house. Clearly they had been intending to stay. Where were they now? The Campbells guessed, or so they told the Lemreway men the next day, that once the boys had got round the corner at Stocanish, they had thought they had better run for home. As soon as the fathers heard this from Donald Campbell, they knew the boat was lost, and without pause set off for the Lewis shore. They searched loch after loch there, hoping to find the boys sheltering from the storm, or driven in there perhaps with their gear broken. They nosed into all the corners of Loch Claìdh, into Bagh Ciarach, Loch Valamus, Loch Bhrollúm, at Camas Thomascro, at Mol Truisg and in the further reaches of Loch Sealg. Their sons were in none of them.

It wasn't a stupid exercise. The Lewis coast has always provided shelter from the Stream of the Blue Men but in 1881 the boys from Lemreway were never seen again. The rudder of the boat was found a little later washed up on the *Mol Bhan*, the blond beach, near Orinsay, a few miles west of Lemreway. Timber was scarce in the Hebrides and the rudder was used for more than forty years as a foot-bridge across the stream that runs down over its pale pebbles on to the beach there. It was the way people took back to the village from the peat-bank and nothing was more welcome, when loaded down with peats, than to find the stream properly bridged, an easy step or two across a difficult passage.

A few weeks later, a rudderless Orkney-built boat was found drifting around Cape Wrath, seventy-five miles away to the north. It was recognised by the Lewis fishermen who came across it as the boat that had been lost at the Shiants. There were sickles stowed away in the gunwale. Shortly before the boys had taken the boat to the islands, it had been used for gathering the seaweed that was to be spread on the fields just before the spring sowing of the oats and the barley. The sickles had been left aboard, jammed between the gunwale and the stringer. The sea had clearly turned the boat over twice: once to drown Murdo Macmillan, John Macinnes, Angus Ferguson and Donald Macdonald, and once to set it on its way again to Cape Wrath, with its cargo of sickles intact.

In 1910, another generation of boys, this time from the village of Gravir, just north of Lemreway, set off on the same summer expedition for the Shiants. The party included fourteen-year-old Donald MacPhail. It was the 'last sad summer of my boyhood', as he wrote as an old man, before he was sent away as a scholar to the Nicolson Institute, the secondary school in Stornoway, to fulfil his father's ambitions for him to have 'a gentleman's job, chained to a desk, a school room, pulpit or doctor's surgery.' He was going to make the best of his last weeks of freedom.

One fine day, with three other boys, I decided to make a hail and farewell trip to the Shiant Islands. My father was away fishing, and my mother did not like the idea very much; however my heart was set on the trip and after getting up early and packing some food and drink in a small cask, we set sail, swathed in the calm early morning sunshine.

When they arrived, they 'roamed all over the island, collected a lot of eggs and watched the thousands of birds that assembled on the cliffs. We had taken shotguns and ammunition and passed the time away shooting at the puffins.'

Only on the way home from their puffin-shooting trip did the schoolboy crew find themselves in trouble. As they left the Shiants, the wind that day seemed suddenly to get up from the north-west – almost precisely the direction they needed to go – and the boat had far too little weight in it to push itself into the wind.

The bright calmness of the morning gave way to a darkening moody sky and we began to have difficulty beating against the wind in our light, unballasted boat. As the sea got choppy we shortened the sail and had to take it in turns to bale out furiously as the spray washed over the boat making it harder for us to steer and retain control.

Eventually, after many hours, late in the evening, they managed to get into the shelter of Kebock Head, tucked in under its big brutish cliffs, which could protect them from the northwesterlies. A little pool of still water lay under the lee of the headland itself. There they had to wait on their oars, unable, with this wind, to sail up Loch Odhairn into Gravir. At midnight, the boys heard the thudding note of a propeller. They set light to a tarred rag and attracted the attention of a trawler which towed them home. Their parents were out searching on the headlands and nobody noticed the trawler coming into the loch bringing their sons in from the sea. The last hope, so they guessed, was that the boys might be sheltering under Kebock Head, and the Gravir families made their way there across the moor. 'When they arrived at the Cabag [the Gaelic spelling of Kebock Head] and discovered that there was no sign of our whereabouts they feared the worst.' Donald MacPhail put the experience behind him. 'The menacing mass of the Shiant Islands,' he wrote many years later, 'never again held any mystery for me. Only a painful memory. My father saw to that.'

A famous and beautiful Gaelic song, still sung at ceilidhs and in the great annual competition, the Mod, can stand for all the laments over those who have drowned in the Shiant seas. In the spring of 1786, the young and handsome Allan Morrison, a shipmaster from Stornoway, who usually traded between Lewis and the Isle of Man, took his boat down the coast of Lewis to Scalpay, where he was to be engaged to Annie Campbell, Campbell of Scalpay's daughter. In the Stream of the Blue Men, off the Shiants, the wind turned, as it does, his boat was swamped and he and all his crew drowned. Annie Campbell, broken with grief, wasted away and soon died herself. There is no burying ground on Scalpay. The soil is too thin and still today the Scalpay dead are carried over to the sandy soils on the Atlantic side at Luskentyre to be buried. Annie Campbell's father took her body in a coffin by boat to the most distinguished of all the burying grounds in Harris, at Rodel, in the south-eastern corner of the island. On the way there, another storm came up at them and to lighten the boat, the coffin had to be thrown overboard.

Soon afterwards, the body of Allan Morrison was found washed up on the shore of the Shiants and a few days later Annie's body was found at the same place.

The song – this is the Shiants' only brush with Hollywood: it was sung in the film Rob Roy – is in the voice of Annie Campbell, grieving on Scalpay for her lost lover. It survives in many versions, some of them still sung in Cape Breton, in Canada, where the descendants of emigrating Hebrideans took it in the nineteenth century.

Brown-haired Allan, *ó hì*, I would go with thee;
hó rì rì rì u ho, e o hùg hoireann ó,
Brown-haired Allan, *ó hì*, I would go with thee.

I am tormented,
I have no thought for merriment tonight
but only for the sound of the elements
and the strength of the gales . . .
And brown-haired Allan, my darling sweetheart,
I heard you had gone across the sea
on the slender black boat of oak . . .
Brown-haired Allan, my heart's darling,
I was young when I fell in love with you.
Tonight my tale is wretched.
It is not the tale of the death of cattle in the bog
but of the wetness of your shirt
and of how you are being torn by the whales.
I would drink a drink, in spite of everyone,
of your heart's blood,
after you had been drowned.

4

I TAKE THE BOAT SLOWLY in to the beach. Her iron-shod stem slides, grates and then halts on the stones. I jump ashore and push the small grapnel anchor between the shingle. It is a way of pinning the boat to the island. However seasick I feel, this of course is the moment. I am walking at last on the familiar shore, awash with the familiarities of the place: the slip of one stone against another, the smell of the seaweed rotting in the nostrils, knowing without even watching them the flickering presence of the birds as they take this route between the islands, the great inviting wings of land spreading out on all sides, the surge and draw of the sea on the shingle. And above all that, the core sensation of island life: knowing the world is held at arm's length by that sea, afloat on the privacy, buoyed up by the knowledge that here I am alone. It can, oddly enough, be a shared feeling. I remember arriving here one morning with John Murdo Matheson, the young shepherd from Gravir, a man, if this is possible, more in love with the Shiants than I am. We were waving goodbye on the beach to the fishing boat that had brought us, watching its wake curve around the rocks of Garbh Eilean, and he said to me, not looking at me, but our shoulders rubbing,

'It's as if the world's been cut off with a knife, isn't it, Adam?'

But now I am alone and I inspect the place, the first time I have been here since the previous autumn. It is like looking through old letters, a slowly growing recognition of a well-known thing, its atmosphere stealing up on you, enveloping you like the smell of bread from an oven. Your body remembers the movements of island life: the hauling of the boat up the beach, the tying it on to the mooring ring, the touch of sun for a moment, the endless wind, as if you were listening all day to the whispered roaring in a shell held up to your ear.

But the beach looks odd. In summer, it extends between Garbh Eilean and Eilean an Tighe in a smooth and well graded expanse of pebbles, cleanly sifted and sorted in a shallow grey arc between the rocks of the islands on either side. Now, in April, it looks as if a team of bulldozers have been at work over the winter. The enormous volume of stone which in summer makes up the centre of the beach, one hundred and fifty yards of it, thirty feet high and a hundred across, has been shouldered aside, roughly barged into mounds which are humped up against the rock buttresses of the islands. This is the work of the winter storms, an unthinkable battering. A third of the fence posts along the cliff edge are broken off at their base, pieces of perfectly good square-section timber, four inches by four, snapped and held now by the wire they were meant to support. Posts don't last long. After they have been here a year or two, the winter wind has so picked away at the wood that they have returned to younger versions of themselves. The little side stems of slightly harder timber which had been buried by later growth as knots, have withstood the eroding wind and now stand out from the shrunken post as truncated branches. Each post looks like a fossil tree.

I unload *Freyja*, piling my belongings on the beach above the rising tide. It takes half an hour. Then I row *Freyja* out to a depth where she will not ground at low tide, anchor her there, inflate the dinghy, row ashore, pull the dinghy up the beach and tie it fast to the wrought iron rings which are hammered into cracks in the rocks.

The landing beach is two hundred yards or so from the house and everything must be carried up over a small rocky rise and then along a level grassy platform to the door of the house. It is, through sheer repetition, the most familiar two hundred yards of the islands, as known to me as the knots in the desk on which I write or the feeling of my teeth to my tongue: the slightly awkward shuffles across that rock step; the point where the path crosses a smooth piece of turf, next to the boulder on which a pincushion of thrift produces two or three blooms in the summer; the little spring, just beyond the small ridge that separates it from the beach, where the path curves round above the shore. The spring is stone-lined, with rushes fringing its edges and a flat stone placed at its lip, on which a bucket can stand while you fill it. Past two ruins of abandoned houses, through a patch of nettles and there, on its little coastal shelf, with the silverweed thick around it, and all the pens and fences in which the sheep are gathered for the marking of the lambs in May, the shearing in July and the autumn cull, you come to the house.

Although I love the building, it is in truth, little more than a shelter in a storm. This is, at heart, the house occupied by the Campbells at the end of the nineteenth century, built for them by their landlord, Patrick Sellar, the Mathesons' tenant, in the 1870s. The Campbells left the Shiants in 1901, and in the next twenty years or so the house partially collapsed, losing a gable. In 1926, the novelist Compton Mackenzie, who owned the islands at the time, rebuilt it. Mackenzie only ever stayed here for a day or two at a time and the house remains almost exactly as he left it: primitive. Its stone walls are pebble-dashed – 'harled' is the Scottish term – and have been painted over and over again with Snowcem, a white cement-based paint. It has a tin roof on which the rain patters and across which the wind for some reason roars. Perhaps the attic space makes a kind of sounding box. There are two small rooms, one to the north, one to the south, each with a fireplace in the gable-end wall and both panelled with tongue-and-grooved lining board. It is, from time to time, rat-infested. The rats skitter across the roof, climb down the chimneys and make their nests between the panelling and the stone behind it. There is no electricity, lavatory or running water but it is possible with a good fire going, and a glass or two of whisky, to make the house feel snug and happy, a glow of inner warmth and outer on the faces of everyone around the table. And it can be beautiful on a summer morning, with the day bright outside, to sit in the kitchen, writing at the table there, the thick walls keeping the house cool in the heat, the light coming through the open door, the quiet self-sufficiency of the house a measure of contentment and containment. If it is always a little severe on arrival – cold, ratty; not much of a human habitation – an hour or two of a lit fire, of cleaning the surfaces, lighting the paraffin lamps, somehow driving out the sense that you are not entirely welcome here, in other words rehumanising the shell of it, and the house begins to acquire a certain friendliness. People have often been happy here and the walls have absorbed some of that delight.

I don't mind this crudity. It is quite unfeminine. There are no curtains. I am afraid to say that the smears and scrabblings which the rats have left on the walls since they were last painted four or five years ago are still there. The hook from which my father suspended his bags of food in the 1930s still hangs from the ceiling. The guttering candles and smoking lanterns have coated the ceilings with a film of grey soot. Women don't like it much. Compton MacKenzie could never persuade his wife to stay there with him. My own mother only went once and never again. Sarah, my wife, has braved it twice but not with much enthusiasm and will not, I think, return. Although in the 1930s, and again after the war, picnics of fishing families from Scalpay went out there for the day, the women sitting on the grass in their floral prints and their cardigans, this is not now a female place. Of course, for centuries it must have been as much woman's as man's country, but the islands' modern isolation has masculinised them, as though they have become part of the sea, which is the male domain. 'You see that hill there?' Joan MacSween, the widow of a fisherman on Scalpay said to me, 'That's as near as I would ever like to get to the sea.' She was pointing at a rock outside her front door. The shepherds now never take their wives or girlfriends.

After dumping my belongings in the house, and gathering some driftwood and lighting a fire, the first task is to collect some water. I keep a bucket and a shallow dish in the house. There are five or six wells along the foot of the cliff that lines the landward edge of the island's coastal strip. One or two have beach cobbles arranged around them, to make them easier to use. Others are scarcely more than scoops in the turf, in which the water seeping from the hill naturally gathers. None is datable. A friend of my father's relined one with the stones he found nearby twenty years ago. Now, although the water-level in it is for some reason a little lower than before, there is no telling it from the others. It might as well have been done a thousand years ago.

The best well at the moment is about a hundred yards from the house. A large piece of driftwood acts as its cover. Silverweed fringes it and a flake of the lichen on the rocks sometimes falls off into the water where it floats as a shallow scooped raft. Water boatmen skid in from either side. It is no good if you plunge the bucket deep into the pool. All you are left with is a brownish and unappetising bucket of stirred-up, peaty soup. But if you take the shallow dish and allow no more than a sixteenth of an inch to slip in over the brim, filling the dish with no disturbance to the body of the water in the pool, you will slowly acquire a bucket of clean, fresh spring water filtered from the hill above.

This gathering of the Shiants' sweet water, which has never, even in the driest summers, run out, always feels to me like an engagement with one of the oldest layers in the place. Where the materials like this are constant, and the uses to which they are put will always be the same whatever your beliefs, or language, or habit of mind, history collapses. It is as if time has not passed. This delicate sipping at an island spring is the same now as it must always have been. That is the key to something central about the Shiants. History does not move here in a single current, sweeping everything up into one comprehensive pattern of change, but in a laminar flow, different sheets of time moving at different rates, one above the other, like the currents in the sea. At the lowest level, the coldest and oldest, there is virtually no movement. Life down there is still. Gather the water at the well and you are performing a Bronze Age act. Dig over the peaty soil in the vegetable garden and you are doing what has been done here in the Middle Ages. Call Sarah on the mobile phone and you are doing something that wasn't possible until the late 1990s. This is not, as people so often say of a landscape, a manuscript on which the past has been written and erased over and over again. It is a place in which many different times coexist, flowing at different speeds, enshrining different worlds.

In early spring, the place is paddled flat by the flock of barnacle geese that live here in the winter. The grass lies down where they have trampled it and looks like the hair of a teenager; unwashed, brownish, greased. All over the surface of the islands – particularly on Eilean Mhuire and the southern end of Eilean an Tighe, called Mianish – lie the goose droppings from the flock. Most of them, according to Calum MacSween, Compton Mackenzie's grazing tenant here, only arrived after the Campbells had left in 1901. Their droppings, MacSween said, 'spoiled the water in the Mary Island pools, which until then had been sweet all year.' They certainly aren't now: foetid, sour to look at, too pea-green even to be tasted. But the geese themselves are worth it. Walk down to Mianish along the western shore of Eilean an Tighe, past the lazybeds that rim the first bay, across the little burn that runs to the shore in one of the dips between the ridges, clamber carefully across the black-lichened rocks – a lichen that grows only in the splash zone where the storms can reach it and the grass will not grow for the saltiness – keep your head down, out of sight of the flock, not disturbing the sheep either, which would alert the geese, and try to come on the birds at their grazing. A dog, of course, with all its carelessness, would be a disaster and cannot be allowed. Previously, without much of a shift in mentality, I would have had a gun with me. Certainly the early twentieth-century shepherds, Calum MacSween, and his nephew, Donald Macleod (DB as he was known, Donald Butcher), shot their goose dinners when they came to the Shiants early in the year, when the geese were still in the Hebrides, and again on the final visits in November, before the winter closed in, putting the tups on the islands. Then the geese had returned from their breeding grounds in the far north. The barnacles made a better roast, I am told, than the greylag, but were downier. The man plucking them, or so Hugh MacSween maintains, would emerge 'looking like Father Christmas', the mass of fine white feathers clogged in his stubble.

I am here to look. I feel more protective of the barnacle geese than of any other animal on the Shiants. They are the winter-spirits of the place. Hardly anyone else comes here in March or early April. The place is more private then. None of the modern train of yachts which anchor in the bay on summer nights dares cross the equinoctial Minch. The private winter islands are the realm of the geese. Come on them slowly. They are scattered across the grass, black and white – white chest and head, a black bib and neck, a black back next to which the wings are barred with grey and white stripes which from a distance gives the effect of moiré or ruffled silk, as elegant and concordant a crowd as the racegoers in *My Fair Lady*, perhaps four hundred of them, relentlessly pecking away at the ground beneath their feet, looking up now and then, a wary eye, but then face-down again to the grass, tugging at the stems, eating, eating. They are busy. This is no holiday. There is none of that standing around, displaying to each other, socialising, or looking bored, which the puffins and other fish-eating birds do later in the year. The goose's life is dictated by its intestines. Even these barnacle geese, a smaller and more delicate version of the Canada goose, need to eat all the hours the day gives them. They are flying herbivores and that is their difficulty. Fish-eating birds can acquire the protein hit they need in a few sharp, efficient dives. A cow can invest in an enormous set of stomachs, through which the tough grass stems can be serially fed, slowly digesting the cell walls of the plant within which the most nutritious proteins and sugars are locked. But as the American naturalist David Quammen has written, 'A Hereford is not obliged to cope with the delicate physics of flight.' A goose can't afford all those voluminous stomachs. It can't even afford to have a stomach that is full. Overladen, it would never fly. As a result, most of what a goose eats passes straight through it in a couple of hours. That's why a goose is as loose as a goose, and that's why the Shiants in the early spring-time are carpeted in their droppings.

They are as innocent and flighty as deer. The flock moves in its grazing like a shoal, a turn of a few degrees communicated somehow at the same instant throughout the pack. There is an ever-present suggestion of a tremor even in the way they stand and walk. But for all the beauty of that sight, that million-fingered responsiveness, this land-life on the grass seems to be no more than an interruption to their favoured state. They belong in the air. Lift yourself for a moment, so that more than your eyes and

hat appear above the geese's horizon and it is as if you have blown a breath of wind across the flock. The four hundred of them rise and shimmer like a single piece of cloth lifted by the breeze. The edge of the crowd nearest you moves first, and that beautiful supple sheet of the rest of them follows on with the same ripples in their white heads and black necks, the same slow crooner's elasticity in the muscles, and same ineffable languor, all synchronised as if tied by invisible threads. A human crowd, suddenly made aware of a threat or danger, would shatter, each shard dispersing as if shot. The flock of geese does the opposite, more whole in the air than it had been on the ground, turning on the wind, a single wing, before beating out over the Minch, down over the small, grassless rock at the southern tip of Eilean an Tighe, Sgeir Mianish ('the rock of the middle headland' in Gaelic-cum-Norse) before flogging over into the wind to the equally inviting grass on Eilean Mhuire, a mile and a half away to the east, a coughing, guttural chatter as they pass.

I may be drawn to them but they don't care for me. They are only here because people like me so rarely are. I have pursued them once but once only. Having disturbed them down on Mianish, I walked the mile back to the beach where the dinghy was tied up, launched it, rowed the mile across the bay to the landing place on Eilean Mhuire, hauled the dinghy up the beach there, climbed the two hundred feet up to the top of that island, walked the half mile down to its eastern tip, the promontory called Seann Chaisteal, the Old Castle, only to see the flock which had been grazing happily there for an hour since I had last disturbed them, lift with that wonder grace, a slow-motion departure, back across the tide-rippled sea to the headland where I had first encountered them.

Sometimes looking up from digging the garden, or sorting out the boat, or collecting firewood from the beach, I will see the flock of Shiant geese strung out against the sky, or wheeling in the gusts that ripple and billow off the back of Garbh Eilean. It is only a question of time before they leave, at some time in April. This is the gateway to summer and I have never witnessed it. All that I have ever noticed is a sudden absence. The paddled turf, the ubiquitous droppings, even the weather, all seem the same, but the geese have gone. It is like a death, or the descent of Proserpina into Hell, a removal of that life-presence which animates a place. The Shiants, then, are like an island from which the inhabitants have been cleared. Nothing has changed except the thing that changes everything.

Not until the nineteenth century did anyone understand this disappearance of the goose and its sudden re-emergence at the end of the year. There was a general belief that the birds hibernated somewhere or other, an idea that went back to Pliny and Aristotle before him. The barnacle goose was thought, but only by the credulous, to retreat into and later emerge from the goose barnacle, a crustacean which attaches itself like a mollusc to the rocks and has a shell which resembles the beak of goose. There is no need to be too condescending about this: still no one has any idea, for example, of what happens to the basking shark in winter. They disappear every autumn only to reappear the following spring. Whether they go out into the mid-Atlantic, or swim south to warm waters or hibernate on the sea floor, it remains invisible to us, and unknown.

There is a strange connection between the Shiants and the question of disappearing birds. According to the late-nineteenth-century Roman Catholic priest and folklorist, Father Allan McDonald of Eriskay, 'the corncraik and stonechat are called *eoin shianta* on account of their disappearance in winter. The opinion is that they are dormant all winter, and that they should be so and not die makes people consider them eerie or uncanny or *sianta*.'

Certainly, that word runs true to the experience of a bird that departs without warning. The emptiness it leaves is haunted by the retinal image of its presence. You feel for a few days that the geese must still be there and that you are simply failing to see them. It is then that the Shiants come to feel like eerie islands.

The Gaelic word probably lies behind the Shiants. 'Si' in Gaelic is pronounced 'sh' and *'sianta'* transliterates as 'shanta'. The 'i' in the modern spelling of the word, which is a phonetic transcription of the Gaelic, is a mistake. Either 'Siant' or 'Shant', not 'Shiant', is the way it should be spelled and pronounced. Only those reading from maps ever say 'Sheeant'. The Old Irish word *sén*, meaning 'a blessing' or 'a charm', derives eventually from the Latin *signum*, meaning a sign of any sort, especially the sign of the cross. From that comes the verb *sénaim*: 'to bless', 'to make holy'. Its passive participle in Old Irish is *sénta*, a word which evolved in modern Irish Gaelic into *séanta*, meaning 'consecrated', 'hallowed' or 'charmed', with a haze of meanings hovering around its outer edges meaning 'haunted', 'spooky', 'otherworldly'. This is the word which is often spelled in Scottish Gaelic *sianta*.

Examples of the name are scattered across Gaelic Scotland. There are sacred mountains in Jura, near Callander and in Ardnamurchan, all called Beinn Sheunta. There is a Loch Seunta, 'Holy Loch', in Cowal, and a cave, an Uaimh Shianta, 'the hallowed' or 'the sacred', in Applecross. There is a Shian Wood north of Oban and a stone circle at Shian Bank in Perthshire. In Skye, Martin Martin described a Loch Siant in the seventeenth century, of which the water was thought to cure diseases. There is a brackish Loch Shient in North Rona, although the derivation of that may be different, describing the sea spray with which the pool is filled. Most curiously of all, there is a record, in one of the Irish Chronicles for the second half of the fifth century, of the Isle of Man having its name changed 'from Inis Falga to "Ellan Shiant", that is "The Holy Isle"'.

The Shiant Islands, full of magnificence and strangeness, protected by the Stream of the Blue Men, standing out in the Minch tall, mysterious and beautiful, a challenge and an invitation to any man with a boat and a modicum of courage along hundreds of miles of coastline from Sutherland to Skye and from Ness to Barra, said, as so many of these islands are, to have been the hermitage of a Celtic saint in the Dark Ages: these are the Holy Islands of the Minch.

Most of the names of places on the Shiants are Gaelic and not particularly rich in association or significance. They describe parts of the islands in the way a Crusoe would, by looking at them, by saying what they are, rather than by associating them with anything that might have happened there in the distant past. So there is a Big Beach, a Beach with Boulders, a Washing Place, a Cormorant Head, some Rocks of the Bay, a Seal Point, the Kittiwake Rocks, the Hole of the Seals – the natural arch at the north-east corner of Garbh Eilean – and the Point of the Fank (the gathering place for sheep on Eilean Mhuire). Most of these still have the attributes by which they are named. Sheep are still gathered on Eilean Mhuire at the Bid na Faing. The seals do indeed lounge and wail on the point that is named after them. There is a kittiwake colony not far from their rocks, and there are shags (the Gaelic word *sgarbh* does not distinguish between a cormorant and a shag) forever standing with their arms outstretched, drying their feathers on the point named after them.

Almost certainly, most of these names are quite recent and do not embody a long tradition. They may well have been given by the shepherds who came here seasonally in the early nineteenth century, after the old Shiant population had left. The Ordnance Survey officers, when recording these names in the 1850s, used as their authority a Neil Nicolson or Nicholson (he couldn't spell) from the village of Stemreway in Lewis. He may not have known the place very well. The surveyors could speak no Gaelic, and so in this way, here as elsewhere in the Gaelic world, much of the information that might have been gathered was lost. The Shiants must once have had a rich suite of names in which the lives of its inhabitants were folded into the landscape and recorded there, but they will never be recovered. A Harris woman, Christina Shaw, when interviewed a few years ago by the ethnographer Morag MacLeod, told her: 'There wasn't the length of between here and the gate that we didn't have a name for, which is not the case nowadays. Every ben and every mound and every hill ... I could name them all.' All of that has been lost from the Shiants.

Here and there, something older can be traced. The islands are set in a Viking sea. Every prominent headland and inlet around them, every stretch of water, and village after village, township after township on Lewis, were named by the Norse. There are three identifiably Norse place names on the Shiants themselves: Stocanish on Garbh Eilean ('the Headland near the Sea Stacks'), the mile-long line of the Galtas offshore (perhaps 'the Sea Gables') and Mianish on Eilean an Tighe, meaning either 'the Narrow Headland' (which it is) or, more intriguingly, 'the Middle Headland', which it also is when approaching the islands by sea from the south. A Dublin Viking, making his way back north, would see Mianish stretching out towards him in the haze, the Middle Head, around which the flood tide rips. All three of these Norse places on the Shiants are precisely those which any sailor would need to mark and remember. Other than that, apart from one glowing exception which I shall come to in later chapters, the place-names of the Shiants record not memories but forgetfulness, the washing away of human lives, the fragility and tissue-thin vulnerability of human culture to the erosion of time.

When I realised that the geese had finally gone, I went to stand on the heights of Garbh Eilean, nearly six hundred feet above the Minch at its most languorous and seductive. The sky was draped with the weightless trails of evening clouds. They were the colours

of the prayer flags which Buddhists leave on mountain passes and their brightness had been bleached by wind and sun. Below them, in the stillness of the evening, every inch of the horizon was rimmed with distant sunlit mountains. My eye travelled them like a fell runner. Even to name the hills is a roll-call of ancestors, the Shiants' own king list. In Sutherland, eighty miles away to the north-east, Foinaven and Ben Stack. Going south, Quinag above Assynt, Suilven and Stac Polly. Above Loch Broom, Coigach matches the ragged notches of An Teallach on its southern side. Behind Gairloch is Beinn Eighe in Torridon, south of that, Beinn Bhan behind Applecross. Each mountain in what Martin Martin called 'the opposite Continent', is the bass note to the human settlement at its feet. The eye swings around to Rona, Raasay and northern Skye, each wrinkle in the rock picked out by the last of the light. In the distance, with only their upper reaches appearing over the foreground, are the Cuillins and the strange flat summits of Macleod's Tables above Dunvegan. On the clearest days, Heaval, the mountain on Barra, is visible past the headlands of

Waternish and Dunvegan. Hecla and Beinn Mhor follow in South Uist; a gap and then the shark fin of Eaval, the unmistakable signpost for anyone sailing south in the Minch, the islands in the Sound of Harris; then Roineabhal, the hill above Rodel, which for years was under threat of removal by the workings of a super-quarry. If the catastrophe should happen and permission were ever granted, five hundred and fifty million tons of it would be dug out over a period of sixty years and this wrinkled horizon would have changed for the first time since the Ice Age. North of it come the mountains of North Harris, the round bull-seal head of The Clisham, the hills of Pairc and Eishken, before the eye swings up to the north-west, to the low mound of Muirneag, north of Stornoway, and the long flat headlands of Lewis beside it. Only then is there a gap in the list, an opening in the ring, and there you look out to the North Atlantic. Nothing till Spitsbergen.

Compton Mackenzie said when he stood here that he felt 'swung between heaven and earth'. No place I know feels more like the centre of the universe.

5

SOMETIMES, EARLY IN THE SPRING, around the middle of April, before any true signs of summer arrive, when the grass on the islands is still dull and tawny from the rigours of winter, when the sheep are poor and thin and an air of exhaustion hangs over the place, a break can come in the weather which seems like a gift from Heaven. Stillness is wrapped around the Shiants for a day or two and the sun bathes their cold, bruised limbs. Once, ten or twelve years ago, I was there on my own when one of these openings came. I watched it in the sky, arriving from the south. The clouds folded back towards me, like the ravelling up of a screen, leaving behind them a sky as pale as an eighteenth-century ceiling, in which the colour went from blue to pale blue, and at the horizon scarcely blue at all.

I could feel the islands sighing in the light, their pores expanding, the vegetable life reaching out from its winter retreat. It seemed to me then – it is the only time I have ever witnessed it – that as the days went on, opening each morning to another new brightness, I could see the Shiants beginning to move towards their summer condition, like the pelt of an animal as it regains its health, the big flanks of Garbh Eilean greening between the ribs of rock, the tight winter-bitten surface of Eilean Mhuire softening under the millions of grass tips and sorrel shoots prodding up into the light, the body of Eilean an Tighe turning towards the vivid luxuriance of its summer life.

I only had a small dinghy with me then and the calm meant I could take it around to the north side of Garbh Eilean. For weeks at a time when the weather is bad you can't visit that northern face, because in any kind of sea it is terrifying, thrashed at by the Minch and merciless in the way it would deal with any boat. When the calm descends, that is the place, more than any other, to which I am drawn. It is where you can sense the Shiants' power, a place of turbulence only ever encountered in tranquillity.

I rowed the boat around, slipped easily through the natural arch at the corner of Garbh Eilean, where, every time you pass, a black guillemot drops out of the cracks in the ceiling on to the sea and then panics and flusters away to the north. The boat slides out across the liquid glass of the Minch. The seals asleep on the skerries wake, stare, shuffle seawards and plunge horrified into the water. The boat rounds the corner of those rocks and then the Shiants reveal their heroic heart. A curtain of columns half a mile long, five hundred feet high and each column up to eight or nine feet wide, drops into the Minch. The black lichen of the splash zone coats them to a height of a hundred feet or more. They bend slowly as they rise from the sea, a wonderful subtle elasticity in the mass. On calm days you can take a dinghy right up to the cliff foot, the boat just nosing and brushing at the giant forms. Afloat on the ink of the green sea, it is like being in the elephant house at the zoo, intimate with hugeness, pushed up next to a herd of still, alien, unembraceable bodies.

This was how William Daniell, the early nineteenth-century topographer of the British shore, portrayed the Shiants in his pair of 1819 aquatints: a vastness of form, a solidity and scale of presence, a tranquil sea passive at their feet.

I had this picture on the wall of my room at school and it remains a consoling image for me. Daniell does not attempt any heroics, any wild dynamism in the picture. He portrays the islands as a place of quiet, with a glow in the light and the huge, brooding stability of the cliffs behind them.

It never lasts. The Atlantic drives its next weather system on towards the islands and that sullen, lit beauty is taken up and twisted into a new and familiar frenzy. The Shiants' temper is like a child's: unbidden, unexplained rage; sudden quiet; a new paroxysm as total as the one before. Awake at night in the house, I lie listening to the weather. I see the Shiants as if from above, laid out beneath the storm. The cloud shadows beat across them. The swells cram themselves, one after another, through the natural arch, filling it, forty feet high and thirty wide, a tube of white water a hundred yards long, squeezed in there, until they burst out on the far side, released into huge, disintegrating flowerheads of surf. The cliffs and the islands are unmoved. Besieged by the Minch, they remain there, black, impassive and irreducible.

It is tempting to see the Shiants in that way. Perhaps any island owner would like to think of his property as a hedge against erosion but it couldn't be more wrong. I once spent a few days on the Shiants with a pair of geologists and under their steady rational analysis all idea of the island fortress was soon whittled away. It was a highly enjoyable experience. Fergus Gibb, the Reader in Igneous Petrology at Sheffield University, and his friend Mike Henderson, now Research Professor of Petrology at Manchester University, both know more about the Shiant rocks than anyone on earth. They have been studying the islands since the 1960s and in a small dinghy they guided me around the cliffs and shore, pointing out to me where the story of the Shiants was to be found.

It was a charming, affectionate and mutually impatient double act. Fergus – Mike calls him Fergie – is the more bullish and macho of the two. He plays tennis for the Yorkshire Veterans, talks with fervour about 'stonking great sledge-hammers', likes to give things 'welly', wears dark glasses and short-sleeved tartan shirts, and looks after Mike, whose balance on the rocks is uncertain. Fergus's big seamen's stockings are always pulled up over his trousers to his knees. He takes charge and one falls into line. Mike – knitted wool tie, glasses, green V-neck, baseball cap well down on the brow– plays the complementary role. He and his wife Joan are keen on organic food, a certain kind of witty late nineteenth-century novel and the finer of the performing arts. Mike must be the only geologist in the world who has had a ballet dedicated to him and the first thing he asked me, as I sat him down to a supper of roast lamb in the house on the Shiants, was what I thought of *Giselle*.

Neither talks of immovability or irreducibility. They are engaged with something richer and deeper: the huge, slow dynamism of this extraordinary place. Everything in the geologist's mind is a symptom of something happening. We layman landscapists may see the thing itself, the immovable rock, the huge columns, the stand of swaying bamboo, the Elizabethan ruff, the clustered organ pipes; they see the process, the mineralisation, the conductive cooling, the developing faults. 'Don't think of what it is,' Fergus said to me. 'Think of how it came to be.'

The Shiants, or at least most of them, are about fifty-eight and a half million years old. They are formed from a series of hot, intrusive magmas, giant plugs of molten rock rising from deep within the Earth's mantle, which squeezed between much older fossil-bearing rocks above them. The process is about as dramatic, and as unlocal as it could be. The 'emplacement' of the magma was part of an event of planetary scale. About sixty million years ago, a whole zone of the Earth's crust began to come under immense strain. Whether the weakness in the crust caused the upwelling of hot rock from deep below; or whether the upwelling of the magma, a huge bubble of heat and energy in the mantle, caused the weakness in the crust, is not certain. What is sure is that this was a stretched, tensed time. Heavy convection currents in the mantle, rising in a plume beneath this spot, put the whole of the Hebrides under pressure. A boil covering half a continent wanted to burst. The whole depth of the Earth's crust was being stretched here, one part being pulled south-west, the other north-east. The result was one of the most cataclysmic episodes in the history of Britain. The precise geography of this is still not quite clear but it is certain that the enormous volcanic outpourings would have been visible from another planet. Signs of the rift system run from Disco and Nunavik on the west coast of Greenland, to Kangertittivaq on the east coast, out to Jan Mayen Island, deep within the Arctic Circle, besieged by drift ice, across tens of thousands of square miles of what is now the North Atlantic, through Iceland, the Faeroes, Rockall and St Kilda, down through the Shiants, all the way through Skye and the Inner Hebrides, to Staffa and the Giant's Causeway in Antrim, on to Slieve Gullion and the Mountains of Mourne, before ending in the granite of Lundy in the Bristol Channel.

The rift may perhaps have been the first attempt at the opening of an Atlantic Ocean. If so, the Hebrides would have been pulled apart. Floating in *Freyja* between the islands, I am directly above one of the world's great might-have-beens. From within the centre of the Shiants, America and Europe would have moved slowly away, eased apart on giant conveyor belts of hot rock in the mantle. The Galtas and Garbh Eilean would now be off the coast of a New England shore made principally of the old and twisted rocks of Lewisian gneiss which form the Outer Hebrides. Eilean Mhuire would be the westernmost island of Europe, looking out not to the screes and green puffin slopes of Garbh Eilean, a mile away, as it now does, but across three thousand miles of grey Atlantic.

It didn't happen. The rift never opened beyond a slit. The Atlantic opened to the west of Rockall and the Hebrides remained whole. All that is left of this cataclysmic episode now are the roots and the remnants. Nearly sixty million years of erosion has done its work and almost nothing of the surface landscape which this vulcanism produced now survives. The great mountain punctuation points of the volcanic province, Slieve Gullion and Mourne themselves, the hills of Mull and Ardnamurchan, the Cuillins of Rum and Skye, represent only the hardened footings of the enormous volcanoes through which this spasm of the Earth's intestinal juices were vented on to the surface.

The Scotland into which the lavas poured was tropical and paradisical. America, Britain, and the Europe of which it was a part, would have been unrecognisable then. Lotus lilies, magnolias and several species of proteus, the tender plant which now flourishes in South Africa, were all thriving in the Hebrides. After each eruption there was a pause. Earth and life accumulated on the ragged, fissured surface of the lava before the next eruption destroyed and enclosed it. In Morvern, one can see the upper parts of each flow stained red where the weather had broken down the rock and turned the iron in it rusty. Each of these red layers is buried under the basement of the flow that came after it. On Mull, at Rudha na h-Uamha, John Macculloch, the fiercely opinionated geologist who was one of the first to give an account of the Shiants' rocks in 1819, discovered the fossil of a tree still standing embedded in a river of lava, twenty feet deep, which had overwhelmed it. You can still see it there today.

The Shiants themselves, though, can never have known any of this. They never had their Hawaiian period and parakeets never flitted along these shores. These islands – or what are now these islands – came into existence two miles or so underground, perhaps under another volcano which has entirely disappeared.

That much was known in the nineteenth century. Since World War II, the understanding of the Shiant rocks has developed enormously, largely in the hands of Fergus Gibb and Mike Henderson, who, in five visits and with extensive laboratory analysis, have, quite extraordinarily to my mind, been able to establish a sequence of events that occurred here over a few decades about sixty million years ago.

It is a vast poem written in heat and liquidity. Remove the sea from your mind. That has nothing to do with it. You are in the dark of the Earth's crust, several miles down. About a hundred and twenty million years before, in the Lower Jurassic, enormously thick accumulations of mud, silt and sand had built up in layer after layer on the floor of an earlier sea. These mud stones and shales have become rock. Beneath them, a huge bubble of hot molten rock starts to rise. The pressure it exerts opens fissures and ruptures in the overlying layers and it is between those laminations that the magma wants to squeeze.

This is the moment of the Shiants' creation. The liquid rock, deep underground, probably took the form of what geologists call 'a cedar tree laccolith', a set of leaf-like chambers arranged around a central stem like the boughs of a cedar tree. The magma, pulsing from below, still hot from the energy generated when the planet first formed, runs into each chamber and beyond it into new leaves, new extensions of the form. The idea of a single tree is wrong: more likely a forest of them, the forms connected through the bough tips or a branching of the stem. The growth of this red-hot forest, each tree fifteen miles high and its canopy spreading as much as ten or fifteen miles wide, was moving north from the southern Hebrides. The whole floor of the Little Minch is covered in the leaves of that infernal cedar grove. In the far more recent past, glaciers have gouged hollows between them in the softer Jurassic sediments, leaving a family of submarine Shiants between here and Tiree. Occasionally they break surface, in the islands of Staffin Bay, the Ascrib Islands, Fladda-chuain, Eilean Trodday, all off the northern tip of Skye and in Sgeir Inoe, the lonely and vicious rock off Scalpay. Most are unseen, apparent only in the kicking of the tide.

Deep inside those ancient layers, the Shiants came into being in an orgasm of incandescent liquid. It was enormously hot: the greatest heat reached in the most violent fire in a burning building is about 850°C. That can melt bricks, turning them into pools of liquid glass. The Jurassic mudstones melt at about 900° but the heat of the magma itself was about 1150°C.

The Shiant intrusion would have been pulsed, the impulse coming and going, like a breath, an exhalation, pushing at the rocks above it and distending them. That dynamism is now fixed in the form of the rocks. You can find precisely the point – it is revealed on the shore in the bay next to the house – where the inrush of radiant magma came up against the cold mudstones in the roof of the cavity. Pull away the kelp and the serrated wrack. The little green crabs scuttle for the dark, the tiny transparent shrimps wriggle like rugby players in a tackle, and you can see the instant of creation frozen and preserved in front of you. The raging heat of the magma meets the old, cold mudstone and that meeting has had a double effect.

Elsewhere on the islands, you can see in the mudstones the layering of the sediments as they had settled onto the Jurassic sea-bed

and you can find many fossils of ammonites and belemnites embedded in them like meat in a cold pie. Here, though, that has all been
lost in the cataclysm. The mud stones have been baked hard into
the solid grey stone called hornfels, without layers in it and without
fossils. If you break the stone open, though, as Mike Henderson
showed me, you can find the ghosts of the life once preserved here.
Heat and pressure has transformed everything that was once in
them and a faint, coppery, gilded sheen coats the inner surfaces
of the rock. These are what Mike Henderson called 'the pyritised
remains', the only evidence of the fossils which the rock once held,
reduced in the furnace to this undiagnosable inkling, a breath of a
suggestion, like the ash of an abandoned hearth. But the mud stones
also exacted their price from the magma. Where the hot, molten
intrusion came into contact with the country rock it was suddenly
chilled. The semi-crystalline mush of the liquid, a kind of hot
granita, was shocked into solidity by the old, cold stones. In suddenly becoming solid, the minerals in the magma are small, almost
instantly formed and so the rock is as smooth and as fine-grained
as cheese. That analogy is curiously exact: where you have broken
the rock open, the fracture marks are exactly like those you find on
the open face of a piece of broken Parmesan. 'Chill' or 'chilled
margin', as this frozen magma is called, sits all alongside the
hornfels on the beach, the twin products of intense heat meeting
ancient cold, fifty-eight and a half million years ago.

Many things are still not clear about the making of these
islands, nor is the precise order of events certain. Broadly though,
it seems that several blades or 'sills' of magma were intruded here
over a period of perhaps a century or two. One fairly narrow
one, having cooled quite quickly, can be seen in the Galtas.
Another makes the rib of rock through which the natural arch
passes at the north-east corner of Garbh Eilean. A third forms
Eilean Mhuire and the fourth, by far the largest, 537 ft. thick,
created the vast bulk, about four hundred acres, of Garbh Eilean

and Eilean an Tighe. No one has yet found how these sills are related to each other, nor how they are connected to the huge feeder pipe along which the magma arrived from the south, but it is obvious that some of the old Jurassic rocks, the mudstones and shales, were caught up in the process. Most of the top of Eilean Mhuire consists of a huge raft of those older rocks buoyed up like a baulk of wood on the flood of magma which poured in, mostly below but some also above it. Another slab of old rock crosses the north-east corner of Garbh Eilean and has been eroded in the bay that stretches out below the puffin slopes there. Those soft and crumbly rocks, full of the nutritious minerals which accumulated on the Jurassic sea-bed, make far better soils than the hard, solidified magma of the sills. These Jurassic rocks, richer than almost anything in Pairc or Harris, and comparable in Lewis only to equivalent rocks around Stornoway, have been the basis for most of the farming on the Shiants. Without the wealth of Eilean Mhuire and the beautiful meadows at the Bagh on Garbh Eilean, it is difficult to think that life on the Shiants would ever have been possible.

For the professional geologists, this story is only the introduction to the book. They seek to penetrate much further into the arcana of chemical detail, above all into the diagnostic mineralogy of the different sorts of rocks to be found on the islands.

Previously it had been thought that the different minerals that can be seen in different places were the result of large crystals settling towards the bottom of the sill as the magma cooled. That was the old orthodoxy developed in the 1930s but Fergus Gibb and Mike Henderson have over the last four decades pushed most of that aside and discovered a quite different process.

As they have revealed, the enormous main sill of Garbh Eilean and Eilean an Tighe is itself made up of at least four different pulses of magma. These were not violent events but of great scale and immense power, slowly applied; a slow squeezing apart of an abscess the size of fifty city blocks. The Shiants laid on Manhattan would stretch from Wall Street to Times Square. These successive pulses are not, as you might think, laid one on top of another, in the way you would assemble a sandwich: mustard on top of the ham on top of the cheese on top of the butter on top of the bread. Not at all: each new one inserted itself, in a hot, licking tongue of new magma, within the body of those that had come before. They could only have done that if the preceding magma was still quite soft. In other words, here in this main sill, they must have followed, one from the other, quite quickly. The picture is of a gradually fattening sandwich, made in something like a piece of pitta bread. You begin with the bread alone, and one by one, butter, jam and peanut butter are squeezed inside it. The sequence you end up with, then, is: bread, butter, jam, peanut butter, jam, butter, bread.

In the Shiants, although the sandwich is 537 ft. thick, it is almost precisely like that, made up of four interleaved layers. The first, of a rock called teschenite, was 6 ft. thick (the top and

bottom of this layer are now 531 ft. apart), the second (picrite), 78 ft. thick, the third (crinanite-picrodolerite), 440 ft. and the fourth (granular olivine picrodolerite), just 13 ft.

Beyond that, I fear, it becomes difficult for a layman to follow. I could tell you about the mineralogy of these islands, with the intriguing differences between picrite (which cooled slowly, so has big crystals and looks wormy, with an eroded surface like the mottled, liver-spotted skin of a toad or like penne in a pesto sauce) and picrodolerite (quicker cooling, a fine, granular porridge), or about the beauty in freshly broken rock of the tiny grape crystals of the olivine and the big black glitter of the pyroxenes, about the evolution of the magma over the years of its emplacement, so that the last spurts of it produce a strange, white, open-structured, vast-crystalled rock called syenite on Eilean Mhuire – but I won't. This is not the place.

After the magma from the vast chambers below had finally exhausted itself, the Shiants, still deep underground, began to cool. From both above and below, the chill started to reach inwards into the heart of the semi-liquid mush, like the hemlock in the limbs of Socrates. It might have taken a century or so for the rock to become solid. As it cooled, it shrank, and that is the origin of the columns of which the Shiants are made. Any large body of shrinking material, contracting over its entire width, pulls apart from itself internally. Shrinkage cracks develop in the body of the rock identical to the network of polygons that develop on the floor of a drying lake. The columns are nothing more than a network of cracks extended into a third dimension.

If this cooling had been conducted in laboratory conditions, where the magma sheets were of equal thickness throughout and both upper and lower surfaces of the intrusions were level, then a structure of complete regularity would have emerged. All the columns would have been straight, the same size, and parallel. But this is not a laboratory. Some of the intrusions were clearly thin (in particular the one that formed the Galtas) and cooled more quickly. This has meant that the columns are themselves much thinner there. More intriguingly and beautifully, it is clear that the opening into which the magma squeezed was uneven. The columns would have formed by growing perpendicular to the cooling surfaces and here the unevenness of those surfaces has created columns that curve, twist and bend, are waved like the hair of art deco statuettes, fixed in the elegance of a geological perm, Jean Harlow turned to stone, Madonna having glimpsed the Gorgon.

Others, such as the upper sections of the north cliffs on Garbh Eilean, cooled so quickly that whole slaggy masses of rock became solid before columns could develop. Below them, deeply buried in the huge Garbh Eilean sill, the magma cooled very slowly indeed and here the Shiant rock-forms attain the great magnificence of the giant columns. These were the forms over which John Macculloch, the early geologist, enthused in 1819:

> The lover of picturesque beauty will here, as in many other
> parts of the Western islands, be gratified with a display of
> maritime scenery combining the regularity of Staffa with

the grander features of the coast of Sky. Towards the north it exhibits one continuous perpendicular face of naked rock. This face is columnar throughout, and forms a magnificent scene for the pencil; spreading in a gentle curve for a space of 1000 yards or more, and impending in one broad mass of shadow over the dark sea that washes its base. In simplicity and grandeur it exceeds Staffa almost as much as it does in magnitude; offering to the tourist an object as worthy of his pursuit as that celebrated island, and of no very difficult access from the northern extremity of Sky.

The Shiants languished in obscurity, while their more famous, and more accessible cousin-rocks off Mull became ever more visited. Perhaps the open waters of the Minch protect the Shiants from fame. Perhaps the nearness of Staffa to Iona creates its public success. And having witnessed, from the deck of a boat, Staffa sagging one summer's day under the weight of its geological trippers, I can only say; 'Thank God'.

A Gothic fate awaits the Shiants. There has been a steady geological drizzle over the millennia which has created the huge scree slopes at the feet of the cliffs. Giant pencil stubs the size of small houses lie tumbled like the aftermath of an earthquake. Sometimes, groups of them still hang together as if thrown in a clump on the rubbish heap. The birds live in many-storeyed tenements among them. If you walk across them, the lorry-sized rocks wobble and creak beneath you. Shiant dynamism is not over. The cliffs themselves are a symptom of the slices being taken out of them and the hard edges of the islands are signs of destruction in progress. 'The upper millstone heaven,' Ted Hughes once wrote, 'Grinds the heather's face hard and small.' It isn't only the heather. Fergus Gibb reckons that 'a million years or two should see the Shiants off.'

Every spring, I look for the new scars, the beds from which

the lumps of rock have broken away. They are unnerving places. Where the splits have occurred, the remaining edges are as sharp as knives. You can cut your hands on them. For some reason, the bare unlichened stone smells of iron or even blood, because blood smells of iron too. The smell is one of deep antiquity, a release into the nostrils of elements in the rock which have not been volatile since the rock was made. It feels as intimate as poking your fingers into a wound.

I have never witnessed something which I have spent hours in a boat waiting to occur: the collapse of an entire column from a cliff. Fergus has only seen it once, and then not here but in the similar rock formations in Trotternish, the northern wing of Skye, twelve miles or so to the south. He too was in a boat on the quiet sea. Alerted by a shuffling, a distant rumbling in the silence which on still summer days hangs around these places, Gibb looked up from his notes. Across the bay, an entire thin pencil, perhaps three hundred feet high, six or eight feet across, was slipping in slow motion into the sea. The base of the column, like many of them, must have been eaten away by the sea. Incredibly, the columns of which the islands are made are scarcely more bound to each other than pencils in a box and once the base has gone, knocked out by a winter storm, there is nothing to withstand the force of gravity. That morning, the column slid down, buckled and then fell, not like a felled trunk but with the shaft snapping in two places in mid-air before the three giant sections crashed like stone hail into the stillness of the Minch. The birds clattered away from the impact, the wash ran up to Gibb's boat and on past it and the silence pooled back in. Fergus said it was like a glacier calving.

These rocks are killers too. In 1796 the Reverend Alexander Simson, the Minister of Lochs, described the Shiants in his statistical account of the parish:

There is one family residing on the largest of the islands. The head of this family has been so unfortunate as to lose, at different times, his wife, a son, and a daughter, by falling down great precipices; the mother and son met with this catastrophe in following sheep, and the daughter, by going in quest of wild-fowl eggs.

There is no further explanation of why they should have fallen. It is easy enough to slip on the dew-wet cliff-top grass, or to be blown away in a sudden gust, or for a rope to fail, but it seems likely enough to me that the collapse of part of a cliff might be to blame.

More recently, the sheer instability of Shiant rocks killed a boy. On 28 June 1986, a party of teenagers and their teachers from Cranbrook School in Kent had just arrived for a summer expedition to the islands. It was a beautiful evening, and as they were putting up their tents, one of the boys, Simon Woollard, an experienced alpinist and gifted climber, decided to climb the small cliff just behind the house. It is no more than twenty feet high and I have often climbed it myself, pushing up past the bunches of wild thyme, the purple knapweed and the hart's tongue ferns, without ropes, for fun. We had given names to some of the routes – 'Grassy Chimney', 'The Squeeze', 'Crab Lunch' – 'a naughty little climb with pretentious reaches', as I wrote in the visitors' book when I was seventeen.

That evening in 1986, Simon Woollard did it by the book. He was belayed from below, wearing a harness and a helmet. His friends were watching him from among their tents on the grassy level behind the house. The Shiants on a summer evening like this, as the sun begins to drop towards the hills of Harris, and the two Galtas stand out as a pair of black moles against the colours of the evening, and as the birds come in from their fishing for the evening wheel between the islands, is the happiest and calmest of places. It could not hurt you. It was then, at about twenty to nine in the evening, that, towards the top of the cliff, a block of dolerite over which Simon was pulling himself came away in his hands. It was about the size of an armchair. He fell with it for a moment but was then held by the rope and the rock sliced through his helmet and into his head. He died there, at the foot of the cliff where he had fallen, and later that night, after many hours' delay and unspeakable distress for those who were there, a helicopter from RAF Lossiemouth came to take his body and some of his friends back to Stornoway. The others left thirty-six hours later, when Donald MacSween collected them from Scalpay. There is a small plaque at the place where Simon died and none of us has ever climbed there again.

That is not quite true. I came to the islands a couple of weeks after Simon Woollard had died. The evidence was still there: shards of broken rock on the turf at the cliff foot, still sharp, a huge and horrifying stain on the boulders which the rain had not yet washed away. On the evening of the accident, Adam Tozer, the master in charge, had written in the visitors' book that there had been a fatality. With big, slashing, diagonal lines he had crossed out the pages in which we had described the various routes. 'DO NOT CLIMB', he had written across the sketch of the rocks on which the boy had died.

For the first day or two I did what he asked and kept away, but reluctantly. Not to climb what we had always climbed would mean the cliff would be haunted by a kind of denial. These islands were a place in which, if you took care, nothing had ever been denied. You could risk a storm if you knew what you were about, you could happily expose yourself to weather which at home you might have hidden from. I decided to climb the cliff again. I went up to the foot of a familiar route, the Grassy Chimney, an adder's tongue fern in the cleft above me, a cushion of thyme on either side. I reached up for the first hold, pulled my body up six inches, perhaps a foot, and as I did so, as I applied my weight, I felt the block, a cubic yard of dolerite, ease out a little from its bed. I let go of it as if it were a burning coal and dropped those few inches back to the turf. Never again.

6

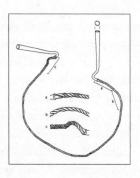

I HAVE SAT FOR HOURS on the bench in front of the house – it's a plank of driftwood on a pair of stones – watching Donald MacSween trawling for scallops (or clams as they are called in the Hebrides) in the waters a mile or two away just south of the Galtas. He has a new boat now, the *Jura*, but in the 1980s, it was the *Favour*, a steel thing, not, it has to be said, the greatest beauty that Scalpay has ever known, painted red and white, with its name in huge letters on the wheelhouse.

Sometimes, he and Kenny Cunningham, his crewman also from Scalpay, went on deep into the night and on a quiet evening all you could hear for hour after hour was the groaning monotone of the diesel, a slow surging in its note, as the *Favour* pulled the heavy clam dredge across the sandy floor of the Minch fifteen or eighteen fathoms below them. It was long work and by the late 1980s most of the scallops here had been fished out. Every few hours Donald and Kenny would haul up the dredge and pick one or two of the valuable shells from its heavy metal mesh. Money was short.

The dredge always brings up other things: boulders, wreckage,:the odds and ends with which the floor of this littered sea is covered. Early in 1991, they spotted a piece of straightish, gold-green wire about two feet long. It had been caught up in the gear. Kenny picked it out and thought little more of it. It was a curiosity.

The length of wire spent a year or so alongside the spanners and heavy screwdrivers in the toolbox of the *Favour*. Fishing boats are high-maintenance creatures. Donald leaves for sea at four every morning, a little later in the winter, and is back in the North Harbour at Scalpay by early afternoon. But that is not the end of the day: there is always several hours of mending and maintenance to be finished. The tool box is as critical as the rudder. Month after month the wire was shoved aside by hands looking for a wrench or a jemmy. At one point it was hung on a hook in the wheelhouse, remaining there for the summer.

One Sunday evening, Kenny happened to be watching the *Antiques Roadshow* on the BBC. A woman produced a piece of jewellery which seemed to resemble the wire that had been dredged up the previous year. Cunningham was going to Glasgow for a wedding and so thought he might take it to an auctioneer's to get a valuation. At Christie's, he brought the wire out of the deep, inside pocket of his jacket. It was in the shape of a walking stick, a long straight section with a curve at the top. Miranda Grant, Christie's gemologist, who had done a thesis in early Celtic jewellery, was called to the desk. She was mesmerised by what she saw and took it in her hands. Kenny said he thought it might be gold because it had been in the sea but was quite uncorroded. It was only gold, wasn't it, that could lie in the sea and remain unaltered? Without thinking quite what she was doing, on automatic pilot, as she says, Miranda Grant grasped the object and bent it into the shape she thought it should have, a looped circle. The wire was of very pure gold, probably between twenty-two and twenty-four carat, and in her hands, it was softness itself. 'It went like butter,' she said. She suggested quite calmly that it should go straight away to the National Museums in Edinburgh for a further view. Cunningham left it with her and the next morning she took it there in a briefcase.

Trevor Cowie, the curator in the National Museums, 'almost died' when Miranda Grant brought the object out of her briefcase. The piece of soft gold wire was the only surviving late Bronze Age gold torc ever to have been found in Scotland. Another three had been recorded in the nineteenth century (from Edinburgh, Culloden and Stoneykirk in Wigtownshire) but were now lost, one certainly and the others probably melted down for their gold. This was the only Scottish survivor of a kind of body ornament, probably made in about 1200 BC, for the neck or, if twisted into a double spiral, the upper arm, of a prince or priest or chieftain. It is a kind of jewellery which in a sparklingly twisted golden trail has been found scattered throughout Celtic Europe: one or two from near Carcassonne in the stony world of the Mediterranean, another in the Pyrenean foothills south of Toulouse, one from Jaligny in the wide, flat meadowlands of the Bourbonnais in central France, one from the orchards of Calvados in Normandy, another from the bed of the Seine in Paris itself. The trail runs on through Brittany and the Channel Islands, across wide swathes of southern and eastern England, one found in the Medway at Maidstone, another at Mountfield in the Sussex Weald and a cluster of them in the Fens. Their heartland is in Wales and across the Irish Sea. Two were found at Tara, in County Meath, the capital of the Irish High Kings, and one at the Giant's Causeway in Antrim. The gold of this torc is probably from Wales or Ireland, or perhaps a combination of the two. Throughout the Bronze Age the metal was extensively recycled.

Excitement rippled through the archaeological community and the MacSween and Cunningham households. (Although scarcely beyond them: this is not the kind of news which is immediately shared on Scalpay.) But whose was it? The proprieties had to be observed and the assumption made by the authorities was that this object came from a wreck. The wreck might have been more than three thousand years old but it was still a wreck. The government employs an officer in ports all around the British shores with the title 'Receiver of Wreck'. Wreck, in this instance, is not a description of a ship but of a category of goods, a cousin to flotsam (goods washed off a ship at sea and floating) and jetsam (goods deliberately thrown off a ship to lighten it in a storm).

'Finders,' the Receiver of Wreck's official document states, 'should assume at the onset that all recovered wreck has an owner.' Finds must be 'advertised as appropriate to give the owner the opportunity to come forward and claim back their property. If no owner is found within one year from the date of the report, the material becomes unclaimed wreck. In the majority of cases the finder is then offered the material in lieu of a salvage payment.'

For a year, the torc discovered by Kenny Cunningham and Donald MacSween remained in the custody of Her Majesty's Receiver of Wreck, Stornoway, waiting for a naked, dripping Bronze Age chieftain to walk into his office, next to the Fishermen's Co-Op a few yards from the town quay, and claim it as his own.

He never did and the torc became the possession of the fishermen who had found it. There was a symbolic struggle between museums. The National Museums of Scotland, then in the process of creating the new glamorous Museum of Scotland in Chambers Street in Edinburgh, wanted it for their new displays. It was of national importance, they could argue, and so should be shown in the national capital. The Museum nan Eilean, the Museum of the Western Isles in Stornoway, forever feeling that whatever was marvellous from the Hebrides was whisked off to Edinburgh, whatever second-rate left behind, also wanted it for their own exhibition. In the end it came to money. The Western Isles Council was still recovering from the financial catastrophe they had suffered in 1991 when £23 million of ratepayers' money had been lost. The Council's funds had been deposited with the high interest, high-risk Bank of Credit & Commerce International. When the bank collapsed, there was certainly no money for archaeological acquisitions. Stornoway couldn't afford the torc and nowadays there is a small photograph of it in the Stornoway museum on Francis Street. The real thing was bought by the Edinburgh museum, for a sum which Donald has asked me not to mention, which was split half and half between him and Kenny and which was substantial enough to have 'paid off the debts'. It was certainly the best day's fishing either of the men had ever had. Their catch is now in a high glamour setting in Edinburgh, shut behind glass in a display case made by Sir Eduardo Paolozzi in the form of an aggressive automaton, his hands raised and his aspect fierce, the torc both displayed and protected by his strange and armoured body.

Can one say any more about this wonderful and mysterious object, the most valuable thing ever to have come to the Shiants? Certainly you can tell nothing from the form in which it is so carefully preserved in Edinburgh. That is simply the shape given it by Miranda Grant in her moment of ecstasy. It has no historical significance. But you can at least see that the torc is beautifully made. A square, golden rod, a single ingot hammered to the correct length, has been fluted on each of its four sides so that the four ridged edges of the rod stand out. It has then been held at both ends and carefully twisted, so the four edges of the bar now spiral around it as a continuous decoration. To the ends of this twisted rod two long plain terminals have been welded or soldered, although the junction is carefully concealed within a tiny gold cushion. Those terminals are made so that they will hook around each other, the torc itself providing the spring and elasticity which keeps them locked together on the neck or arm of the wearer.

It is a delicate thing. Alongside it in Edinburgh are examples of neck ornaments from other times and other parts of Scotland.

Many of them take the form of vast money display: the huge, early Bronze Age golden collars from Dumfriesshire, which are positively Incan in their scale and vulgarity, or the extraordinary Pictish silver neck-chains from the centuries before the Vikings' arrival, heavier than dog-collars, perhaps made from melted down late Roman silver, paid to the Picts as protection money; or even the massive Norse brooches and neck rings from the hoard stumbled on in the nineteenth century at Skaill in Orkney, in which the brooches are six inches across, normal objects inflated as a display of power.

The Shiant torc is not like that. There is a simplicity and subtlety to it which perhaps means that it is not intended as a form of dominance. It is meant to decorate rather than to impress and would have graced the body which wore it. One might even have taken a moment or two to recognise that the person was wearing it. This is, in other words, a civilised and not a violent thing, as subtle as scent. Its presence here seems to me as exotic as a silk dress on a cliff face, Audrey Hepburn, somehow, en route to the North Pole. No torc of this kind has ever been found this far north.

What is it doing here? Were the Shiants themselves in the Bronze Age a place of significance, to which objects of this kind would naturally gravitate? Or was it washed it here from somewhere else by the currents of the sea? Did it go down with a boat that was wrecked on the Galtas? Was it dropped overboard by mistake? Or was it, perhaps, deliberately thrown in?

It seems wildly unlikely that the Shiants in the Bronze Age were a place of any importance but how could I tell? The past is so opaque here. Did I really want to poke around in the body of the Shiants? Wasn't it better to leave things in a state of uncertainty?

For a long time I hesitated. One of the reasons I loved the Shiants was that they were away from the world of definition. When I was a boy, the masters at school would always say, whenever I produced any work, 'Yes, Adam, but have you thought it through?' The answer would invariably be no. I never think things through.

I never have. I never envisage the end before I plunge into the beginning. I never clarify the whole. I never sort one version of something from any other. I bank on instinct, allowing my nose to sniff its way into the vacuum, trusting that somewhere or other, soon enough, out of the murk, something is bound to turn up.

I'm wedded to this plunging-off form of thought, and to the acceptance of muddle which it implies. Something that is not preordained, that hasn't even envisaged the far wall before it has started building the near one, has the possibility, at least, of arriving somewhere unexpected. There's a poem by the American, Denise Levertov, with the marvellous title 'Overland to the Islands', which in four words makes a bright little capsule of that frame of mind. Thinkers-through would never go overland to the islands. They would never expect to find the islands there. But Levertov, drop by drop, takes you out, on a mapless walk full of suddenly grasped fragments, each to be treasured for the way it is stumbled on, out of nowhere, with no context. 'Let's go,' she says, 'much as that dog goes, / Intently haphazard . . .'

And she does, musically, elegantly, chancily, discovering the Mexican light, the iris ripples on her dog's back, and his nose sniffing for the next thing.

> There's nothing
> the dog disdains on his way,
> nevertheless he
> keeps moving, changing
> pace and approach but
> not direction – 'every step an arrival'.

If I were to erect a motto over the Shiants, I could do worse than almost any one of those lines. 'Every step an arrival' should be on the door of the house. Give everything a sniff.

The dogs love the Shiants. It is a dog's world of not thinking through, of beautiful incoherence and the thing seen for itself, the rocks and mud under the dog nose, that travelling to and fro along the margins of a path, an excited 'What next?' as the motivating force in life, a stodgelessness, an inability to plan.

All of this is the opposite of the fashionable qualities. The modern world likes the complete, the systematic, the self-sufficient, the clarified and the unabsorbent. Softness and haze are things to be cleared away. Hard truths are to be revealed by stripping back obscuring surfaces. The landscape you see, with all its fluff and uncertainty, only hides the bones of a lurking reality which archaeology or psychotherapy will all too happily cut back to. Suggestiveness and ambiguity, the half-conditions, in which one thing is not entirely distinct from another, are seen not as something in themselves but as failed or incomplete versions of something else and better. Ignorance is not bliss; it's a missed opportunity.

'Voluptuous as the first approach of sleep,' were the words Byron used to describe one evening twilight. It is a phrase which, with clean-edged condescension, would be considered sentimental now. But what about twilight, dusk and the burnt-out ends of smoky days, as the times in which most understanding is to be had? What about the virtues of ambiguity and the incomparable beauty of a lit sky over a dark earth? Isn't it reflected, and not direct, light that illuminates the mind?

These were all troubling thoughts for me when I was considering the idea of making a long, deep investigation of the Shiants' history. Would all the business of finding out destroy the islands' enveloping magic? Would as much be lost in finding out as was gained? I spent a few days there trying to think it through. Only at the end of the last day did I decide. The blue evening was creeping over from the west. 'Already night in his fold was gathering / A great flock of vagabond stars . . .' And the answer was this: once the questions had arisen in my mind, it would be purely sentimental not to attempt to answer them. For many years I had walked across these islands without a question in my head. I had noticed, of course, the ruins here and there, the short stretches of wall, the cultivation ridges, the lazybeds, on whose ribs the forget-me-nots and meadowsweet grew, with the yellow flags and watermint in the ditches between them. They all had remained, so to speak, in a dusky condition, contentedly ambiguous, a sign of the undifferentiated past.

That had changed now. I had changed. I wanted to know. I wanted to bring this ambiguous sub-conscious of the place up to the level of full consciousness. Why? Perhaps because I felt more social about the islands. In my twenties, they had been somewhere to escape from a fretful marriage and from a fretful job in a publishers' office. They were cut away from the adult world, somewhere a kind of ideal and delayed boyhood could be lived out for a few weeks. Isolation was integral to that. This was a place where I was happy to be alone. The idea of investigating earlier lives, and all the team work that would have involved, would have been an interruption to the pleasures and safety of solitude.

That is what has changed and this book is evidence of it. I have known the ecstasy of being alone here but at least partly I have left that behind. It was fuelled by a feeling that the presence of other people could only be damaging and that islands at least allowed the solitary self to exist without apology. I don't feel that any more. Solitariness now seems to me a diminished rather than a heightened state. It is one way of being alive, with its own rewards, but it is not necessarily the best way and, besides, solitude can only mean anything in counterpoint to sociability. Now I want to people these islands, both in reality, and in that deeper sense, to discover what life the Shiants might have nurtured over the years.

I left with my mind made up. In the University Library at Cambridge I found a series of volumes published by various archaeological expeditions to the Hebrides. One in particular drew my eye. It described the discovery of a Neolithic house, lying just under the floor surface of a late-eighteenth-century house in the obscure valley of a stream called Allt Chrisal in Barra. The excavations had summoned an exact and ancient past, full of ghostly suggestions of hearths and sleeping places, potsherds and flint tools, from a landscape which all others had looked at with scarcely a second thought. Its authors were Keith Branigan and Patrick Foster, from Sheffield University. I rang Branigan. He was too busy and put me on to Foster, now attached to the State Institute of Archaeology in Prague. I rang him there. Would he leave his Hallstatt burials and Neolithic riverside timber halls for a while and come to the stony exigencies of the Shiants? He jumped at it. His Hebridean programme had come to an end. He had been longing to return. When could he come?

Pat is a remarkable man and gifted archaeologist, of enormous, cheerful enthusiasm and a wide variety of experience, (son of a Northamptonshire stonemason, gunner in the Royal Artillery, stationed for two years on St Kilda, mature PhD student at Sheffield University, studying the reuse of Roman building stone in Saxon churches, tyre salesman, collector of postcards, guns from the Wild West and a variety of mementos of the British Empire).

He is passionate, physically strong, full of unstoppable energy and with a commitment to the field realities of archaeology, to getting your hands dirty. He arrived one afternoon on Malcolm Macleod's boat from Stornoway. I went out to meet him and as he stepped down into the dinghy, he was rubbing his hands like a hungry man about to sit down to dinner. I gave him a cup of tea in the house and he began surveying the territory. From morning till night, he walked up and down the islands. You would see him from time to time on the skyline, or peering down at some tumbled stones, or just occasionally, in the lee of an old wall, catching a few minutes sleep in the sunshine. I came with him as much as I could and we walked across the islands together, for many hours, arguing, suggesting, attempting to find coherence in the evidence he was turning up.

The places in which people have lived here are not scattered at random across the islands like confetti after a wedding. Just as the puffins cluster in some spots particularly suited to them – ground good for burrowing, steep enough for easy take-off – guillemots and razorbills in others – room for communal clustering on convenient shelves, access to fishing grounds – people over the millennia have used what the landscape has given them.

As the days went by, I took Pat to the different parts of the islands where I thought people must have lived. We treated the Shiants like prospectors, newly arrived in a new world. What would we make of this? What kind of life could we sustain here? The first place, of course, was around the modern house on Eilean an Tighe. Down there on the coastal shelf is where anyone would choose: near a landing beach and and within a minute or two of both west and east coasts, lots of sweet water in the small seeps at the cliff foot, mounds of seaweed from the bay on the west coast, good growing ground, easy, level, relatively rich, convenient. It is not surprising that the modern house and other early and recent buildings are here. It is where, when I am here with my family, we spend most of our time, moving between boats and shore and well and house, digging over the vegetable garden, cooking sometimes on the flat rocks beside the ruins. It is the most obvious place for a Shiant home. As a result, there is little that is identifiable as prehistoric on the ground. Pat was convinced, though, that it was certain to be there, buried under later structures. Any investigation would have to wait.

A thin, old path leads from that house settlement up into the middle valley of Eilean an Tighe, skirting the upper edge of the cultivation ridges, running between them and the steep screes above. The path is as wriggly as a thread fallen on carpet and after a climb of a hundred and fifty feet or so it emerges on to

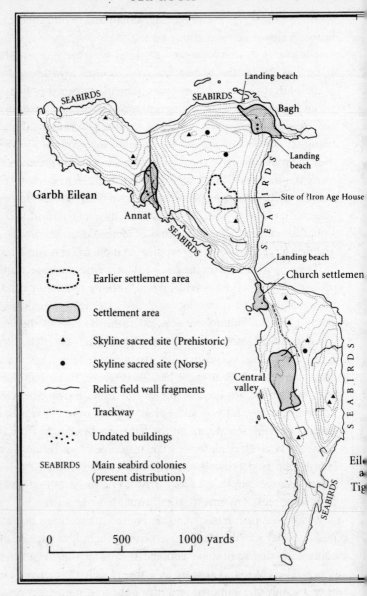

Landing beach

SEABIRDS

SEABIRDS

Bagh

Landing beach

SEABIRDS

Garbh Eilean

Annat

SEABIRDS

Site of ?Iron Age House

Landing beach

Church settlemen

Earlier settlement area

Settlement area

▲ Skyline sacred site (Prehistoric)

● Skyline sacred site (Norse)

Relict field wall fragments

Trackway

Undated buildings

SEABIRDS Main seabird colonies
(present distribution)

SEABIRDS

Central
valley

Eil
a
Tig

0   500   1000 yards

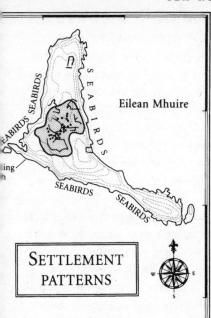

Eilean Mhuire

SEABIRDS SEABIRDS SEABIRDS SEABIRDS SEABIRDS SEABIRDS

SETTLEMENT PATTERNS

?Iron Age House on Garbh Eilean

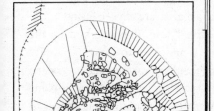

5m

the wide, level plateau of the central valley. Here there is a second cluster of buildings. They do not seem older than the seventeenth or eighteenth century, but with good corn ground here (now undrained and so boggy) and sweet running water, it is nearly inconceivable that these later buildings do not overlie much earlier structures. They are not near the shore, but are within fifteen minutes' walk of the landing beach. This, too, hidden beneath the early modern ruins and the rushes and flag irises that have grown up around them, is another place of ancient habitation. It is the site, as I shall describe later, of the house we excavated.

This was a strange experience for me. Places in which I had only ever walked and looked before were now subject to analysis and investigation. Everywhere we came to I could remember playing football with my children, or lying in the shelter of the walls away from the wind on a sunny day, or going there in the middle of a summer night, with the starlight dropping around us and the snipe fluting in the marsh. I had never, curiously, considered much beyond an idle thought what had happened there before. So this was an intriguing and rattling experience: the archaeologist and the psychoanalyst are close cousins.

Then I took Pat over to Garbh Eilean, dragging him up the steep southern face, Sron Lionta, and over to what has always been to me one of the most lovely places on the Shiants, tucked into the south-west coast of the island. It is called Annat, a name whose resonances I will explore later. A stream comes down to the shore there, dropping from one peaty, basin-sized pool to another, running between little meadows and then tumbling over the black rocks into a deep, seaweed-lined pool, where on calm days a boat can be brought in as if next to a quay, and where you can swim with twelve feet of water below you, glass-clear to the red of the dulse and the fretted lionskin of the wrack, while the fresh, cold moorland water drops through a beard of green weed on to your head. There is ruin after ruin here, one laid on top of another. The soil is not particularly rich, although it is not as sour as the moor above and has obviously been improved. A huge, round stone platform, perhaps a hundred feet across and up to eight feet deep, has been built here next to the place where the stream falls into the sea. Pat thought that it might well be the foundations of a large Neolithic house. There are vestiges of other buildings, including what might be a small, round Bronze Age house, and a large, mysterious D-shaped enclosure, perhaps for animals. In the nineteenth century, shepherds built a fank here, a sheep-gathering pen, using the stone they found on the surface, and little of what had been there before is now obvious.

Annat, too, awaits its excavation. It may well turn out to be the richest place of all the places on the Shiants.

Up from there, over the heights of Garbh Eilean and down at the far north-eastern corner to the place now known as the Bagh, the Gaelic for 'Bay'. It was like showing Pat my treasures, opening box after box. Here, around the lush and bright green slopes there is another set of tumbled and ruined buildings. This, too, feels like a favoured place: the best shelter from the southwesterlies in any part of the islands, in under the lee of the big north cliffs; a supply of fresh water seeping from the rocks, which I have never known run dry; luscious red and pink campions grown from the turfy cushions; highly productive land on the underlying band of Jurassic rocks, some of the best soils not only in the Shiants but in the whole stretch of the Outer Hebrides from the Sound of Harris to Stornoway; a convenient landing place in the bay below; plenty of easily harvested seaweed to enrich the soils; and the enormous quantities of sea birds which nest in the surrounding screes and grassy slopes, in their hundreds of thousands.

One of the miracles of the Shiants is that a place like this, no more than a few acres, and no more than a mile from the modern house and the landing beach, feels as if it is in a different world. Perhaps because of its shelter from the wind, perhaps because of the sweetness of the turf in which the daisies grow like on a southern lawn; perhaps because of the way the puffins wheel across this corner, their shadows cast onto the grass like the revolving patterns of light and dark on a Fifties dance floor; perhaps because from here the Shiants are spread out before you to make an auditorium, cupping the bay of the islands in their arms; perhaps because from here there are such wonderful views across the Stream of the Blue Men to the long, tweed-coloured coast of Pairc, blue in its prominences, black and brown in the depths of its crevices, so near on a bright day you think you could touch Kebock Head; perhaps because a long habit of occupation is so obvious here, this, I think, is where I would have lived.

It is not surprising that here, among the more ambiguous heaps of stone – fowling shelters, summer huts or shielings from the nineteenth century, whose corner cupboards raised above the earth floors were intended to keep the dairy products cool – is something which seems to emerge from an extraordinarily distant past. Like almost every other structure noticed by Pat, no one had seen it before. Some way up from the beach, settled into the grassy slope below the cliffs, a few yards away from the edge of the enormous screes into which the tumbled blocks of columnar dolerite have collapsed, are a pair of rock shelters.

A many-tonned lump of rock, about ten feet across, has fallen so that its two edges rest on other rocks, leaving an irregular hollow beneath it, six or eight feet across and about four feet high. Its floor is very crudely but quite unmistakably paved with small, flattish slabs. Where the boulders do not quite make a neat seal around the place they enclose, small lengths of dry-stone walling have been built to fill in the gaps. Inside the shelter, structures which look like stone shelving have been built.

Although it is a little sheepy now, and there are rats that run in and out of the place, it is not at all difficult when you crawl in there to imagine this as a kind of home. It is a tent made of boulders. As my son Ben said to me, it is the sort of shed Fred Flintstone might have built.

There is another slightly smaller one just downhill from the first and alongside them, where the sheep have kicked open the turf, limpet shells and pieces of crude, undatable pottery tumble down the slope: the midden, the rubbish heap, of those who used the shelters. It is not possible to date them yet. Extremely careful, microsurgical excavation might do that in the future and all Pat Foster will currently say, once again, is the careful non-commitment of the archaeologist: 'multi-period'.

We went over to Eilean Mhuire, but here the mystery remains as profound as it has ever been. Most of its upper surface is made up of the soft Jurassic rocks which are also to be found at the Bagh on Garbh Eilean. The rocks have meant that nowhere on the Shiants is more luscious than these soft, easy slopes. It is salutary to remember that almost the entire history of the Shiants would have been shoeless. Even in the early twentieth century on Lewis there were families living without shoes. That understanding transforms your idea of the way in which people lived here, their canny, prehensile toes, gripping the rocks with an assurance and a fittedness which we have now lost. And after climbing up from the beach on Mary, a stiff, crumbly climb on a narrow path through the igneous rocks that underlie the sedimentaries of the upper surface, you can feel today, if you do this shoeless, the beautiful relief of arriving at Mary's luxuriant pastures. This is the island of fertility and welcome. It is all too easy to imagine these Atlantic islands, as Yeats said of the Arans, as places 'where men must reap with knives because of the stones'. That is not true on Eilean Mhuire. It would always have been the Shiant islanders' granary. It was their garden island and the sheep that graze here are still the fattest that either the Shiants or anywhere else in Lewis can produce. It is and always has been good land.

Did people live on Eilean Mhuire in prehistory? That question cannot yet be answered. There are the remains of seventeen houses here, two or three of them making mounds that stand seven feet above the surrounding land.

Such an accumulation of material surely indicates long occupation. But there is a difficulty. Because the Jurassic rocks crumble so easily there is almost no building stone on the upper surface of the island. These house remains are made of turf, which has itself broken down to soil. There is, in other words, no hard structure which archaeology can interrogate. So how old are these buildings? How many of them were in use at the same time? Were they permanent or temporary habitations? Certainly this is the richest place in the islands, but it is also one of the windiest, and its water supply, from a deep, rushy hollow on the southern side, is not entirely reliable. Would people have lived here if they could have chosen to live at the Bay or at Annat or at either of the spots on Eilean an Tighe? Probably not. Eilean Mhuire would have been of central importance for the Shiant Islanders' food supply but would not have been a favoured place to live, particularly in the winter, when gales from all quarters would sweep across it.

These were the five places in which people would have lived on the Shiants, at least in the last few centuries: two on Eilean an Tighe, two on Garbh Eilean and one on Eilean Mhuire. Pat found one other cluster of what looked like prehistoric houses. It was the most intriguing. On the high ground of Garbh Eilean, some four hundred and fifty feet above sea-level, in an area which is now no more than acid peat bog (with the marks of some nineteenth-century peat cutting still visible in it) are one or two rushy pools and sour, reddish moor grasses. This is the area now occupied most densely by the great skuas. They have only been there since the mid-1980s, spreading south from their breeding grounds in the northern isles. In early summer, when defending their young, they are terrifying birds, an imperial presence on the heights of the island, carefully shadowing your arrival on their ground, making an admonitory 'kark' at first from a distance, sometimes accompanied by a beautiful, high-winged display, as two birds fly one above the other, both with their wings lifted in a steep-sided V of victory and viciousness. If you persist with your trespass, the skuas come for you, flying as adroitly as hunter-fighters in a mountainous battle zone, concealing themselves behind the natural mounding of the island until the last minute, when they emerge, feet from your head, with a rushing of air in wings. I have never been hit but Kennie Mackenzie, John Murdo Matheson's uncle, knew a man who had his scalp split open by a passing skua. 'It was the shock more than anything,' Kennie said.

Here, in their territory, are several stony mounds which are likely to conceal some form of prehistoric habitation. Many of them, all now visible from hundreds of yards away because their better drainage and the enrichment of the soil allows sweeter, greener grasses to grow there, had summer huts or shielings built on top of them in the nineteenth century. And that is where the skuas make their surveying stands. It is a Hebridean stratigraphy: possible Bronze or Iron age houses, nineteenth-century shielings in which the girls and boys would stay in the summer, tending to the cattle, making the cheese and butter, and above them the skuas, Viking birds, heroic, bitter northern, aggressive, magnificent modern invaders. Bits and pieces of puffin and kittiwake litter their nests.

No one of course would think of living up there now. The conditions would be intolerable and there would be nothing to draw you there. You could grow nothing in those waterlogged soils. But if you wanted a demonstration of the deterioration in the climate, this is it. What is now peat bog might, in the Bronze Age, have been freshwater pools. What is now sour moorland through which the sheep pick to find their sustenance might then have been arable fields. On Lewis itself, near the stone circles at Callanish, archaeologists from Edinburgh University have cut through the peat, sometimes five or six feet deep, to find Neolithic fields, complete with stone walls, houses and the marks of primitive ploughs lying underneath, exactly as they were abandoned, the people retreating through the thickening of the rain and wind. Up here are the remains of what may well be ancient habitations and, under the ruin of a nineteenth-century summer shieling, the remains of the largest structure ever built on the Shiants. It is an Iron Age house, sitting on a mound or platform fifty feet across and six feet high. The house itself is perhaps thirty feet in diameter, able to accommodate perhaps as many as fifteen people, and with clear marks of radial dividing walls still poking out between the nettles. That too awaits excavation.

Apart from that ancient anomaly, high on Garbh Eilean, there is distinct pattern here. It seems that the Shiants – like many parts of upland Britain – divide into two sorts of landscape, which are inter-dependent and can broadly be defined as 'core' and 'margin'. In the cores, you have arable ground, fresh water and easy access to the shore. In the margins you have rough grazing, bogs or stagnant pools and a great distance from boats and beaches. People build their houses and live permanently in the core areas. In the margins, they go in the summer, building shelters and temporary lean-tos, but little more.

Pat also discovered a fascinating extra dimension to this relationship of core to margin. Arranged on the skylines, as seen from these core settlement areas, are a succession of prehistoric ritual sites, deep in the sour and marginal country. On Eilean an Tighe, a series of Bronze Age cairns stand sentinel on the high ground to the east and south of the settled areas. On Garbh

Eilean, there are other Bronze Age cairns on the heights, while, above the north-western cliffs of Stocanish, the Shiants' own diminutive menhir, standing only eight inches high on a mound about four feet across, perhaps marks a Bronze Age grave.

As will emerge later, when the Norse arrived, they too seem to have made use of the dramatic skyline for their own burials.

Tentative, uncertain and provisional as it is, not making any firm distinctions between different periods of prehistory, a kind of answer emerges from the survey. The place was occupied in prehistory with evidence of Neolithic, Bronze Age and Iron Age houses. The Shiants are a microcosm, if a slightly impoverished one, of the Hebrides as a whole. There are armies of ghosts here. One can make a guess at how many Shiant Islanders there have ever been. If each of the core areas could accommodate a family of, say, five people; if the islands were occupied from, say, 3000 BC until the mid-eighteenth century, a length of about four thousand, eight hundred years; and if people lived on average until they were thirty, that would give you about three and a half thousand people who would have known the Shiants as home. This is not an empty rock; it is soaked in memory. At the moment little more than that can be said.

My question remains nearly unanswered. Would the Shiants have been the sort of place in the Bronze Age to which an object such as the golden torc dredged up off the Galtas would naturally have belonged? Probably not. It is not rich enough. The island group is too small, too poor and too difficult to access for any great or rich man ever to have made it his headquarters. In prehistory, as ever, the Shiants were in the shadow of the bulk of Lewis to the west. The torc, in other words, came from somewhere else.

Was it, then, somehow wafted here? Perhaps. Because the seabed in the Minch is extremely lumpy, the passage of anything across its floor would be difficult, but it is not inconceivable that a light metal object such as this might be drifted from one place to another. Stones of all sorts are to be found on the Shiant beaches. There are always one or two cobbles of black and white banded gneiss from Lewis to be found among the cool grey of the Shiant dolerites. Some of those will certainly have been dropped here by glaciers. There is a large lump of gneiss sitting on the turf at the eastern end of Eilean Mhuire, brought here by glacier from around Stornoway, twenty miles to the north. But other stones, red granites, green cupric metamorphics, even the occasional tiny natural flint nodule, all of which you find on the beach and all of whose origins can only have been to the south or east, could not have been brought here by the ice sheet, which was travelling in the other direction.

So the torc might have been washed here by the tide or by the slow underlying current which pushes slowly north, year in, year out, up the Minch. The existence of that current was only detected in the 1980s when the movement of radiocaesium from the Sellafield nuclear reprocessing plant on the west coast of Cumbria was tracked up the Minch and out into the North Atlantic. Thanks to the persistence of radiocaesium, that current, it is now known, moves at about two and a half miles a day, nine hundred miles a year. The torc has had three thousand years to get here – it is contemporary with Greeks laying siege to Troy. It had time enough to have come here from anywhere.

The simple wafting of the torc must remain a possibility, although perhaps an unlikely one. So did it, then, go down in a Bronze Age wreck? Divers and marine archaeologists have asked Donald MacSween exactly where he found the torc. He will not say. Not that he can know precisely. On the trawl which picked it up, the scallop dredge had been down for several hours as the *Favour* followed its usual spiral path round and round the sea-bed. He has gone back himself but nothing else of the sort has yet emerged from the spot. But perhaps there is a Bronze Age wreck down there. Evidence is accumulating that the Bronze Age seas, while not exactly crowded with shipping, would not have been an utterly alien environment to man. Bronze Age boats have long been known from the Humber Estuary, where three have been dug out of the clay ooze. Their heavy oak planks were laced together with lashings made of yew, part of a sewn boat tradition that extends around northern Europe, through the Baltic and across the Kola peninsula to northern Russia.

The Humber boats were probably only used as ferries across the estuary but more relevant is a large sea-going Bronze Age boat, about forty foot long, found in Dover in 1992. The boat, which was about the same age as the torc, was partly pegged together and partly stitched with yew withies. The seams had been made watertight by squeezing moss between the huge oak planks. John MacAulay knew a man whose father was still doing the same in the Hebrides early in the twentieth century, the only difference being that he soaked the moss in Stockholm tar. The bottom of the Dover boat had clearly been run up again and again on stony shores and been grooved and scuffed in the process. And inside it the archaeologists found part of its ancient cargo, a piece of shale from Kimmeridge, a hundred and eighty miles away along the south coast of England.

No one has found any convincing evidence of a Bronze Age sail, at least outside the Mediterranean, but it seems likely that early journeys across the Minch would have been under sail. It was a case then, as now in *Freyja*, or any craft with vulnerabilities, of picking your day. Surely to the south of here, the large paddle-driven boat would have aimed to make a crossing, perhaps from Ireland, perhaps from Wales, both possible sources of the gold in the torc, to the Scottish or English shore. It would have felt good, as ever, when they set out. The boat would have seemed large and capable in the calm and the sunshine. People have surely always laughed at this moment, when the sea seems kind and the future a sequence of possibilities? Then the weather turns wrong, and the experience is one only of fear. The boat was surely driven north in the storm, rather than making its way here. For what could a man or woman who had in their possession such a torc want with this northern place? Perhaps for a day or two, they were driven before the wind. It is two hundred miles to the Shiants from Malin Head, the nearest point of Ireland. It would take a day and a night at five knots, suffering the cold of hell, baling hard as one roller after another came aboard, to cross that sea. Suddenly, out of the storm those bitter rocks would materialise, and the people would die as the surf threw them at the pinnacles. One piece of geometry is significant: Donald and Kenny found the torc on the southern side of the Galtas. That was the side from which the Bronze Age boat was slammed into them. Those rocks, a bar set by the Shiants, mark the northern limit beyond which the golden torcs of Celtic Europe never reached.

The experience of shipwreck would have been the same millennium after millennium and almost every one would have gone unrecorded. Only after the Merchant Shipping Act of 1854 were the Receivers of Wreck in every port around Britain obliged to make an Examination on Oath of the master of any ship that was lost in the waters for which they were responsible. Finally, in the last few decades before marine combustion engines changed for ever the relationship of man to the sea, the pitiable condition of ships in a storm are recorded.

There is an account taken down by the Stornoway Receiver in January 1876 which goes some way to re-enacting the loss of the Bronze Age boat. The *Neda*, a large, wooden barque, three hundred and seventy-four tons, registered at Newcastle, had as master Joseph Clark, a Newcastle man. His wife and child were on board and there were ten crew, including the Irish mate Patrick Brady, an illiterate. The *Neda* had been at Dublin and cast off from the docks at noon on 17 January, destined for Newcastle, the tide at half flood and the wind blowing a fresh breeze from the west. The intention had been to go by the Irish Sea and English Channel but because of the wind backing into the south-west, it was, as Brady told the Receiver 'decided to go north about'.

All went well until they passed the light on Skerryvore, the shipwrecking rock, one of the richest of all British graveyards, standing ten miles out into the Atlantic south-west of Tiree. They had passed the light at nine o'clock on the morning of the 22nd, and soon afterwards 'a heavy gale, accompanied by drizzling rain and a high sea sprang up'. Half-way through that afternoon, in steadily deteriorating conditions, the Master laid the ship to, under nothing but her reefed main topsail. The storm worsened and visibility sank. Constant watch was kept for any land. At three o'clock the following morning, land, somehow, was sighted and they stood in towards it. Only at six did the day lighten enough for them to recognise it as the south-west corner of Skye, dominated by the heights of the Cuillins. (That is the reason all mountains in the Hebrides have Norse names: they are the only seamarks in foul weather.)

Immediately, Clark put the *Neda* onto the other tack and headed for the western side of the Minch. About ten o'clock that morning, Sunday 23 January, they sighted an island to the north but it could not be identified, 'the wind at the time rising in the SSW and blowing a gale and the weather very thick with rain.' They had no idea where they were. For safety's sake, he brought all the crew on deck and turned east again, away from the Harris shore. The wind had shifted a little, now south by west, and was shrieking in the rigging. Mrs Clark and their child were cowering below. Quite suddenly, 'a quarter of a mile ahead, a little on the port bow', the Shiants came at them, out of 'the thick rain gale'. The ship was immediately 'hauled to the wind and every effort made to escape the land', as Brady told the Receiver of Wreck, 'but this being found impossible Master ordered said ship to be run ashore on the largest of the Shiant Islands.'

I have often wondered exactly where the *Neda* struck. There is no easy place for which Clark could have aimed on that south-western shore of Eilean an Tighe. The whole extent of it is a series of craggy little inlets and intervening shards of rock. The reporter from the *Oban Times* had heard that the Shiant shepherd, Donald Campbell, was instrumental in saving the lives of all on board. He noticed the barque coming to a place where she would have been dashed to pieces and all lives lost, and from the shore he waved to those on board and guided them so that they were able to run the vessel ashore, clear of sunken rocks.

Wherever it was, it can have been no gentle landing. The huge seas driving in from the south-west picked her up and slammed her on to the rocks. Her masts collapsed forwards and the rudder was soon gone. The keel soon broke and the decks, as they always will in a ship whose whole frame and body is rupturing, began to 'start' – the planks springing away from their housing. The ship had gone ashore starboard side to, and the hull was soon stove in on that side in the bilges. The hull, which had been insured for £2,500, was later sold as a lump of partially salvageable timber, for £68 and its contents for £246.

All thirteen of the lives on board the *Neda* were saved. One of the crew swam ashore through the surf as soon as the ship struck, the other twelve remained on board until the tide fell and 'were lowered over the said ship's side on to the rocks by means of a rope and were afterwards sheltered in a shepherd's cottage.' As the *Oban Times* said, 'To the shipwrecked crew – especially to the captain's child, who was much injured – the shepherd and his wife showed every kindness and attention, and all speak highly of the efforts which this poor and lonely couple made for their comforts.'

On Friday 28 January 1876, the attention was drawn of a Harris boat out fishing on a still-wild Minch and the Master was taken to Stornoway. His wife, child and the rest of the crew stayed with the Campbells until the following Thursday, when the storm had abated.

The wreck of the *Neda* is still remembered in Harris. Uisdean MacSween once described to me the moments after the ship had gone ashore. He thought that the Campbells had been alerted by the single crewman who had swum through the surf. They hurried down to the western side of Mianish and stood open-mouthed at this sudden irruption into their lives. Once the tide had dropped, most of the crew were indeed happy to leave the splintered ship for the security of land, however windswept. But Mrs Clark, the Master's wife, was not keen. Sheltering her child in her arms, she looked at the Shiant Islanders, monoglot Gaelic speakers, the men vast and hairy, with their beards, Hughie said, 'reaching down to their waists', drenched in the rain and wind, their hair plastered to their heads, their feet probably naked, and thought of her parlour in Wallsend, its polished iron range and cretonne furnishings. Mrs Clark screamed above the wind, 'I'd rather stay here than put myself into the hands of men such as those!' Her husband was having none of it. He ordered two of his crew to tie up his wife and have her carried ashore, in Hughie's words, 'like a bale of ticking'.

Without question, there would have been people living here when the Bronze Age torc somehow arrived off the Galtas. It is not inconceivable that the same kind of welcome might have been extended to them.

But there is another possibility. The torc may not have come to the Shiants from a wreck. It might have been deliberately dropped into the sea here. This is, perhaps, at the outer reaches of speculation, but it is not outlandish. There are arguments to be made, and precedents to be brought from elsewhere towards the end of the Middle Bronze Age, which suggest that this piece of gold may indeed have been deliberately thrown away.

The Bronze Age, beginning in Britain at the start of the second millennium BC, had marked a change in human consciousness. No longer the giant communal monuments, the New Granges and the Stonehenges, nor the communal graves in which individual bodies were dismembered and all parts of all people scattered together. In one of the neolithic tombs of the Orkneys, at Isbister, the remains of the people were mixed with the bones of another animal: at least eight and maybe ten white-tailed sea eagles were also buried there. This may be chance; the eagles may have used the tomb as a cave-like eyrie. But it has also been suggested, more intriguingly, that it is the eagles whose grave this is, a place which the human beings were allowed to share as a privilege. At the time, with the average height of men no more than five feet, six inches, and the average life expectancy in the mid-twenties, the eagles would have been both larger and longer lived than almost every person. The human bodies may even have been exposed at death for the sea eagles to consume as their royal food.

That frame of mind, a certain Neolithic humility, disappears in the Bronze Age. The hero arrives. Agamemnon and Achilles are the Bronze Age archetypes and hubris becomes their governing sin. The human person is glorified and with his egotism comes his guilt. He carries remarkable weapons. He wears jewellery. His body becomes the arena of his glory. Bronze itself requires travel, exchange and communication because tin and copper are almost never found together in nature. The idea of the exotic – amber from the Baltic, faience beads from the eastern Mediterranean, silver from Bohemia – becomes the individual's mark of splendour. In the Bronze Age, with his marvellous things alongside him, the individual man is buried alone.

Metal was the means for this glorification of the person. Its emergence from rock to burnished strength was itself marvellous and that transformational quality, that birth of the precious from the dross, was symbolic of potency and magic. This material was not for use but for beauty. It was a jewellery culture. The standing of important people was bound up with it. The tiny socketed bronze axe heads that have been found in Scotland, the symbolic spears and shields, too thin to be used in battle but as perfect in their making as the breastplates now worn by the Household Cavalry, or those tiny medallion hints at a breastplate which officers wore throughout the nineteenth century, a hint of manhood in the candlelit halls: this is an understanding of metal not in the huge material sense of the Victorian engineer, but in the amazed and delighted vision of the jeweller. That is why this torc is more important than it seems. It does not matter because it is pretty. It matters because in its incorruptibility and rustlessness, the very qualities which drew Kenny Cunningham to its value, it is a denial of death, a sketch of perfection and eternity.

Conditions started to decline towards the end of the second millennium BC. The weather worsened. The land which had been taken in for agriculture throughout this Atlantic fringe of Europe started to become difficult. And in difficulty, life became violent and frightened. The amount of metal, whether bronze or gold, that was in circulation on the European web of connections, along the river valleys and the western seaways, began to decline. But this was no democracy. There was no trimming of the top end to help the people at the bottom. Far from it. The number of pieces whose purpose was elegance and display actually increased. Beautiful shields, large cauldrons made out of sheet bronze, gold torcs: as the weather thickened and the crops diminished, more and more of these nearly useless objects were made. Social stress produced not an arms race but a beauty contest.

Slowly, one needs to approach the idea of the gold torc being thrown into the sea off the Galtas. And to do that one needs to understand the idea of the gift. It remains true that the giver of a gift exerts power over its recipient. The recipient remains in debt to his benefactor. And he can only absolve himself of that debt by giving in return. This leads without much interval to a generosity contest. Give and you shall ordain. Give back and you shall conquer. In pre-capitalist societies, it is not the accumulation of wealth which is the mark of standing but the ability to dispose of it in the form of gifts.

Consider for a moment that the torc might be a gift to the world. If it had been thrown into the Minch, it would be, as Trevor Cowie, its curator in the National Museums of Scotland, has written, 'a means of accumulating prestige without the risk of the original gift being returned or "trumped" with the loss of status that would ensue.' If you can give something of such enormous value to the Minch, the Minch will be forever in your debt. Such gifts to the world are found all over Europe in the Bronze Age and later. The hoards, which earlier generations of archaeologists interpreted either as the hurried concealment of treasured goods or the nest eggs of travelling merchants who failed for some reason to collect them, are now starting to be seen in this different light.

The golden torcs are often found with other precious objects. The one in the fen at Stretham in Cambridgeshire had with it a golden bracelet, some rings and human bones, although that is exceptional. Another in the Fens was accompanied by some bronze adze-axes called palstaves. The one in Calvados had with it a bracelet, a spear, a razor, a small anvil and a hammer for working the metal. In Lewis, such a hoard was found in 1910 at Adabrock, in Ness, just beyond the Shiants' northern horizon. Bronze axes, a gouge, a spearhead, a hammer, three razors, two whetstones and some beads, one of glass, two of amber and one of beaten gold, were recovered from under three yards of peat. The Bronze Age acts with unparalleled generosity to the earth as the earth grows meaner.

The Shiant torc fits. It is on the very margins of the Europe in which these practices occur. The place in which it was found is as dramatic as landscape comes. Intriguingly, another torc, similar to this one in its tapered terminals but without the twisted decoration, was found at the Giant's Causeway in Antrim, the columnar dolerite sill whose structure so closely resembles the geology of the Shiants. That is perhaps no more than a coincidence, but it is a suggestive one: the brightness of the gold against the dark near-architecture of the columned rock, a bringing together of opposites which once seen would not be forgotten. The Shiants are also the most northerly example of this sort of rock. Is it a coincidence that the most northerly golden torc was found at this most northerly extension of the British volcanic landscape? Was there a Bronze Age recognition that the Shiants marked a sort of frontier? Certainly no rock is more easily identified by a non-geologist than columnar dolerite. It continues to have the air of divine or diabolical sculpture. And the Norse may have recognised this too. Another possible derivation for the name is *Galt*, the Old Norse word for 'magic' or 'charm'.

The northern boundary of their world would have been important to the middle and late Bronze Age. As the weather worsened, it would have been seen to have been coming from the north. Looking from the south, was this, I wonder, the outer margin of the world as it was known, the frontier between what was theirs and what they feared and needed to resist and control? The Galtas, the most sculptural of all the columnar formations in the Shiants, are like a giant's causeway that has been set adrift, afloat on the tide. As Thomas O'Farrell, the Ordnance Survey man, saw in 1851, the tide run is savage between them 'at all times especially at Spring tides there is a rapid current. About them the tide flows exceedingly strong, flowing the same as a large River.'

The gift of the torc here – and perhaps of other objects which have yet to be found – was an act not of propitiation but of dominance. The Bronze Age chieftain gave away what was most precious to him and in doing that showed his standing in the world and his control over its nature. The Shiants marked the frontier of that golden world and the throwing of the torc into the teeth of the Galtas was an act of symbolic empire.

I have often taken boats through there. You need a quiet day but, however quiet the weather, the sea still bumps and ripples around you. Small spiralling eddies break off from the corners of the stacks and for a few seconds adopt a life of their own. Little insucking constellations of bubbled water waltz and veer across the liquid floor. Sometimes there is a succession of them, a troupe of whirling water-dancers strung out before you, making their way from rock to rock, formation-dancing in the tide. The hull tips with the turbulence as you squeeze past them. Some of the channels are no more than ten or twelve feet wide, and as deep as that, square beams of running water below you, as wonderful as liquid steel for their concentration of energies. It is a place which can never be the same however often you return and I have gone back there for year after year. If there is any kind of swell you have to be careful with the boat, holding it back on the surge, pushing it forward as the swell sucks away again, choosing the moment to be swept on through, suddenly leaving the Galtas behind, out again in the widths of the Minch. Occasionally in a corner between the rocks you can find a still backwater pool where the boat can rest and slowly turn and you can watch, beside you, the long fronds of the kelp billowing in the channels like hair. Underwater, it is a swept world. No sediment, but a place of endless movement, recognised as magical three thousand years ago, still magical today.

7

THE GEESE LEAVE AS the spring comes. Their absence marks the opening of the days. I have never seen that visionary moment, as the flock heads north, but whatever it is that the geese sense in the air, I know it too. Crossing the Minch with *Freyja* again in early May feels like my own migration to summer pastures. John MacAulay had given me at first too small a sail, reluctant to overpower a boat in the hands of a novice, but I had put it to him that she needed and could carry something bigger. He had a larger one made for me, at a sailmaker's in Tarbert, Loch Fyne, and its clew now reached back almost to the stern. Filled with wind, the fabric made a sickle curve three-quarters the length of the boat itself. I could sit back in the sternsheets and look up at the wide scimitar of my sail above me. *Freyja* thrived with the new potency, lifting to the lighter breezes, heeling a little under them, so much at home, and so motherly for me, that I felt I had never been happier on sea or land. Seas which had always alarmed me in smaller dinghies now felt like *Freyja*'s natural element, and mine.

Crossing from Scalpay in May, the Minch was sparkling in her spring-time clothes. The water lay glittering around the boat as though sugared, a frost of beneficence across its surface. You had to squeeze your eyes against its little shafts of sun. A pair of white-headed Risso dolphins, moving south, passed me off the Sound of Scalpay, arcing together, breathing twice. Twenty yards from the boat, a Minke whale slid its long black back above the surface for a moment, as seamless and as faceless as a U-boat, before easing away again as the sea washed over its tiny fin and water-swept stern. A great skua flashed its two white-wing streaks overhead and went on. The Shiants were in the distance, ten miles away, just big enough for different weather to fall on the three islands, and I watched the slow, soft stroboscope of sun and shadow moving on their greenness.

One enormous swell after another, each a hundred yards long and about six or eight feet high, was creaming into the Minch from the north. It made a billowed downland of the sea. From the crests, all of Lewis and Harris was visible, and its troughs cut off the shore. The sea ridges were so long and certain in their movement that there was nothing alarming here, just a steady breathing of the water, as if the Minch were buried in sleep.

The tide, at springs, was running at the flood, perhaps as much as three knots in places, bubbling occasionally in one of those flat mushrooms of upwelling sea, breaking into unexpected riffles as the submarine topography disturbed the flow. The sea itself was sliding and sidling me to my destination. It was my travelator, and the winter Minch was nowhere to be seen. Pick your moment and the sea will do what it can for you, however small the boat and however unpractised the helm. The wind was steady on the beam, and as it says in an old Gaelic song, it felt as if *Freyja* 'would cut a thin oat straw with the excellence of her going.'

This moment of ecstatic ease is the significant historical fact. Anywhere that can be reached on a calm day will be reached. What matters is the invitation, not the threat, and if there is an opening, people will take it. That is why the Shiants are as much part of the human world as anywhere else. The entire population of Europe is descended from a maximum of ten people, some arriving thirty thousand years ago, others arriving perhaps from the Ukraine only after the end of the Ice Age, thirteen thousand years ago. Those late arrivals, five or six of them, brought with them the ancestor of the Indo-European languages we now speak. The children and grandchildren of those ten filtered along the capillaries of Europe and filled it. In fifty generations we have spread everywhere.

Seen on a planetary scale, it is an extraordinarily short and rapid event, a peopling of a continent as quickly as weeds can colonise rough ground. The movement for a while comes to a halt at the Atlantic shore but resumes a couple of thousand years later, when the technology is up to it and first the Norse and then the other Europeans continue to spread westwards and on around the globe. There is a temptation to imagine the past as essentially static and the present as essentially mobile and disrupted. Nothing could be further from the truth. The peopling of the Shiants is only one fragment of an endless chain. That is why this crossing of a potentially alarming sea, at a moment which is picked because the weather is kind and the spring is coming, because the tide is running with you and the sun is out, when you can see where you are going and you have everything you need, is one of the deepest of all historical experiences. Don't imagine the past as a place full of catastrophe and horror. This is its colour: a chance fairly taken, a sense of happiness in the light of spring. The Minch is laced with the wakes of the ancestors and this wonderful, easy-limbed stirring of *Freyja* on the long Atlantic swell is a stirring of the past. I smile in the boat now and open my face to the warmth of the sun and the shining of the sky.

Allowing for leeway and the northward drift of the tide, I am aiming for Sgeir Mianish, the rock at the southern tip of Eilean an Tighe. The heading is eighty-eight degrees magnetic, in effect due east. Slowly enough I gain on the Galtas. The shore of Harris retreats and greys. The stripes of the lighthouse on Scalpay fade with the distance. The bulk and reality of the Shiants grows with each yard. The enormous swells coming down from the north were breaking across Damhag in a band of surf half a mile long. In the sunshine it looked Hawaiian; a steepening of the wave along that full broad front, a blueness as deep as a new-born eye, and then above it the absolute white of the wave-cap, tumbling and breaking the whole length of the wave wall, a rippling as the sea crossed the rock bar hidden beneath it. Donald MacSween, the Scalpay fisherman, the tenant of the Shiants for many years after his cousin Hugh MacSween had retired, and now my mentor and guide to the waters of the Minch, had told me about Damhag in a swell: 'That's when it'll be wearing its crown,' he had said. 'Crowned white from one end to another.'

The islands are flushed with greenness and colour. My heart expands at the Shiants' spring-time welcome. On the bigger Galtas, where there are now no sheep to graze, the sea mayweed, which is like big, luscious chamomile, and the thrift, the sea campion and the rock rose have erupted into flowering cushions of newness. The winter outlines of these islets have changed. Now they are sprouting lumps of new growth, soft-edged warts, coloured carbuncles on the faces of familiar friends. On Galta Beag the sea pinks are so thick that the whole island, even from a mile away, has a pink flush, as if the rock were blushing.

Once ashore in the spring-time, it is difficult to imagine that the islands could ever be unkind. Winter does not exist. I walk through the new grass with my shoes off. The geese have left it paddled flat but it is already, quite literally, springing back. There are primroses in the clefts of the rock and violets as big as pansies next to the well. Thrift makes its cushions on stones where it seems impossible to derive any sustenance, and next to them, where the sheep cannot reach them, the sea campion or bladder campion makes white gardens in the wilderness. There are forget-me-nots growing by the stream and the first dark, hairy leaves of watermint have gathered at its edge. The lichen glows like cracked lacquer on the cliffs. Big, lush, red campions, some pinker, some paler, grow in the clefts between the columns. English stonecrop, only just lifting its head above the modesty of a lichen, encrusts the grooves and shallows of the boulders. The spear-tips of the flag irises have begun to prod above the surface of the bog, sharp but still flowerless, a stipple of brighter green among the tweed of the marsh plants. The orchids too are now just poking above the grass, and in the marshes the kingcups glow like cartoons of marshland flowers as the snipe flick away from your footstep, a jittering into new life.

This is what I have come to the Shiants for, year after year, at just this moment. It is a half-season. The new lambs all have the same little bony body, the same strange combination of fragility and resilience, the same jumpy immediacy. On their suddenly vast green grassy playground, they perform from time to time a startling leap, all four legs in the air, a quiver along the tensed back, a sudden blowing off of the synapses, for no real reason and always followed by a look of bemused horror. Why did my body do that? What is this sensory, neural life I have acquired? Am I me? What is this shocking, jerking, stuttering of which I am a part? Where's my mother?

Spring here is always beautiful for those uncertainties, for its hesitations and incongruities laid alongside each other without comment or context. 'I will be fed,' the lamb's cry says. 'I will not be fobbed off. But help me, look after me, I need you.' And spring replies, 'I will freeze you and cosset you, I will be everything you have hoped for and nothing you could desire, I will be banks of primroses open to the sun and the reticent, denying face of the vernal squill in shade.'

It is the season of discontinuity. The other three have a sort of wholeness to them. All of them have something at least of unbroken length and continuity. Think of the summer and what drifts into your mind – or mine anyway – is languor, the breadth of the grass banks on Eilean Mhuire where the thick summer growth stretches unbroken from cliff to cliff, the length of days, the sheer extent of summer; autumn hangs on like an old tapestry, brown and mottled, a slow, long slide into winter, unhurried in its seamless descent into death; and winter itself, of course, has persistence at its heart, a long, dogged grimness which gives nothing and allows nothing and becomes more dreadful each year, one long, wet, dark, hard day after another.

There is none of that in spring. Its music is broken and jerky, moving backward as much as forward, offering gaieties and delicacies only to withdraw them, with frost as much as warmth in its heart. Botticelli's *Primavera* does not belong in the Hebrides but it is the true image of the Hebridean spring. Among the crowd in the picture, it is Flora who commands your attention. She walks barefoot through a meadow. The flowers are brooches on its cloth. Her dress, arms, neck and hair are garlanded with flowers. Her manner is delicate but definite, like a Grace but more tentative, or like the Venus behind her but newer, less knowing. There is nothing lush here. Flora is in the process of becoming: the embodiment of life as life actually emerges. That is why, like spring, she is still slightly withdrawn. She still has something of the winter in her. And every time I walk around the early spring-time Shiants, I see her on the path ahead of me, picking her way between the stones and the flowers.

The Barnacle geese are on their way to Greenland. They follow the spring north, catching the wave of new grass as it sprouts under the sunshine. The birds are tuned to the world, to the planetary fact of the northern hemisphere tipping towards the sun and their journey is an elegant and perfectly measured surfing on the breaking wave of greenness that ripples towards the Arctic with the spring. From a satellite you could see them, long skeins of the goose bodies, sewn like stitches into the air, travelling in family and in island groups, flogging north with the lengthening of the days. From offshore islands along the entire length of the west coast of Ireland, clouds of them from the coast of County Clare and the Arans, a huge concentration leaving from the Inish-keas at the tip of County Mayo, others in Sligo Bay, a scattering all along the coast of Donegal, up to Malin Head, over to Islay and Tiree, from one island after another the flocks have lifted away.

The Shiant birds have joined them. Day and night they are making their way to the Faeroes and then on to the valleys of north-west Iceland, concentrating in the spring-time in their tens of thousands, descending en masse to the wet river pastures of Húnavatnssýsla and Skagafjarðarsýsla before heading off again, across the Denmark Strait to the breeding grounds in north-east Greenland, between Kangertittivaq and Orléans Land. There, at last, in a savage stretch of country, whose hinterland is one enormous glacier, sliced with deep fjords and glacial valleys, and on the islands that lie offshore, they arrive for the nightless summer months to breed. The Shiant geese, it is thought, will remain together there, recognising each other, a flock within a flock, and will return together in the autumn with their young.

The geese are en route for a few weeks each spring and again each autumn. If you could watch the North Atlantic over the centuries, you would see their passage flashing on and off twice a year. From the west coast of Ireland, across to the Inner Hebrides, up past the Shiants to Rona and Sula Sgeir, on to the Faeroes, Iceland and Greenland, this is a line creased into the palm of the world's hand. It is also a map of something else. These were the paths taken by the Celtic hermits between the sixth and the tenth centuries. Is it possible that they, in search of 'a desert in the ocean', followed the track the geese had blazed for them? It is often said that the wild goose became a symbol in the early Celtic church of the Holy Spirit. There is no evidence for that. But this is a separate question. Did these wonderful birds lead the churchmen, by example, to the north?

Whether in the wake of the geese or not, the idea of holiness clings to the Shiants, as to other islands. Remoteness from the world looks like a closeness to God and intriguingly, it turns out that the association of islands and holiness predates anything Christian. There was an important Christian moment on these small Hebridean islands but it was part of a much longer continuum. There is some evidence that, in Britain in particular, islands were thought of as holy places long before the Christian idea of the hermit arrived here from Egypt in the sixth century. Three pieces of evidence coalesce. In Plutarch's essay 'On Oracles that have ceased to function', the Athenian scholar and philosopher reports a conversation that occurred in Delphi in about AD 83. A

traveller called Demetrius of Tarsus, a *grammatikos*, a literature teacher, had just returned from Britain. The traveller told the priests at Delphi what was happening at the far end of the world:

> Demetrius said that many of the islands off Britain were uninhabited and widely scattered, some of them being named after deities and demigods. He himself had sailed, for the sake of learning and observation, to the island nearest to the uninhabited ones, on an official mission. This island had a few inhabitants, who were holy men, and all held exempt from raiding by the Britons.

At just this period, another man called Demetrius (or perhaps the same one: there are few Greeks mentioned on Roman inscriptions in Britain) left two small bronze votary tablets at a temple in the Roman city of York. One was dedicated to the 'Gods of the Governor's Praetorium'. The other 'to Ocean and Tethys', the male and female deities presiding over the wildness of the outer sea. And again, at this same period, the last years of the first century AD, Agricola was conducting large-scale sea-borne explorations of the west coast of Britain, sending a fleet around Cape Wrath and through the Minches. It is at least a possibility that Demetrius was describing the situation in the Outer Hebrides and the Shiants may well have been holy for millennia. And were these islands once, I wonder, named after a Pictish deity, as Demetrius described?

What can only be called a pagan sense of the holiness of islands lasted well into the historical period. When Martin Martin in the 1690s asked a man of Lewis

> if he pray'd at home as often, and as fervently as he did when in the Flannan Islands [a group to the west of Lewis], he plainly confess'd to me that he did not: adding further, that these remote Islands were places of inherent Sanctity; and that there was none ever yet landed in them but found

himself more dispos'd to Devotion there, than anywhere else.

Because of this sense of 'inherent sanctity', a whole set of superstitious rules applied to the language people could use on the Flannans and to the way they could behave.

Customs of this kind are not recorded for the Shiants but the same conditions apply. They, too, are never given their true name in Gaelic but are called 'the Big Islands' or even simply 'The Islands'. What is it about islands that summons this tiptoeing around them? This is difficult and speculative territory, but it is worth considering why, outside any Christian framework, islands have for so long felt holy. The Christian experience is centrally shaped by the experience of Christ in the desert, and by the idea that Satan and the flesh can be overcome by exposure to the dangers of a desert place. That idea is important in the history of hermits in the Hebrides, but leave it aside for a moment and other aspects of islandness move to the foreground.

For want of a better word, the holiness of the Shiants, their numen, the inherent spirit which the Lewisman described to Martin, is tangible enough. Only once in my life have I felt it strongly enough to be disturbed by it, but that single experience has entered my own private understanding of the place and it remains an underlayer which shapes everything I know and feel about the Shiants. The first time I was there on my own, I was nineteen and an undergraduate at Cambridge. Donald MacSween had dropped me on the beach and I had with me no more than my one or two boxes of supplies, books and candles, a small canoe and a dog. I had waved goodbye to Donald's boat, the *Favour*, as it disappeared around the rocks on its way back to Scalpay and I spent the day of my arrival arranging everything I needed. I collected wood from the beach and water from the well, I unpacked my stores into the house's cupboard and laid out my sleeping bag. I was there alone with a dog. I had three weeks' literal isolation in front of me.

Even then, before I had learned what I know now, I knew the islands had a reputation. Their name in Gaelic could mean 'haunted' as well as 'holy'. And there was a more recent story. In about 1911, a man was said to have gone to live in the house which had been finally deserted by the Campbells only a few years earlier. He had his furniture delivered by boat and his stock of sheep. He set everything up in the two simple rooms, one for living and cooking, the other a bedroom. He lay down to sleep and in the middle of the night woke to find an old man at his bedside. 'Do you realise,' the figure said in a straightforward and conversational tone, 'that you are sleeping on my grave?'

As soon as he could draw the attention of a passing fishing boat – he was said to have set fire to the heather on the top of one of the islands so that its whole upper surface sprouted a blazing head of flame – he left again, taking with him his furniture and his pots and pans. Except for visiting shepherds and lobstermen, the islands had been deserted ever since.

I knew the story but I didn't want to pay attention to it. I did not want to be alarmed at the prospect of being alone on this big, remote and empty place. I had been here before with others and loved its many uncompromised beauties. The idea that it was haunted lay somewhere in the background, in the basement of my feelings. More, I was filled with a deep underswell of excitement and pleasure at being out there, exposed and unfettered, at the feeling of being dangled in a solution of such richness, so uninvadable. But perhaps, now, looking back on it, these twenty years later, I can recognise that those are the pre-conditions for an awareness of the metaphysical.

I know I was frightened because I moved the bed from one room to the other. I moved it in other words away from the grave and went to sleep there, deeply ensconced in the red, downy sleeping bag. The dog, a terrier, was curled up on the mattress beside me and the fire was well stoked, flaming and then glowing.

Nights are not long in northern Scotland in mid-summer. Real dark only lasts for three or four hours, but when it comes it is as black as night ever is. There is no sodium haze. There is no electricity on these islands, but I had a torch with me. Right in the middle of this dark darkness I suddenly woke up. The dog, a terrier, keen to dig any rat out of any hole, not a fearful creature by any account, was standing on the bed next to me, shaking, utterly alert, staring at the far side of the room. I shone the torch over there. Nothing to see beyond my own pots and pans, the washing up bowl, my own coat hung on the back of the door.

His fear infected me. I felt at that moment colonised by terror. There was nothing to see, but my torch made the places where it wasn't shining even darker. The dog would neither move nor relax. There was no sound beyond the swell on the shore fifty yards away. I began to shake, dragged the dog down into the sleeping bag with me and then pulled its hood over the two of us, the torch still in my hand, cocooned from that fear. I couldn't sleep. The dog and I shook together. From time to time I would make a little eyehole of an opening at the top of the bag where I was holding its rim gripped in two fists, waiting for the light to come, for colour to drain back into the shapes and blackness of this room.

The length of short nights! Again and again that eye, opened on to the world beyond the downy warmth of the dog and the cotton of the sleeping bag, revealed only blackness. It became a matter of patience, of out-waiting the night. At three or four o'clock, the world started to grey. I could put my head out into air. It felt as though the room and I had been through something deep and long together, that used-up sensation of exhaustion and a world clarified because some of its deeper possibilities had been seen.

I realised, as I cooked breakfast over the fire, that I was exhilarated. Perhaps this was some physiological effect, a drained, post-adrenaline high, but it felt more than that, a new intimacy with a place that went beyond the purely aesthetic. I had somehow met its soul. But at the same time I knew I didn't want to go through it again. It was too frightening. That day, after the sleepless night, I did everything I could to exhaust myself, walking from end to end of the islands, rowing from one to the other, setting pots, collecting firewood from the shore. By the time the evening came, my whole body was slack with tiredness, my limbs drooping like eyelids. The dog had come with me here and there, to and fro, and by early evening it was asleep.

I drank beer in front of the dropping sun. I knew I would sleep and I did, straight through, waking to find a beam of sun pointing its finger through the window and across the room in a diagonal on to the floor. From my bed I could reach out and put my hand into its light, which felt warm, like sun in a greenhouse. The morning was calm and the sea slick in its stillness. I spent the whole day out in the boat, the dog curled up on a rope in the bow, and the sun plunging through the green water, lighting the guillemots diving there for fish. That was a morning not to be forgotten. Whatever had frightened me that first night now seemed to embrace me. I lay adrift in the boat and felt the arms of the islands around me. They could never frighten me again. If there was a tutelary spirit here, I could live with it, I could love every aspect of it, however bitter its moods, or harsh its treatment of me and that love would, in a way that I cannot properly describe, be returned and sustain me. From that moment I can date my love and affection for this place, an attachment to it beyond the touristic. In the course of those nights and days, the Shiants became a kind of home, a place which would never desert me wherever I might be, the touchstone of reality.

Years afterwards, I read a remark by Jung to the effect that if ghosts are said to be 'nothing but projections of your own unconscious thoughts and fears on to the outside world, no intellectual acrobatics are needed to turn that sentence around and describe your own fears as ghosts that have taken up residence in you.' That permeability of the skin, the flippability of inner and outer, seems to me now like a true description of that experience and perhaps of island experience more generally.

Islands, because of their isolation, are revelatory, places where the boundaries are wafer-thin. My sons tell me that night after night, asleep in their tent on the island, they have heard footsteps beside them in the grass. Not the pattering of rats, nor the sheep but something else. And although I have never heard anything like that, I am inclined to believe them. These remote islands are 'places of inherent Sanctity' and the footsteps are perhaps some of the last modern echoes of an ancient presence.

Everyone who comes here responds to it. This is not the preserve of outsiders or holiday-makers. The shepherds acknowledge it conversationally enough. For them all it is a kind of dream country, a place over which the mind can roam, to which your thoughts always turn at a spare moment, walking with your mind's eye across the loved contours of the place. Both Hugh MacSween and John Murdo Matheson, the young shepherd from Gravir, who since 1996 has had the sheep on the Shiants, have talked to me about the Shiants with an intensity outsiders would never credit. We can have entire conversations about hollows in rocks and pools in streams. It is a bond for anyone who comes here, or at least for anyone that allows the islands to envelop them, to be the encompassing limit of their world, even for a while.

That is a strange but perfectly real effect: after a few days here, the place seems to expand. The Shiants no longer seem, as Compton Mackenzie described them, like 'three specks of black pepper in the middle of that uncomfortable stretch of sea called the Minch' but a world in themselves. To walk the mile or so from one end of Garbh Eilean to another becomes a day-long expedition. Eilean Mhuire is another continent. The details of rocks and plants, of the little alders growing in the rock clefts, the honeysuckle twined around them, the acre after acre of dwarf willow growing on the marsh, the wrinkles in the turf which might or might not hint at previous lives: all of this becomes as varied as America. The Shiants have no wood but they have hidden places, tucked among the rocks. They have no rivers, but they have streams in which the watermint and the forget-me-nots grow. They have no lakes, but pools around whose margins the turf luxuriates into neon green and across whose still, dark surface the water boatmen paddle like Polynesians between their archipelagos. And they have of course the richness of the sea.

Something of the sense of holiness on islands comes, I think, from this strange, elastic geography. Islands are made larger, para-doxically, by the scale of the sea that surrounds them. The element which might reduce them, which might be thought to besiege them, has the opposite effect. The sea elevates these few acres into something they would never be if hidden in the mass of the mainland. The sea makes islands significant. They are defined by it, both wedded to it and implacably set against it, both a creation and a rejection of the element which makes them what they are. They are the not-sea within the sea, standing against the sea's chaos and erosive power, but framed by it, enshrined by it. In that way, every island is an assertion in an ocean of denials, the one positive gesture against an almost overwhelming bleakness. They would not be what they are without the bleakness. The state of siege is creative and an island, in short, is life set against death, a life defined by the death that surrounds it. Like the peak of a mountain, or perhaps more like your own presence on the peak of a mountain, it is an image of salvation and of eternity.

It has long been thought that a hermit once lived on the

Shiants. On Eilean Mhuire, the tradition is that one of the ruins there was a chapel to the Virgin. That is, I think, mistaken, as will emerge, but what can be said for certain is that the island's Gaelic name, Eilean Mhuire, is the name given to the mother of God, and is quite distinct from Mairi, the name used since the Reformation by Protestants for their daughters. This, unequivocally, is the Virgin's island. The men and women of Scalpay, strict church people, when referring to the island in conversation nowadays, call it not Eilean Mhuire but Eilean Mairi, avoiding any taint of Catholicism. The Ordnance Survey officers in 1851 were told that Eilean Mhuire had been a refuge for a priest 'in the time of Knox'.

That seems unlikely, although the island might conceivably have sheltered one of the Franciscan missionaries who evangelised the Hebrides from Ireland in the early seventeenth century. Perhaps the name of Eilean Mhuire is a thread leading to a more ancient past. The church in the centuries before the first millennium, the age of Columba, not only in Ireland but in the whole Christian world from here to Syria, was deeply devoted to the

cult of the Virgin. Hymns to the Virgin were composed on Iona, sung antiphonally there in the timber-built choir. Mary was the embodiment of fertility and hope. She had made good everything Eve had spoiled and the cross to which she gave her son restored everything the tree in Eden had destroyed. Without Mary, the world could never have been redeemed.

Dedications were made to the Virgin all over the Ionan world. But the Mary of Iona was not the keening figure at the foot of the cross which the later Middle Ages would make of her. Instead, the focus of the Columban devotion was on Mary's gift to the world, the remaking of the universe in her womb, her conceiving and delivering of the Kingdom of Heaven. She was, in other words, the image of holy fertility.

Eilean Mhuire is an island of astonishing richness set in the middle of the wild sea, where the grass even today clogs your feet as you walk across it in midsummer, seventy-five acres of extraordinarily fertile pasture, a rolling meadow two hundred feet above the sea, surrounded by cliffs, where the lambs fatten so quickly that, as John Murdo Matheson, the shepherd, says, they are always 'ready for the hook by the end of August', and the sorrel grows in miniature, heady-scented forests. It is not difficult to recognise the resonance of that fecundity for the early Christians. You can quite literally roll in it, wrapping yourself in the fullness of life on Eilean Mhuire.

Is this a key to the attraction of the Shiants – and of other equally fertile islands – for the Dark Age saints? Those early Christians would have absorbed from the Gospels and from the writings of the Desert Fathers in Egypt and Syria what has been called 'the theology of dispossession'. This was the doctrine which, as the Celtic scholar Dr Thomas Owen Clancy has written, 'lay behind the Irish attraction to *peregrinatio*, in which the ascetic would leave home, lands, family and wealth, and seek salvation on a distant island.'

In a fallen world, redemption could come only by abandoning the everyday and by finding in the desert the pearl of great price conceived in the Virgin's womb. No Hebridean island I know fits the description of a desert pearl better than Eilean Mhuire. It is in itself an icon of the Christianity that held sway here a thousand years ago.

There is a long-standing confusion that must be clarified. In the late seventeenth century, Martin Martin said of the Shiants that 'Island-More hath a Chappel in it dedicated to the Virgin Mary'. Since then, this has been taken as a reference to a building on Eilean Mhuire, because of the coincidence of the names. That is a mistake. The chapel was not on Eilean Mhuire but on what is now known as Eilean an Tighe and was until the mid-nineteenth century known as Eilean na Cille or Church Island. The passage runs as follows:

> Island-More hath a Chappel in it dedicated to the Virgin Mary, and is fruitful in Corn and Grass: the Island joining to it on the West is only for Pasturage. I saw a couple of Eagles here ... those Eagles are so careful of the place of their abode, that they never yet killed any Sheep or Lamb in the Island ... so that they make their Purchase in the opposite islands, the nearest of which is a League distant.

Apart from Martin's muddle over 'West' – Garbh Eilean is in fact north of Eilean an Tighe – he is describing a situation in which Eilean an Tighe contains the Chapel and Garbh Eilean the eagles. Eilean Mhuire is the place in which the eagles 'make their Purchase'.

Several times in the nineteenth century, travellers in the Hebrides had pointed out to them the 'cell' of the hermit on Eilean an Tighe. The artist William Daniell saw it in 1815. John Macculloch, the geologist, saw it four years later and TS Muir, visiting on 21 July 1859, while conducting the research for his

'Ecclesiological Notes on Some of the Islands of Scotland etc.', found after landing on the beach and coming to the shelf of ground immediately to the south of it on Eilean an Tighe, that 'on this level space, there are traces of a burying ground, and the foundation of what seems to have been a chapel of small size.' By the 1850s, then, at a time when the islands were empty for a while, the site of the chapel had virtually disappeared.

The archaeologist Pat Foster re-identified the cemetery in the summer of 2000. It is a hundred yards or so north of the present house, a low mound on whose surface there are still one or two fragments of Lewisian gneiss, which might or might not be grave markers. The mound has been dug into at some time and there is a story still current in Scalpay of a woman finding a skull here in the 1930s. There is the ruin of a building within the western side of the mound, which has some squarish masonry in it, but has clearly been built up and adapted since Muir saw the chapel reduced to a 'foundation' in 1859.

A hazy folk-tradition of a saint or hermit, an ancient island name, ruins which certainly don't sound earlier than medieval, a burial ground which cannot be dated: that until the summer of 2000 was the limit of the muddle and the knowledge.

A discovery made by Pat Foster's archaeological team changed that. The excavation of the house, whose larger findings will be described later, had reached its final day. All fortnight, one intense squall after another had moved up the Minch. The sun had shone brilliantly in the intervals, but those dark, cold showers were like little patches of night travelling through the mornings. A cold wind blew them in from the south. As Pat had indefatigably stalked the islands, mapping out all the early sites, Petr Limburský and Linda Čihakova, had taken charge of the excavation. Both are among the most brilliant of young Czech archaeologists, the most careful of excavators, patient beyond belief, able to sift, it seemed to me, the brushings of one eighteenth-century week on the house floor; the peat ash and charcoal, the fragments of broken pot, the odds and ends of daily life; from those of the week after and of the week before. As the final investigation of the year (a party from Prague would be returning each summer for perhaps another five years) Linda had decided to cut a trench – 'sondage' was the more glamorous word she used – through the floors of the house to see if there was anything immediately beneath them. In the trench, about half-way along the house, immediately next to the northern wall, she slowly uncovered a smooth, flattish round stone about twelve inches across, deeply buried in the clay and peat ash of the mid-eighteenth century.

We all came to look at the revealed upper surface of the stone. Even *in situ*, it had an air about it, simply through the perfection of its shape: not the knobbled awkwardness of most of the wall stones, but this organic circularity, this fullness and shapeliness. It looked as yeasty as a loaf. Jana Žegklitzová, the draughtswoman from Prague Castle, had been baking bread for us every day in the oven in the house, and Linda's stone looked like one of Jana's loaves. 'She must have been up here this morning!' Linda laughed, sitting back on her heels on the clay floor, reddened with the peat ash trodden into it two hundred and fifty years ago, and pulled her hair back from her face.

Linda approached the stone with her trowel. On her hands and knees she cleared the soil from around it and then with her fingers slowly turned the stone over to see what was underneath. It was heavy and as the stone rolled over on to its upper side Linda jumped back and away, shrieking at what she saw, holding her hand to her mouth. Deeply carved on the underside, the side which had been set down and buried in the floor, was a four-armed cross set within an equally firmly carved circle, just in from the outer circumference of the stone.

The four quadrants left by the cross stood proud, doughily pillowed like scones. Clay clung wetly in the carved grooves. An encircled cross, buried face down in the floor of the house: clearly this was something that had been significant twice, once in its making and once in its burying. I carried the cross stone down to the house and we photographed it there against the silverweed and the grass. It was the culmination of the dig, the conclusive find, a reorientation of this place, its history and meaning.

I sailed back to Harris with the stone beside me in *Freyja*, a touchstone, the most beautiful man-made thing the Shiants had ever known, heavy and perfect, radiating significance. It belonged, like everything else recovered in the dig, to the Queen, but she graciously allows excavators to hang on to their finds for a while so that their origins and meanings can be understood. It will eventually end up in a museum, perhaps in Stornoway, perhaps in Edinburgh. Feeling like Little Jack Horner with my plum beside me, I travelled Britain with the stone. I wanted to know what it was and I wanted to know what it meant. I showed it to Professor Charles Thomas, the first of the modern excavators of Iona and one of the leading experts on early Christianity in Britain. He was definitive. 'It's a grave marker, a primary grave marker. They put them either in the grave or on the grave. Not before the seventh century AD; probably somewhere between the seventh and tenth centuries. You can't date them more precisely than that. They didn't exist before AD 600 and they became more elaborate after 1000.' And what was it doing in the early-modern house where we had found it? 'People, at least until the modern reform movement, would always have been very receptive to these things,' Professor Thomas said. 'They would have taken it there from the grave. They would have liked it in the house.'

At one stroke, the Shiants had acquired their early Christian reality. Columba, the prince-poet-bishop-saint who in the mid-sixth century had founded the monastery on Iona and an archipelago of related monasteries and outlying hermitages in Ireland and the Hebrides, had been an ascetic himself. According to

Adomnan, his biographer and the abbot of Iona at the end of the seventh century, 'He returned to his lodging and reclined on his sleeping place, where during the night he used to have for his bed the bare rock; and for pillow a stone which even today, stands beside his burial place as a kind of grave-pillar.'

Here then on the Shiants was the pillow stone of a follower of Columba. Here his head would have rested in life and with this stone his grave would have been marked in death. I took it with me to the Primary School in Scalpay, and asked Mrs MacSween, the headmistress and form mistress of the upper form, and the other Mrs MacSween, the form mistress of the lower form, if I could conduct an experiment. The children of both classes had to lie down with their heads on the stone as a pillow. It was a holiness test: whoever could treat it as a pillow would be a saint. The beautiful children of Scalpay, their pale, freckled skin and thick black hair, their dark, observant eyes, lay down one by one on the classroom floor. Most of them gingerly and carefully lowered their heads on to the stone, tentative at its hardness. Only two boys passed the test, lying down as if going to bed and believing so easily this was their pillow that they banged their ears into the unyielding stone and were rubbing them for the rest of the day. They were the true heirs of Columba.

The pillow stone's transforming presence was doing what archaeology was meant to do: the hazy and uncertain were now pinned to the incontrovertible material fact. What had only drifted before in half-imagined half-memories was now suddenly concrete and alive. The legend of the Shiant hermit was true. And the discovery, of course, enhanced the astonishing fact of that memory. With no other sustenance or confirmation, over a thousand years or so, the presence on these islands of an early Christian figure, perhaps bringing Christianity to this part of the world, had, it now turned out, been accurately remembered.

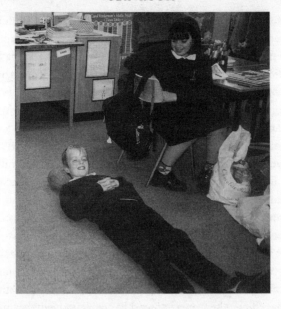

The stone, sitting beside me on the front seat of the car, dwelled in its silence. It was a window on another millennium. Everyone who saw it said 'What's that?' A woman at the toll booth outside the Dartford Tunnel said 'That looks nice.' A man in a garage thought it was a fossilised meat pie. This most private of objects was making acquaintances. I took it to Dr Fergus Gibb, the Shef-field geologist. I had never been to his office before and as I walked in I stopped. It was exactly like my work-room at home. Its walls were lined with maps and photos, diagrams, sections and analyses of one thing only: the Shiants. It was like a teenager obsessed with Britney Spears. Fergus got out his eyeglass, exam-ined the crystalline structure of the cross stone and pronounced that the rock certainly did not come from the Shiants. It was a nodule of Torridonian sandstone of which there is none on the islands. Its surface had been pecked and battered as if it had been in use for a long time, dropped and knocked and some of the larger crystals had fallen out leaving a skin pored and dimpled like an orange. But almost certainly the stone had been picked up as a largish beach cobble. There were cobbles on the big beach on the Shiants now which in form, if not in substance, resembled the cross stone. So if not from the Shiants, where did this stone itself come from? That was almost impossible to say. Torridonian sandstone outcrops all along the west coast of Scotland for two hundred miles. There is even a submarine exposure of it ten miles or so north-east of the Shiants under the Minch. It could have been washed up on this beach, as cobbles of other alien rocks are. Or it might have been brought there.

Scanning with Fergus the geological map of the west coast, I saw with excitement that Torridonian sandstone outcrops on Iona. Frank Fraser Darling had found a piece of what he thought was 'Iona marble' in the chapel in North Rona (although that identification is now thought to be suspect). The foundation of new churches in the ancient world often involved the pioneer taking with him, in a bag blessed by his bishop, soil or stones from the mother church. According to the Icelandic *Placenamebook*, compiled in the twelfth century but collecting far earlier traditions, an Irishman called Orlyg was sent by St Patrick to Iceland 'with wood, suitable for building a church and a meeting house and an iron bell, a golden penny and consecrated earth, to put under the corner pillars.' Sanctity inhered in objects that had been blessed. Was this stone, by any chance, a piece of Iona, made blessed by its carving, carried out into the far north by the hermit who came to settle here? Sadly not: the Torridonian on Iona is too 'flaggy' – it makes big paving slabs and not cobbles. This wonderful object had not come to the Shiants from Iona.

I then took it on to one of the world's leading experts in early Christian sculpture. Ian Fisher works at the Royal Commission for the Ancient and Historical Monuments in Scotland and he has, among other multifarious interests, made a lifetime's scholarly study of the crosses which are littered around the lochs and islands of the west coast. Many of them are free-standing grave markers, the entire stone cut into the shape of a cross. Others are carved on to boulders or cliff faces, above landing spots or next to wells, sanctifying the daily acts of existence. Ian is known to have a buzzard's eye for these things, spotting them in obscure mossy declivities where no one has thought to look before. The map of early Christian presence in the Hebrides has thickened and grown thanks to his years of labour.

When I brought the Shiant stone into his Edinburgh office, Ian's eyes quite literally shone with delight. 'Ah yes,' he said, his hands grasping it, moving his palms carefully over the roughened surface. 'Yes, yes,' as if it were a home-coming. The stone had only been out of the ground ten days and had already found a godfather.

Straight away, of course, he knew the provenance. 'This reminds me very much of the stones on Inishmurray,' Ian said, half-cradling the stone, allowing his fingers to explore its rough and dented surfaces. A book came down from the crowded shelf, was flicked open to the relevant page, and there was a photograph and an engraving of this very stone. But it wasn't this stone. It was its near twin, along with a large collection of about sixty others, in a Columban-age monastery on the small rocky island of Inishmurray off the coast of Sligo. 'What is Inishmurray made of?' I asked Dr Fisher. 'A sandstone, I am told.' I rang the office of the Geological Survey in Dublin. 'Hallo, Solid,' the Irish voice answered. The Solid Geology department could provide the information but it was disappointing. The Inishmurray sandstone is part of the Mourne series, grey and fine-grained, quite different from the Shiant stone.

Nevertheless, the connection was undeniable. In form and in atmosphere, the Inishmurray stones, from a tiny, bare and windswept rocky island three hundred and fifty miles away in

Donegal Bay, were, apart from the material itself, indistinguishable from the one we had dug up on the Shiants. The route
between them was, quite simply, along the flyways of the barnacle
geese. Given good weather, and favourable winds, even *Freyja*
could do it inside a week, or certainly two. And the Inishmurray
stones had been long known as beautiful. Many were in the
National Museum in Dublin. Another, very like the Shiant stone,
had ended up in the Duke of Northumberland's collections of
antiquities in Alnwick Castle.

The stone then went on for yet another interview with another
Edinburgh archaeologist, the Irishman John Barber, who has
excavated extensively at Iona. He too took the thing into his
hands like a doctor with a patient, a stroking investigation in his
handling of the relic. He runs a private archaeology company
now, hired out to developers, but he was treating this like a
sculptor with another man's work. The ring around the cross had
clearly, he thought, been 'pecked' with some pick-like tool. But
the arms of the cross, had at least in part been made by grinding,
perhaps with a piece of flattish stone and some water and a little
sand, rubbed backwards and forwards along the chosen line. Very
slowly, it was perfectly possible to grind away the lines of which
the cross was made. You could see where the inner parts of the
v-shaped incision had been polished in the very process of grinding. The work, Barber thought, looking down through his half-
moon glasses, might not be entirely finished. One of the arms
had been ground deeper than the other. It was 'country work'
and so was not something, you could safely say, that had emerged,
as had the high-figured stone crosses of Iona or the sculptures
and illuminations of the great monasteries of Ireland, from a rich
and powerful centre. 'It's a cross all right,' he said, 'no two ways
about that. But it is such a simple thing. You couldn't found a
monastery on the basis of this.' Instead, the Shiant stone had all
the other virtues: naivety, simplicity and the unadorned directness

of work done by a man on the margins of the known world. This looked, in other words, like the work of a hermit and as likely as not had been done on the Shiants themself.

Still no one knew where it had come from. The sheer spread of Torridonian sandstone made sourcing it a near impossibility. But I needed to know. This thing was the most resonant object ever found on the Shiants and I continued worrying at the problem. Eventually, I realised that if I could find the right person, I could ask one intersecting question which might throw up the answer: was there any place in the Highlands where cobble-making Torridonian sandstone coincided with an early Christian presence? Ian Fisher didn't know. John Barber didn't know. I asked John Wood, Senior Archaeologist at the Highland Council in Inverness. He didn't know but he passed the query on to Patricia Weekes, archaeologist at the Inverness Museum. She didn't know but asked her colleague, the natural historian Stephen Moran. Moran remembered something, a place he had last seen in 1979, on a footpath along the coast between Applecross and Coillegillie in Wester Ross, on the mainland opposite Skye. There, a few of miles south of Applecross, was a section of the coast on which, as he told me on the phone, 'the Torridonian outcrops in lovely cushions, in large piles of brownish, pinkish cushions, heaps of them on the shore. They are all sizes, six or eight inches thick, any length you like. I think that might be where your stone comes from.'

It is the best possibility. The monastery at Applecross was founded by the Irish prince and saint Maelrubha in 673. He had been born a Derry man, was educated at Bangor in County Down – no direct connection there with Inishmurray on the Sligo side – and came north with his following of monks to Ross when he was thirty. Having founded Applecross, Maelrubha became the Apostle of Skye and perhaps of Harris and Lewis. The Shiants sit in the very centre of his province. Did a follower of Maelrubha's, seeking his hermitage in the desert of the ocean, bring a holy stone with him from the founder's monastery on the mainland and keep it with him at his island hermitage as a symbol of sanctity in a wild world?

As that stone sat in the car beside me and above all as it rested with all my other gear in *Freyja*'s bilges, acting its part as holy ballast, leant on by the dogs and cushioned by my sleeping bag as I sailed to and from the Shiants that summer, I came to see in it a focus of the kind of eremitic Christianity which had produced it between ten and thirteen centuries ago. As a talisman and companion, I carried the stone with me every time I crossed the Minch. It is a wonderful and powerful object. Its symbolisms are highly concentrated and it sits beside me, now as it must always have done, as a capsule of sacred intensity. It came with a halo of questions. Could I, in any way, approach the mind of the man who had made and treasured it? I could feel his presence on the islands, but could I know in any way what he was like, what ideas filled his mind, what his reasons might have been for being in this place at all? Could I, in other words, draw this individual out of the silence of the past?

8

ISLANDS FEED AN APPETITE for the absolute. They are removed from the human world, from its business and noise. Whatever the reality, a kind of silence seems to hang about them. It is not silence, because the sea beats on the shores and the birds scream and flutter above you. But it is a virtual silence, an absence of communication which reduces the islander to a naked condition in front of the universe. He is not padded by the conversation of others. Do you want the padding or do you feel shut in and de-natured by it? Do you love the nakedness, or do you shiver in the wind? Do you feel deprived by your island condition or somehow enabled and enriched by it?

Those are the questions for the solitary, now or at any time. Nothing is as envelopingly total as aloneness in a place like this but the silence, paradoxically enough, is far from empty. Whenever I have been alone on the Shiants, it has been a continuously social experience. If I am scrubbing the floor of the house, or out in the boat trying to catch some pollack or cod for my supper, or taking water from the well, or trying to make sense of the perplexing fragments from the past which litter the ground like the remains of a party no one has bothered to clear up, the whole time, in my mind, I am discussing with people I know everything that is going on around me. Isn't it frustrating, I say to them, how when you wipe lino, you can never get it clean? Isn't that wonderful how the water boatman sits within the meniscus of the well head pool? Do you see how that surface bows down to the pads of his feet? Think in the past how people must always have sat here in their boats, just at this point, hauling out the coleys where the flood tide rips on the unseen reef. Do you think the wind might be getting up? Is the darkness of that cloud a signal of the gale tonight? Is the mooring safe? Will the boat survive the storm? What, in the end, am I doing here?

All the solitaries of the past have lived with that intense inner sociability. Their minds are peopled with taunters, seducers, advisers, supervisors, friends and companions. It is one of the tests of being alone: a crowd from whom there is no hiding. It is tempting in these circumstances to turn Crusoe in the face of loneliness. A hermit will force himself to confront that crowd of critics. The followers of the great St Antony, the third-century founder of Christian monasticism, who immured himself for twenty years in the ruins of a Roman fort in the Egyptian desert, could hear him groaning and weeping as the demons tested him one by one. Defoe's hero does the very opposite. He is endlessly busy, endlessly adapting the world as he finds it, building new shelters or planting new crops or finding new aspects to his island. He fills his solitude with business. He constructs boats and digs canals. I have spent weeks on the Shiants like that, making enough noise in working on, mending and setting creels, repairing fences, digging a vegetable patch in one of the old lazybeds, setting up winches on the beach, putting wire netting on the chimneypots to keep the rats from scampering down them, painting the house inside and out – all this, in the end, to keep the silence away.

Always at the back of that hurry is the knowledge that it is a screen against honesty. More than on anything else, Crusoe expended his energy on fences. He built huge palisades around both his island houses, the stakes driven into the ground, sharpened at the top, reinforced, stabilised, all designed to keep the world out. It was not the world he was fencing out but his own profoundly subversive and alarming sense of isolation.

That crowd of critics is the reason that even now, in the Orthodox church, which is the most direct descendant of the universal church of the seventh and eighth centuries, the life of the solitary is seen as the higher calling. A monk needs to qualify to become a hermit, through years of discipline and training, and of social acceptance within the monastic community. The hermitage, in other words, is only ever occupied by a profoundly cultured mind.

That is the first step towards understanding the man who lived in the Shiants a millennium ago and who made the stone. The hermit is no primitive. He may be primitivist – in his engagement with essentials, in his exposure to extreme honesty – but primitivism is one of the more sophisticated forms which civilisation can take. One needs to leave behind a great deal of eighteenth- and nineteenth-century thinking about these early churchmen. Gibbon thought monks as a whole a 'race of filthy animals, to whom [one] is tempted to refuse the name of men.' Compared with the elegance of Roman paganism, Christianity, with its filth and self-abasement, its adoration of nauseous relics and its elevation of the criminal to the holy was, Gibbon thought, a descent into barbarism.

In the summer of 1841, a reader of Gibbon, or of his followers, dropped anchor at the Shiants. James Wilson, Fellow of the Royal Society of Edinburgh, Member of the Watercolour Society, was cruising the Hebrides as the future author of *A Voyage around the Coasts of Scotland and the Isles*:

> On Eilan-na-Killy (the Island of the Cell) are the remains
> of some ancient habitation, the supposed dwelling of an

ascetic monk, or 'self-secluded man' possibly a sulky, selfish, egotistical fellow, who could not accommodate himself to the customs of his fellow creatures. Such beings do very well to write sonnets about, now that they are (as we sincerely trust) all dead and buried, but the reader may depend upon it they were a vile pack, if we may apply the term to those who were too unamiable to be ever seen in congregation.

The Enlightenment saw only the vulgarities of asceticism, the disgustingness of existing, for example, on the Eucharist alone, or limiting oneself to a daily ration of a single fig, or even one small piece of dry bread every other day. A fourth-century Egyptian called Evagrius lived in a cell, in isolation for fifteen years, 'eating only a pound of bread and a pint of oil in the space of three months.'

The Syrians, as Gibbon delightedly described, went further. Chains were worn around the neck and loins, often hidden beneath a hair shirt or a tunic made of wild animal skins. Others had themselves suspended from ropes so that they could never lie down or sleep in comfort. Some endlessly reopened wounds in their bodies or shut themselves in skin sacks, with an opening only for the nose and mouth. Still others lived as beggars, prostitutes or transvestites in the cities of the eastern empire, as holy fools, or famously on the top of columns for decades at a time.

These practices would almost certainly have been known to the Shiant hermit whose stone we found. The example of the early monks and hermits, through the hagiographies and collections of sayings which were held in the large library at Iona and other monasteries, would have been constantly in his mind. But it is scarcely the whole picture. The marginalised brutalism of the extreme Syrian ascetics, which held an almost pornographic fascination for Enlightenment rationalists, was not part of the mainstream monastic tradition. Even in Egypt, the wearing of chains, perpetual wandering, or living exposed to the elements without a cell, were disapproved of.

If I think of the hermit who lived on the Shiants, a more humane picture comes to mind. The world from which he emerged was profoundly literate. Most of the monks of whom there is any knowledge were highly educated and usually members of the ruling princely families of Ireland. Much of the standing which they enjoyed, and of the fame which allowed the reputation of the Shiant hermit to last more than a millennium, derived from the fact that they were great people in the world, who had voluntarily submitted themselves to the condition of exile and permanent pilgrimage. Martyrdom was only significant for those who could have chosen an easier path.

The idea of 'a desert place in the ocean', which emerged in Ireland in the sixth century, was fundamentally metropolitan. It is an outgrowth, in the end, of the urban civilisation of Europe and the Near East. No indigenous inhabitant of the Shiants would conceive of the islands in that way. Only a man who knew of the power of cities and the glories of courts would think of them like that. The hermit's presence here is a reaching out of that Roman idea into the margins of the Atlantic. And there is something theatrical about it, self-dramatising. The turbulence of the seas, the visual violence of the cliffs, the way in which the islands stand out so tall on the horizon, 'three lofty and desolate ones' as the young naturalist George Clayton Atkinson described them in the 1830s – all of that makes the Shiants a setting for metaphysical drama.

It was a canny choice, for underneath the surface imagery, there is plenty here that can sustain life, that can ensure the hermit was not going to starve. No hermit chose the near-sterility of, say, Scalpay, which has neither the same visual drama nor the Shiants' richness. Throughout the Hebrides the same pattern emerges: the relics of early Christianity tend to be on the best remote places. They ignore the acid ordinariness of Harris and Lewis and choose instead the fertility of Canna with its Columban sites, Berneray and Pabbay by Barra, the beautiful, easily worked machair of Barra itself and the Uists, Boreray, the other Berneray and Pabbay near Harris, the ecstatic beauties of Taransay, the huge wealth of birds on St Kilda and the Flannans, the Shiants and the rich fertility of North Rona, forty miles out in the Atlantic, north of the Butt of Lewis. Richness *in extremis*: the definition of the Celtic church.

Highly cultured, attuned to the meanings of the landscape, astute, and not, it emerges, radically alone. The Hebridean hermits, much like their models in the Near East, were in touch with each other and with the network of Columban monasteries here and in Ireland. Iona, in particular, was a centre of learning and spiritual civilisation. Greek was known and probably read there. A yearly chronicle was kept. Abbot Adomnan wrote a famous guide to the places of the Holy Land. At Iona, the abbot employed a baker, a butler and gardener. The abbey had lay tenants on the island. The governing spirit of Columba, an Irish prince, while majestic in its power over many centuries, and in the foundation of a holy austerity, was also pastoral, affectionate, social and generous. As they had done in the Egyptian desert, monks and hermits visited and cared for each other. Here, as there, the hermits were never truly independent. All were at least spiritually, if not physically, living with an elder. In the Hebrides that spiritual father, who had proved himself in the discipline by spending many years in solitude, fasting, praying and meditating, would have been the abbot of Iona or perhaps of Applecross on the mainland. As Thomas Owen Clancy has written, 'Even among the early Desert Fathers who valued solitude and were called to "flee women and bishops", there are countless tales told of the futility of a monk seeking mystical union with God if he is not merciful and attentive to his brother.'

Not that the island life was for everyone. There is the revealing story of Declan, a fifth-century Irish Saint, who with God's advice and guidance had decided to settle on a remote western island called Ard Mor. He and his small band of disciples arrived at the beach opposite the island and found that all the boats had been stolen by the local people. The monks were frightened and told Declan that they would prefer to go elsewhere. They had to travel back and forth to the mainland if they were going to survive and that was not going to be helped by the hostility of the local people. When Declan died, as he surely would, and was no longer there to protect them in person, the situation would be even worse. They made an urgent appeal to the saint:

> We implore you with heart and voice to leave that island,
> or to ask the Father in the name of the son through unity
> with the Holy Spirit ... that this channel should be thrust
> out of its place in the sea, and in its place before your
> settlement should be level ground. Anyway, the place cannot
> be well or easily inhabited because of that channel. There-
> fore there cannot be a settlement there; on the contrary
> there could scarcely be a church there.

Declan was angry and told the monks that God alone would know whether or not Ard Mor could support a community. They all prayed and Declan struck the ground with his staff. The waters duly receded. Ard Mor had become a beautiful, habitable and accessible peninsula.

Remote islands, even then, were for extremists. If one has to abandon the picture of the early hermits as a set of filthy tramps, one must also get rid of the idea that they were somehow eco-solitaries a thousand years ahead of their time. The motivation of the hermits (the word derives from the Greek for a 'desert' – *ereme*) was the very opposite of the modern. Nothing resembling a Romantic desire to come close to nature and to see in that closeness a form of salvation can be found anywhere in the seventh or eighth centuries. The extreme and difficult desert of the Shiants (and the Latin *desert* or *disert* was the word used by the Irish churchmen for places such as this) was attractive in the seventh century precisely because of its horrors. Almost certainly, at this period, the Shiants were part of the territory controlled not by the Irish but by the Picts. Any hermit coming here (or for that matter to St Kilda, the Flannans or North Rona) had put himself far out into dangerous territory.

The sea itself terrified them. It was the zone not of divine beauty but of destruction and chaos. Only God and the saints could control it. Others were at its mercy. In the opening prayer of an Irish Mass written in about 800, the sea is the testing ground where God alone can save the pitiable: 'We have sinned Lord, we have sinned. Spare us sinners and save us: You who guided Noah across the waters of the flood, hear us: and who by a word rescued Jonah from the deep, free us; You who stretched out your hand to the sinking Peter, help us.'

The animal world was no better. One hermit, finding himself on an island which would now be thought of as a bird sanctuary, was unable to pray because of the noise the birds were making. Only with God's help was he able to silence them and, in the blessed quiet, address himself to the Creator.

Suddenly you can see the hermit there. He stands on the shore. This island is the only garden he has but the garden is his and it is God's gift for him to use. The first chapter of Genesis is quite explicit and these are verses that are still quoted in the Hebrides:

> Have dominion over the fish of the sea, and over the fowl of the air, and over every living thing that moveth upon the earth.
>
> And God said, Behold, I have given you every herb bearing seed, which is upon the face of all the earth, and every

tree, in the which is the fruit of a tree yielding seed; to you
it shall be for meat.

And to every beast of the earth, and to every fowl of the
air, and to every thing that creepeth upon the earth, wherein
there is life, I have given every green herb for meat: and it
was so.

Life in the seventh- or eighth-century Hebrides was not and
could not be conservationist. Anything less than full access to the
fruits of the earth on these margins of viability would tip life
over from survival to suicide. Again and again, conditions in
which crops might normally grow could turn catastrophic. In 670
a snowfall blanketed the whole of Ireland and brought on a
universal famine. Snow fell again in 760, 764 and 895 and hunger
followed. In 858 a rain-drenched autumn destroyed the entire
harvest. In 1012 terrible rains wrecked the standing crops and in
the following spring farmers had to choose between planting their
seed corn or eating it, leaving nothing for the following year.

On islands it would be worse. The biographer of the Irish
Saint Berach told the story of how in one of these years of scarcity
a farmer on an island decided that he had to leave his wife and
child while he searched for food on the mainland. As he left, he
told his wife to kill their new baby because they could not hope
to feed it.

Of this entire thought-world, only the pillow stone, apparently,
survives on the Shiants. Can the stone itself be interrogated? Can
one read from the stone anything of the mind of its maker? Of
course, in the cross itself, it carries the full burden of Christianity.
It is the symbol of Christ's death, resurrection and continuing
presence. It also carries the faint echo of a Roman imperial
memory. The ring, which on this stone, and in many Irish stones,
either surrounds or intersects the cross, has its origins in the
imagery of the laurel wreath. Early examples found in Germany
show the ring around the cross carved with the laurel leaves that

would surround the head of Caesar. The ringed cross, then, is an elision of empire and the martyred Christ, of the majesty of the father and the suffering of the son, of imperium and humility, of greatness descending to the condition of martyrdom.

More precisely than that, though, it symbolises both the suffering and ambition of the life of the hermit himself. It is an extraordinarily self-sufficient object. It needs no context or frame to achieve its effect and was surely intended to be portable, to be carried from one place to another, to do its work wherever it might be, much as I have driven it around Britain, and sailed it back and forth across the Minch. The stone is a manifestation of holiness carried into the desert. But it also embodies holiness found in the desert. The carving, so laboriously done, not by an expert, draws life and meaning out of the inert lifelessness of rock. It is, in that way, a model of the way in which a man, isolating himself in a stony place surrounded by the sea, arrives at a new understanding of divine power in the world. Like Christ's passion on the cross itself, it is the emergence of spiritual life from bodily death. Its beauty is not in itself but in the transformation it represents.

It may, just, be possible to make that stone speak. By chance, two poems survive in manuscript, one copied out in the sixteenth century and now in the Bodleian Library in Oxford, the other a century later and now in the National Library in Dublin, which are almost certainly the work of a hermit living on a sea-battered island in the Hebrides in the seventh century. The name of the poet-hermit is Beccan mac Luigdech. He is a scholarly man, and an aristocrat, profoundly versed in the ways of Irish heroic poetry, a member of the same Irish family as Columba. Beccan is devoted to Columba's memory, as his leader, his spiritual father and his saint. The poems are themselves a rare enough survival, but what makes them more extraordinary is that they are joined by a letter, addressed to him as '*Beccanus solitarius*', Beccan the hermit. It was written in 632 or 633, by an Irish churchman on the subject of the dating of Easter, the controversy then dividing the Columban from the Roman church.

A richer and more subtle world than one inhabited by 'sulky, selfish, egotistical fellows' emerges from Beccan's verses. His is a landscape and seascape of immense richness and passion and through him the full depth and power of Latin Christendom reaches up into these stormy waters. Beccan may have been on the Shiants, but it is by no means certain that he was. There is, in fact, a possibility that his hermitage was on the island of Rum, south of Skye, halfway between the Shiants and Iona. But if Beccan was not the hermit here (and his connection to Columba points more at Iona than at Applecross), he was exactly contemporary with the man who was, he would almost certainly have known him and would have inhabited the same world. This is, quite legitimately, the voice of the stone.

Looking southwards from his island fastness, Beccan, as translated here by Thomas Owen Clancy, surveys the holy kingdom that Columba has created. Seas surge through the poetry and Columba, or Colum Cille, the Dove of the Church, both ascetic scholar and courageous adventurer, as much prince of Connacht as saint, the light of the world gleaming with sanctity, triumphs over them:

> He brings northward to meet the Lord a bright crowd of
>   chancels –
> Colum Cille, kirks for hundreds, widespread candle.
>
> Connacht's candle, Britain's candle, splendid ruler;
> in scores of curraghs with an army of wretches he crossed the
>   long-haired sea.
>
> He crossed the wave-strewn wild country, foam flecked, seal-filled,
> savage, bounding, seething, white-tipped, pleasing, dismal.

Fame with virtues, a good life, his: ship of treasure,
sea of knowledge, Conal's offspring, people's counsellor.

Leafy oak-tree, soul's protection, rock of safety,
the sun of monks, mighty ruler, Colum Cille.

Age does not diminish this. As passionate as Emily Dickinson and as power-driven as the Anglo-Saxon sea poems, Beccan suddenly vivifies the seventh-century Shiants.

In his only other surviving poem, as Columba appears again, all elements of the hermit world are brought together. Sea-heroism, austerity, skill *in extremis*, persistence, the princeliness of Columba's holy enterprise, the imitation of Christ and the love of learning rise together in a moment of heroic completeness:

> *He left Ireland, entered a pact,*
> *he crossed in ships the whales' shrine.*
> *He shattered lusts – it shone on him –*
> *a bold man over the sea's ridge.*
>
> *He fought wise battles with the flesh,*
> *he read pure learning.*
> *He stitched, he hoisted sail tops,*
> *a sage across seas, his prize a kingdom.*

This poetry is not, as later medieval Irish poetry can be, the wan appreciation of Nature's delicate charms. This man is not looking out of a window. Nor is it mystic. He is not contemplating another world. He loves this one and his love of it and of his patron saint has emerged from struggle. Beccan seems to be purified by his understanding. He has been out in the storm and has felt the waves beat for days and months on his shore. His mind now is as clear, unadorned and direct as the holy ringed-cross stone which this poet, perhaps, may also have made.

I have often walked the Shiants wondering where the hermit may have lived; which of the favoured five or six spots he might have chosen. It might well be at the place called Annat, a soft and welcoming nick in the ragged west side of Garbh Eilean. It is where I would have chosen. The long gentle valley called Glaic na Crotha, 'the valley of the cattle', runs across the island here from the north cliffs to the south-western shore. The little stream in the valley gathers pace as it drops and the buttercups and watermint cluster around it. Down at the bottom, the land flattens out into a little seaside meadowy apron beside a sharp rocky inlet. It would be a beautiful place to live and I have sometimes brought a tent here to spend the night, seeing the last of the light falling on the mountains in Skye to the south (they are hidden from the house on Eilean an Tighe) and waking in the morning to find the sun warming the turf. There's a stony beach here which always has driftwood on it and the smoke from the breakfast fire slowly spirals upwards. All morning you can lie with your nose buried in the tweedy scents which the warming grasses give off. Beccan's seas stretch out in front of you to the southern islands of the Outer Hebrides, trailing off to Barra Head, and you can imagine what this place might have been like thirteen hundred years ago.

It is a numinous place and the feeling here is quite unlike any other on the islands. This is not a wild corner. It is calm but not quite as domestic as the settlements on House Island. It has a sense of privacy and of removal from the peopled world of Eilean an Tighe. Annat bears the same relationship to the Shiants as the Shiants do to the rest of the world. I like to think of it as the place the hermit chose. It has certainly been lived in for a long time and, as Pat Foster showed me, there are clear signs of prehistoric buildings here: a large platform for a neolithic house, a round Bronze Age house and a D-shaped enclosure which may have been to keep stock in. So it might be the ideal place for a hermit: somewhere that had been lived in in the ancient past and was suitable for human occupation but in the seventh or eighth centuries happened to be empty.

It is possible to investigate this quite closely. On the maps it is called Airighean na h-Annaid, which means 'the shielings or summer pastures of the Annaid'. Annaid itself, a place-name which in the form of 'Annat' or 'Annet' occurs throughout Scotland, comes from the early Irish word *andóit*, from the late Latin *antitas*, a contraction of *antiquitas*, meaning simply 'the ancient'. In Ireland, *andóit* acquired the more particular meaning of the oldest church of a local community, founded by the saint who had first brought Christianity there and whose relics this church would often continue to enshrine. Tithes were due to this mother-church and in turn it had a duty of pastoral care over the parish that surrounded it. These significances did not need to be enormous in scale. There is no reason why the Shiant mother-church should have had any influence beyond the Shiants themselves.

The Celtic place-name scholar William J Watson wrote in the 1920s that 'Annats are often in places that are now and must always have been rather remote and out of the way. But wherever there is an annat there are traces of an ancient chapel or cemetery or both. Very often, too, the annat adjoins a fine well or clear stream.'

The stream that runs down at the Shiant annat, trickling between mosses and over the hot rocks, with wild thyme and clover growing in the grass beside it, full of the cool of the moor that it drains, is indeed some of the sweetest of all Shiant waters.

So is this, in its sun-trap warmth on these wind-besieged islands, where the church of Beccan (or his contemporary) might have stood? Maybe. But, as Pat Foster established, the cemetery is on Eilean an Tighe and one might, as William Watson said, expect the cemetery to be in the place where the mother-church was. Thomas Owen Clancy has recently re-examined the question of annaids in Scotland. How come so many annaid place-names, he asks, which should, as the mother-churches, be central to the human geography of Scotland, turn out, as William Watson said, to be on the margins? He provides a possible explanation. Many annaid place-names are combined, as it is in the Shiants, with other elements: the pastures of the annaid, the bank of the annaid, the well of the annaid, the field of the annaid:

> These places need not themselves be the places referred to as the annaid; they may express their relationship, by property, use or general proximity, to the local 'mother church.' We should not necessarily expect to find evidence of church-sites at the location of such names, but perhaps somewhere else, even at some distance.

So the Garbh Eilean pastures of the Annat might have been no more than the church's glebe, a place called 'Church Meadows', and the church itself would have been where the graveyard is, on the island known until the mid-nineteenth century as *Eilean na Cille*, 'the Island of the Church'. A careful examination of that site on Eilean an Tighe does in fact reveal a pair of banks, set at some distance back from the graveyard and its associated buildings, each bank running from the cliff foot to the shore, making an enclosure, as was the norm, around the holy site. Although there is nothing that can be firmly identified now as the ruins of the church, many nineteenth-century travellers had a few tumbled stones on Eilean an Tighe described to them as the hermit's church-cum-residence. It looks, in other words, as if he did not live at Annat but on Eilean an Tighe, near the present house.

That is far from certain, though. The Gaelic scholar Aidan Macdonald has also looked at the annaid question and has come up with precisely the opposite answer to Thomas Clancy's. Macdonald sees in the pattern of distribution of the annaid name – remote, apparently abandoned, never the centre of later ecclesiastical development – evidence not of continuity but of disruption. The technical and legal sense of andoit can never have mattered much. 'Place-names are usually simple, straightforward and descriptive, and specialist technicalities would tend to be forgotten, if ever properly appreciated, by a non-specialist population.' The names mark the sites of 'churches of any kind which were abandoned and subsequently replaced but not, for a variety of reasons, at the same sites.' *Annaid*, in this version, means simply 'old church'.

This, of course, is an intriguing possibility on the Shiants. The lovely Annat on Garbh Eilean is just the place a Beccan might have chosen: good soil, good water, a place where you can bring a boat alongside, even if hauling it up is difficult. People had lived there before and there was building stone to hand. It may be that the prime site near the landing beach on Eilean an Tighe was already occupied by Pictish pagans. Annat was the corner into which the hermit could squeeze, not perfect but not bad either and perhaps separated by a mile or so from the people on the other island.

For some reason, that old church was abandoned, but not forgotten, and a new one built on the island which then became known as the Island of the Church. The consciousness of the 'antique', of what had been there before, survived until the name was recorded by the Ordnance Survey in 1851. It may also have survived in one other detail. George Clayton Atkinson, the Newcastle naturalist, was told in the 1830s that the island now called Garbh Eilean (Rough Island) was known as 'St Culme', a clear corruption of the name of Columba. Rumours of a dedication to St Columba had also reached John Macculloch's ears ten years earlier. The church on Eilean an Tighe was said in the 1690s by Martin Martin to be dedicated to the Virgin. But is it possible that the old church at Annat on Garbh Eilean, Beccan's church, for want of a better shorthand, was in fact dedicated to the saint he loved?

'Annaid' is a term which came into use in the ninth and tenth centuries and Aidan Macdonald is unequivocal about the reasons for its sudden appearance: Norse raids. The Hebrides were first plundered in 798. Raids on Iona continued throughout the ninth century and Norsemen were living in the Hebrides by the 850s. The scatter of annaids were all readily accessible from the sea or river valleys or the routes between them. These abandoned sites marked, Macdonald thought, the terrifying destruction from the north.

Is that what happened here? Archaeology has yet to address that question, if it ever can. But elsewhere in the Hebrides, at a site called The Udal in North Uist, it is quite clear that the Norse arrived suddenly, comprehensively and violently. A settlement which had been there, in much the same form, for five hundred years was razed and immediately built over. Everything which the earlier inhabitants had used in the way of buildings, pots, bonework, metalwork, plates and buckets disappeared overnight in the middle of the ninth century, to be replaced by their Viking equivalents. In the new, high-stress environment, a small fort was built there, the first military architecture in two thousand years of human life at The Udal. The archaeologists looked for the faint, tell-tale traces of sand blown across the earlier levels before the new buildings were erected on the place. That would be the sign of a slow evolution, of natural abandonment and natural recolonisation. But there was nothing. It was a literal physical truth that the Norse buildings were put straight on top of the ruins of their predecessors. 'The Vikings came without apparent cause, provocation or feud,' Iain Crawford, the excavator of The Udal has written, 'and they were speaking an unintelligible tongue, like visitants from outer space.'

You can imagine that at the Shiants: the sudden arrival, the keels on the beach stones, the leaping from the bow, the walk around the corner, and then the careless erasure of lives and meanings, the leaving of bodies for the ravens, as one Norse saga

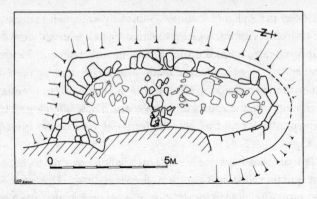

after another describes it, the destruction of buildings, the burning
of their contents, the ridiculing of the odds and ends they might
have found there, the laughter at the easy win, the excitement in
slaughter. 'Agony, death and horror are riding and revelling,' one
English sailor wrote after Trafalgar. 'To see and hear this! What
a maddening of the brain it causes. Yet it is a delirium of joy, a
very fury of delight!' Here on the Shiants, as the blood slopped
on the shore and seeped into the grasses, those would have been
the words in the air. It was a blood culture. Blood was the mortar
of the Viking civilisation.

Soon enough, the Norsemen made their mark. Up above the
coastal shelf on Eilean an Tighe, tucked into a fold in the ground
so that it is invisible from the sea but commands a wide view of
it to the west and the south, not calmly and confidently set on
the domestic bench of flat land but hidden, nervous, aware of
the possibilities of violence emerging from the Minch, is what
might be a Norse house.

It is boat-shaped, using a natural cliff as one wall, and with
the foundations of a dividing wall half-way along it. It has the
look of a Norse building. There is another of the same form, also
tucked into a hidden shelf, also invisible from the sea, two hundred yards or so to the north. Both buildings await excavation

but here, perhaps, are the houses of the people who destroyed the church at Annat and who replaced Beccan's 'bright crowd of chancels' with something that at this distance seems colder and meaner.

On the hillside above what is perhaps the Norse long house, is another enigmatic monument. Mary Macleod, the Western Isles County Archaeologist, who came over to the Shiants for a day to inspect what Pat Foster and his team had done, was reluctant to accept this arrangement of stones as anything more than the fragmentary rubble of a couple of field walls, meeting at a corner. Her professional scepticism was proper enough and any more explicit identification can only be tentative. Nevertheless, the romantic landowner, wanting to see in his islands a reliquary for all that is most glamorous in the past, persists in reading these stones in the best possible light.

They are loosely arranged in the form of a boat, about eighteen feet long, just outreaching *Freyja*, with a wide, flat stone set crosswise at the stern, another for a thwart amidships and a third, taller, at the front, curved up and back in the way of the Viking stem post found on the island of Eigg. Pat Foster will describe this as nothing more than a 'Boat-Shaped Stone Setting'. Similar structures in Scandinavia, if far more precisely and neatly made, have housed Norse graves. This one is aligned on Dunvegan Head in Skye, thirty miles to the south, the seamark on the Viking route to Dublin. There is another Boat-Shaped Stone Setting high on the far end of Garbh Eilean, almost on the lip of the northern cliffs, arranged on rising ground, as if breasting a wave coming down from the north.

That one is aligned precisely the other way, on the dominant outline of Kebock Head in Lewis, en route to Stornoway and the north. In the summer, purple orchids are clustered next to the stones and the fulmars from the cliffs below cut easy discs in the air above them.

Are these Norse graves? I can only say, in the face of professional scepticism, that I hope so. If they were ever excavated, it is unlikely that anything would be found. The acidity in the turf will have eaten away all evidence.

That doesn't matter to me. The Shiants are a place where the deep past seems more nakedly present than any other I know. Perhaps it is because the islands are so pristine in their silence. Perhaps it is this landscape's ability to retain the marks of previous lives. Little here is overlaid, as it is elsewhere, with the thick mulch of recent events. The physical remains lie just beneath the surface, scarcely skinned in turf. Modernity is almost absent, cut off by the Minch. Crossing that sea, whether in *Freyja* or in any boat, pares away the fat. The surrounding sea makes you, for some reason, more attuned to habits and ideas that are unlike all the usual daily traffic of the mind.

This is almost undiscussable. It is a strange effect, existing only at the margins. Try to hold it or define it and it slips away like mercury between the fingers. Sometimes I have felt, especially in *Freyja*, and above all when out on the sea late in the evening, that I only have to look to the other end of the boat for some other figure to be there, sorting out the ropes, wrapping the plaid around them. Of course they never are. Of course not. The world is not like that, but there is often something else in the wind, which is, I suppose, the potential that they might be there, quite ordinarily, without any kind of fuss being made. If this were a film, the camera would move casually past them, panning around the black bodies of the islands, the lace of surf and the green glow of the evening sky, catching the hunched figures on the forward thwart as no more remarkable a presence than my own in the stern or the creels amidships, the tide running with us or the long, haunted wailing of the seals.

Being out on the sea at night brings some kind of connection with an older and more essential world. It is not as foreign as people tend to imagine. Men have been at home on it since the Stone Age. The Hebrides are littered with the remains of Bronze Age farms, whose inhabitants must often have crossed these waters with their implements and their stock on board. Imagine cattle in those ancient boats, how impossible that must have been! At least you can cross the Minch or the Sea of the Hebrides in a day, and you can see your destination as you begin. What amazes me more is the idea of the Vikings bringing their herds of cattle with them in open boats across the North Sea, plunging for days across that hostile grey territory, navigating by instinct as much as anything, with the animals increasingly restless, trussed presumably, longing for the destination.

Stripped as it is of context, and with the modernity of the world sliced away, it is easier to imagine the past at sea at night than in any other circumstances. Fixing the tiller with a length of rope, I leant over the bow late one evening and put my head right down there where the water rose and broke around the stem post. *Freyja* sailed herself in the quiet breeze of the night. The loom from the lighthouse on Scalpay swept out across the Sound, three white flashes once every twenty seconds. The buoy marking Damhag flickered its quick uninterrupted green. The surf on the Galtas came and went, the teeth of a long, white smile, and the boat sailed on as though another hand were on the helm.

9

SUMMER HAS COME. IT is mid-June. I lie on the grass on the
north front of Garbh Eilean and feel the abundance around me.
Shut your eyes and the shadows of the passing birds flicker across
your lids in a film of profusion, each blip another life, another
energising presence. I sometimes dream of the Shiants without
the birds and it is like finding a child dead.

These islands are one of the great bird places of the world,
with so many birds that counting them is nearly impossible.
According to the best estimates of modern ornithologists, strug-
gling with densely packed, mobile, teeming and pullulating masses
of identical bodies, all of which come and go at variable rates
and in undependable patterns, attempting to identify them from
boats below the colonies or with telescopes on distant cliff-tops,
there are between fifteen and eighteen thousand guillemots here,
eight to eleven thousand razorbills, between four and six thousand
fulmars, two thousand kittiwakes, roughly fifteen hundred shags,
a few hundred gulls of various kinds (whose numbers are rising),
twenty-six great skuas, also on the increase, and two hundred

and forty thousand puffins, about one in eight of the British total and two per cent of all the puffins in the world.

There are more puffins on St Kilda, and in one or two offshore islands further north in the Atlantic, but nowhere, it is said, are they more densely packed, or do they make a more extraordinary sight, than on these islands in the Minch.

This is the puffins' summer outing. They begin to arrive in the first days of April. Malcolm MacSween, Lord Leverhulme's, Compton Mackenzie's and, for a while, my father's tenant on the Shiants, told Mackenzie that 'the Puffin comes, always on a Sunday night and remains for a week to clear out his burrow and prepare his nest.' It is a tentative beginning. They have been at sea all winter, dispersed from here to Norway and Greenland, to Sicily and the borders of Morocco with Spanish Sahara, scattered in their unseen millions across the width of the winter ocean, perhaps one puffin per square mile of Atlantic, muted in their winter plumage, with last year's coloured beak fallen away, a safe and wintry privacy on the sea. I have, once, seen a couple of puffins in December off the rocky west coast of Majorca, sullen, grey-faced things. We looked at each other and then looked away.

Now they are back. To begin with they do not come ashore. Crowds of them, increasingly busy in enormous rafts, float in the bay between the islands and in front of the big north cliffs, clustering there in small conversational groups, as engaged, as social as the people in a Canaletto square. You can take your boat in among them. They scatter to start with, but then slowly seep back in, soon enough clustered around you like a crowd waiting for the pub to open.

In little groups the puffins and other auks come ashore, standing around on rocks for a few minutes before heading back out to sea. They are dipping a toe in the land. Suddenly, one becomes aware of it, a repeopling of the islands. All along the back cliff of Eilean Mhuire, the guillemots cluster in their thousands, standing on shelves and sloping boulders down to the very edge of the sea. On Garbh Eilean, the screes of tumbled hexagonal rocks along the east shore, and on the grassy banks around the corner on the north face, and in one or two places along the east cliffs of Eilean an Tighe, everywhere begins to fill with summer birds. The wrens continue to hop about in the screes while the vast number of far larger seabodies gather around them. It is as if a corpse has come alive. The Shiants flutter with their sudden vitality. Now, for months, the place is never still. Look up and it will be filled with wings passing. The air is whisked into life. There is a shared thickness of coexistence here, a palpitating, repercussing, gyrating co-presence. How it must have been blessed in the past! The bird arrival comes at precisely the moment in the year when the crops stored from the previous year would have been running thin. This was manna on wings.

When John Harvie-Brown, the late nineteenth-century naturalist, came in the 1870s, he could scarcely contain his excitement. The puffins were around him

> in countless thousands. The sea, the sky and the land seemed populated by equal proportions, each vast in itself – constantly moving, whirring, eddying, a seething throng of life, drifting, and swooping, and swinging in the wind, or pitching and heaving on the water, or crowding and jostling on the ledges and rocks, arising from and alighting on the boulder-strewn slopes, or perched like small white specks far up in the cliff face amongst the giant basalt columns.

Many of these puffins have been coming here as long as I have. A puffin never moves house if it can help it and soon the returning birds begin to reinvestigate last year's burrow, poking into it, starting to clear it out. You see puffin and wife sharing the labour. The birds are soon spattered and slick with mud, especially if it has been raining and the burrow is leaky. They emerge from their sodden homes like squaddies at Passchendaele. Little sprigs of grass are brought back to line the end of the burrow, or lengths of orange and blue fishing twine.

By the middle of May eggs are everywhere, the most beautiful ones, turquoise-flecked and scribbled in dark brown like a Jackson Pollock, tucked under the feet of guillemots, single white eggs hidden deep inside the puffins' burrows, a clutch of three or four laid in the chaos of the shag nests. (If you alarm a puffin in its burrow, it creeps to the far end, a yard or so, and turns its face to the wall, placing the egg between you and it. It is a straightforward calculation: better to lose the egg than the puffin.)

All of this for the ancient Shiant Islanders was the pulse of wild protein for which they had been longing all winter. As late as the Second World War people came out to the Shiants from Lemreway and Scalpay in the summer to supplement their government-controlled diet. I must confess, I have never taken any of the eggs to eat, not through any sense of its wrongness but having been put off by a famous experiment conducted in the early 1950s by the Cambridge zoologist HB Cott. How tasty, he wanted to know, were wild bird eggs? A panel of heroic gourmets was assembled and presented with plate after plate of scrambled eggs, each from a different species. None was labelled and no salt or pepper added. Cott then asked the tasters to score what they had eaten. The scale ranged from 10.0 for 'ideal' to 2.0 'repulsive and inedible'. Cott, wartime expert on camouflage, later knighted for his services to zoology, ranked the eggs of birds found on the Shiants as follows:

9.0 *Very good*
8.3 Lesser black-backed gull
8.2 Kittiwake
8.0 *Good*
7.9 Herring gull

7.8 Razorbill
7.7 Fulmar, great black-backed gull, guillemot
7.2 Great skua
7.0 *Barely perceptible off flavour*
6.6 Puffin
6.0 *Definite off flavour*
6.0 Common eider
5.4 Gannet
5.0 *Unpleasant*
4.4 Shag
4.0 Off

If the shag egg lurks between 'unpleasant' and 'off', shag meat can make a delicious and healthy soup-cum-stew, or so Kennie Mackenzie, the uncle of John Murdo Matheson, the Gravir shepherd, assured me. The Shiants are the second biggest shaggery in the British Isles – only Foula, the loneliest of the Shetland Isles has more – and so, one day a year or two ago in early summer, I took a large stick with me to one of the headquarters of the shags, high up on the west coast of Garbh Eilean, with the idea of getting some lunch.

I headed off for the colony. The wind was coming in riffles off the sea and swirling under the cliffs. Whiffs of shag life, that ammoniac fug of fish and foulness, the smell of seaweed as rotten as manure and filled with creeping bugs the colour of decay, came to me on the wind in heavy doses. A dead puffin, its body turned inside out by a black-backed gull and the breast meat picked away, was slopping to and fro in the shore surf, its sodden wings flapping as the water stirred. A big grey seal was lying on its back on the pebbled beach, long dead, its jaw twisted open, half sideways as though in mid-chew. The molars looked human. The flesh on the body, where the fur had rubbed away, was half-rotten, half air-dried, bresaola on the turn. On its flippers, the fingernails, which were five inches long, hung stiffly together

like the fingers of a paralysed hand. Involuntarily, my nostrils closed against it. In the nooks of the cliff below the shag-fest, I found a dog-rose in bud the colour of a pink iced gem, bunches of meadowsweet and tall flowering sorrel, the weeds and flowers of sweeter places, surviving here only where shelter allowed them space from the gales. Beside them, the sea pinks and the sea campion were over, the flowers no more than wisps of brown paper on the end of six-inch stalks.

I climbed towards the shag rocks. The turf is a bright skin across the underlying bone. Tormentil and self-heal alternate in a tiny, rich, repeating pattern of yellow and purple among the watermint and the irises. The shags are up towards the top of the big boulder scree. Lower down, there are puffins standing about on the rocks near their burrows in what ornithologists call 'clubs', groups of young puffins, less than five years old, and so not old enough to have a wife or a burrow. Ludicrous and lovable puffins! Their sociability is as stiff and predictable as an evening in an Edwardian London. Gestures of deference are required of any newcomer, and a little accepting dance of stamping feet is made by those already settled with cigars around the fender. They walk around by the mouths of each other's burrows as if on eggshells; or bat their bills in little love displays, one puffin of a pair always apparently keener than the other, his mate slightly bored with this love thing, particularly when he goes on too long; or make little threats with their mouths agape; or suddenly jump into a tussling, angry clinch with a neighbour, bill to bill, turning each other over and over as they tumble down the slope towards the sea, suddenly realising at the last minute what a spectacle they are making of themselves. They are more capable of looking embarrassed than any bird I have seen. So polite is this world, in fact, that most of its members seem struck dumb by their sense of propriety. Puffins remain monogamous (or at least about ninety per cent of them are, because both spouses remain loyal to the same burrow) throughout their extraordinarily long and stable lives: up to forty years of politeness and tedium, the whirring of wings and the ritual stamping of little orange feet.

Resting above them on the steepness of the slope, I watch a gannet out at sea. That is different country. In the binoculars, its hanging, seeking, intelligent head is mobile, looking left and right in front of its swept-back, spotless body. The fuselage rises on stiletto wings, hangs coolly for a moment, a hundred feet above the sea, and then falls, the body twisting as it goes down, a quarter-revolution or so. There is a sudden half-folding of the wings, a darting of the form, and the bird cuts into the water. The sound is of a paper bag being popped, a muffled implosion, leaving behind it on the surface a pool of broken water, a bubbled glaucousness at the point of entry. A gannet can swallow four or five mackerel or herring in a single dive. It is gorging unseen. Then the bird is up, returning to the surface fast like a human swimmer, bobbing up, shuddering, a pause and then the long haul back into the air, a workman-like beat of the wings before returning to the glide, the hunting glide. You can see them three or four miles away, soaring and diving, the repeated search and plunge for prey. The whiteness is part of their armoury. Gannets are intended to be visible at distances so that their brothers, sisters and cousins, can see them on the ocean and can share in the kill. The sea is their savannah.

If puffin and gannets are from different worlds, the shags are from another universe. Nothing can really prepare you for the reality of the shag experience. It is an all-power meeting with an extraordinary, ancient, corrupt, imperial, angry, dirty, green-eyed, yellow-gaped, oil-skinned, iridescent, rancid, rock-hole glory that is *Phalacrocorax aristotelis*. They are scandal and poetry, chaos and individual rage, archaic, ancient beyond any sense of ancientness that other birds might convey. Even an eagle or a buzzard seems slick by comparison. The earliest puffin fossil to have been discovered is no more than five million years old. The oldest shag, identical to its modern descendants, has been found in rocks laid down sixty million years ago, a couple of million years after the cataclysm that killed off the dinosaurs.

As you climb the big broken scree towards their stinking slum, as you hear the honking, guttural hoot of their cry even in mid-flight as they beat against the wind around the headland, you can feel in the creep of your skin that you are somehow, in this coming encounter, penetrating a scale of time that can be measured only geologically. The shag was born half as long ago again as the Alps were made. The shag, or something very like it, flew over seas in which the ichthyosaurs swam. The shag is as old as the Giant's Causeway in Antrim, as Staffa, as the Cuillins in Skye. Here today, it is older than the rocks on which it sits.

You can only have a sudden immersion into the shag world. Your head comes over the lip of rock, and there, jutting and quivering in front of you, perhaps two feet away, defending its young, that guarantee of survival, is the bird whose yellow gape, as yellow as the heart of a pot of yellow paint, hawks and spits at you, its gizzard shaking in anger and fear, its whole head prodding and prodding towards you, like an angry finger. There's nothing neat or controlled about it. There's a fluster of rage, resentment and clumsiness as the big, black, webbed feet stamp around the sticky, white, guanoed mayhem of kelp stalks and wrack-branches that is its nest, in the back of which, creeping for the shadows, you see the couple of young, half-formed embryonic creatures, shag chicks, rat-birds, serpentine, leathery, hideous.

Then, through all the fluster, you see the eye of the adult, a green point of clarity, a distillation of the green that lurks in the black of the bird's damp feathers. But in the light of that eye, the whole greasy body seems an irrelevance. The eye is the source of all that anger, the bright, hard centre of the shag's existence. It's an adamantine green, a mineral concentrate, able to outlast any kind of erosion or catastrophe that might occur around it. It is the eye of animal persistence and the colour stays with you as the bird flogs off towards the ruffled sea. How on earth could anyone have ever clubbed one of these things to death? Hunger would make you do it, but then hunger would make you choose a softer option.

The puffins are prep-school boys beside the shags and it is their innocence that encourages you to catch them. Puffin eggs may be relatively disgusting, mysteriously more disgusting than those of their relatives the razorbill and guillemot, with whites that are a livid blue, but the adult puffin's flesh is delicious boiled, stuffed, roasted, smoked or salted, as it is throughout the lands bordering the north-east Atlantic. There is no doubt that puffins were eaten here in the past: we found clutches of puffin heads in the midden that we excavated next to the eighteenth-century house on Eilean an Tighe. The heads were still clustered together deep in the pile, where they had been thrown, once cut from the bodies being prepared for a stew.

Almost certainly these puffins would have been caught with snares. I have done it myself and it requires little skill. There is a snare preserved in the National Museums of Scotland in Edinburgh and I made a copy of it. It is as primitive and as ingenious as technology gets. Take, first, a length of rope, perhaps six or eight feet long. Tie loops in each of its ends. Then, at intervals of about a foot along its length, tie on short snares made of string. Form each of these little strings into a noose with a mouth about four inches across, so that if you put your finger into the noose and pull, the string will tighten around it. Then pin the rope to the ground at each end in front of some puffin burrows and retire. The puffin is an extremely curious bird. It will inspect and pick up anything of interest on the grass in front of its burrow. They will soon begin to investigate the catching rope. One puffin after another sees it, snaps it up in its beak, shakes it, examines it with one eye like a monocled biologist, thinking perhaps that the string is some kind of land-fish or out-of-element sprat.

This is now illegal. The puffin is protected by law. You can buy them frozen in supermarkets in the Faeroes but there is no eating them here. Besides, there is, for us now, something a little wicked about attempting to catch a puffin. It is – I shudder slightly to say this – amusing in a way of which the modern eco-consciousness does not entirely approve. Where the boys from Lemreway would have taken it with glee and a sense of fun, happy at the abundance of this marvellous summer presence of the birds, we must now stand back, in silence and admiration, committed to non-involvement, to 'respect', to whispered distance.

So this catching of a puffin is a historical experience and a strange one, as you watch the sweet bird getting caught in the trap you have devised. It picks up the snare string and ignores it. It walks to and fro in front of its burrow. It stands for a moment, Chamberlain on the tarmac back from Munich, sniffy-nosed, buttoned up, the chest feathers riffled by the breeze, and as it does so, looking out to the north, it puts its foot inside the noose. I am watching from a hundred yards away on the grassy bank. I see the puffin lift its orange foot, I see the foot within the noose and I see the string tighten around the orange scaly leg. The bird does not know for a moment that it is caught. It stands, a captive on the grass, and examines its identical neighbours. The colony is an almost silent place. A little burred growling comes from the puffins inside the burrows, a slow, creaking note. But my puffin has now felt that it is caught. It wants to promenade a little to the left. It can't. It tries to walk a little the other way. It can, but only for six inches or so. It then, most pitiably of all, goes into its burrow. I see the saddest thing: a single, bright orange puffin leg sticking out horizontally from the mouth of a burrow, the body of the bird invisible, the leg held there by the string of my snare.

It doesn't take much to kill a puffin. I hit it on the head – people often used their tillers for this – and the bird dies. The body is a little longer and fatter than a large and old-fashioned mobile phone. Its chest is thickly and beautifully insulated with a mass of tiny feathers. They have the consistency of felt wadding and you can push your fingers in among them, covering the quick of your nails, feeling for the warm breast flesh underneath. This is what keeps it from dying of cold out in its eight-month-long vigil in the North Atlantic. The bird, in fact, has a wonderful circulatory system, consisting of three separate loops – one for the body and one for each orange foot – which are only connected to each other by the narrowest of necks. This means that the blood in the feet, which inevitably dangle in the ocean, can remain at a temperature scarcely above freezing, while the blood in the body, behind that thick mat of feather-hair, remains beautifully warm. The ornithologist who discovered this miracle of self-preservation described the puffin as 'a hot water bottle with two orange icicles hanging off the end.'

It is a bird whose life has made it useful for human beings. That thick chest down makes for perfect pillow stuffing. So much was it valued in the nineteenth century that on St Kilda puffins were caught by the tens of thousand for their feathers alone. The naked bodies were spread out as a manure-cum-mulch on the fields and gardens. That turns upside-down some of the ideas that people still have of the poverty of life in these places. At times there was glut, far too much goodness to know what to do with because the meat of the puffin, well basted and roasted in the oven for thirty-five or forty minutes at most, is delicious. It is as dark as wild duck, as rich as that, with no more than the suspicion of a life at sea about it. I have eaten puffin with my friends. It is dense with a kind of mineral substance, next to which farmed animals seem vapid and soggy. Eating a puffin is a sudden reminder of the reality of wildness from which we are removed. What we eat is as flaccid as ourselves. And that is the heart of Shiantism: the shock of unmediated life.

The puffin is a chesty creature and there is a curiously large amount of meat on such a small bird. If, as my father used to tell me, the definition of a gentleman is 'someone who can make a grouse do for six', the Shiant Islanders, with their annual puffin bonanza, would have had no difficulty qualifying. The puffin could give them so much breast meat because of the way it lives its life. It must fly but it must also swim and its fore-limbs are a compromise between paddles and wings. The ideal wing for a sea bird, giving maximum lift for minimum effort, allowing easy, energy-conserving glides across the waves, is long and narrow, like the wings of an albatross by which it can be hung around

the mariner's neck. You could never hang a puffin around a mariner's neck because its wings have been trimmed back to make them work underwater. They are feathered fins and I have spent summer afternoons on the Shiants swimming with these birds. They are not frightened. They gather around you, swimming up to you, looking curiously sideways at this new kind of rubber-suited whale. The puffins – and the guillemots, which are braver, beside them – dart in the sea, those wing-fins propelling them suddenly forward, a pulsed movement, more gobbling on the sea than grazing on it.

At sea, the wing-fin is extremely efficient. Ornithologists have attached depth meters to puffins and the deepest dive they have recorded, extraordinarily, is a hundred and eighty feet below the surface. Another was observed making a hundred and ninety-four dives in eighty-four minutes, with an average of only three seconds between each dive, which is a measure either of stamina or desperation or both. In the air, the puffin has to beat his short wings extremely fast. There is not enough lift for any sort of level glide. Only when taking off from the heights of their burrow slopes can they half-glide, a beautiful angel-like position as they drop to sea-level. There they must begin level flight. That involves an exhausting six hundred beats a minute and that is why they are such good eaters. A huge breast muscle is needed to power the wing which life at sea – and under the sea – has designed.

The bird teeters, like most of the auks, on the borders of flightlessness. You see a puffin taking off from the sea and it is a desperate business, a grinding attempt to get airborne, to get up the speed at which those wing-fins will work. It is buffeted in a gale as alarmingly as a Sopwith Camel. Once going, a puffin can fly fast, up to sixty miles an hour, but then the landing can be difficult, less a controlled jump jet settling into place than a managed crash, after which there is a lot of head-shaking and shoulder ruffling by which coherence is re-established and dignity restored.

The birds are here and that's their vindication. Their strategic compromise has worked. There were scares in the early 1970s that the puffins had experienced an enormous crash in numbers. There is some anecdotal but no hard evidence of this. Harvie-Brown's account is more one of amazement than of calculation and it is difficult to say that the numbers there today are less than in the past. The first careful counts ever made, in 1970, were repeated in the summer of 2000. Although the shape of the colonies seems to have changed slightly – an extension here, a retraction there – the overall numbers of puffins on the Shiants seems to have remained almost constant over twenty-five years.

Their presence here, at the top end of a chain that stretches deep into the geological roots of the islands, is a miracle of connectivity. Each step is ripplingly consequent on the one before: because the sea-bed in the Minch is roughened and corrugated with the hard volcanic rock ridges that are the Shiants' submarine cousins, the tides run violently across them; because the tides are so turbulent the nutrients in the muds and sands on the sea floor are stirred up throughout the height of the water column; because the water column is so thick with those elements, the phytoplankton, the lowest level of life, thrives in the enrichment. On those microscopic plants the zooplankton, the smallest of animals, can happily graze. Sandeels and sprats feed on the zooplankton, and both the larger fish, the mackerels and herring, and the birds can, in turn, feed on them. The birds are not here by chance, or by some kind of avian romanticism. They are here because around them is the great hunting ground and marketplace.

It goes further than that. The Shiants are on a frontier. They are the northernmost outcrop of the hard volcanic dolerite sills. Those rocks not only cause the currents and turbulence in the sea. They create the protected place of the islands themselves, away from land predators, the foxes, or nowadays the mink, which would destroy the birds. Isolated cliff habitat plus enriched turbulent seas equals bird heaven. This is an ideal site because just to the north, the nature of the sea-bed changes. There, over an area of about ten miles long and ten miles wide, is the perfect breeding ground for the sandeel, the little silver-flash needle of a fish on which the majority of sea birds feed. Sandeels like a rapid but not too rapid circulation of water above a sandy or gravelly, rather than muddy or rocky, sea floor at a depth of no more than two hundred feet. That is just what the North Minch gives them. There they live for the most of the year buried in the sand, waiting for the glory months of spring and summer.

Everything is precisely timed. With the growing light and

warmth in March and April, the plankton begin to thicken in the sea. Then, and only in the daytime, the sandeels emerge from their sandy beds to prey on that plankton and to lay their own eggs. The sea birds then begin to arrive and, while making their nests and incubating the eggs, prey on the adult sandeels. Each bird has a different strategy: the kittiwakes and gulls dabbling in the surface, puffins (despite their two-hundred-foot depth record) usually diving to thirty or forty feet, shags, foot-propelled, feeding on the fish close to shore, the guillemots, wing-propelled pursuit-divers, plunging much deeper, often to a hundred and fifty feet, and going much further afield.

Each bird is designed for a niche, but each must satisfy the same need. The making of the next generation is the most demanding task ever confronting a bird. Energy expenditure in the breeding season, in terms of building a nest, catching fish, avoiding the predatory gulls and skuas, goes up by two thirds compared with the relatively restful time spent out on the ocean in winter. That energy expenditure needs feeding. For every three fish caught in the winter, five must be caught during their Shiants summer. And for that surge in appetite, each sandeel or small sprat represents a package of high-energy food. They are also, incidentally, delicious. Every morning during the breeding season in the puffin colonies you find sandeels accidentally dropped, many of them bearing the marks where the puffins carried them in their beaks. They make a delicious whitebait. A breeding sea bird requires 2,200 kilojoules a day. A small shrimp, for example, provides only 4 kJ/gram, a squid no more than 3.5 kJ/g, but the rich, oily sandeel packs in a huge 6.5 kJ/gram. Here, in other words, is the concentrated protein pulse on which the entire bird system relies. Without it, this whirring miracle in the air above me could scarcely happen.

The birds are perfectly synchronised with it. When laying and incubating, they feed on the adult sandeels. By late May the young sandeels, which were born in March, have metamorphosed into little fish themselves and are catchable by the sea birds just at the moment when their own young are going through their sharpest growth phase. Baby sandeels provide the food for baby chicks. That is what you see hour after hour as the puffins come in out of the Minch, the tiny glittering fish still wriggling in their beaks: infant prey for infant predators.

If any link in the chain fails to deliver, catastrophe threatens. If the sea temperatures disturb the production of plankton, or delay it, or if for some reason the immense productivity of the sandeels, as ubiquitous as grass in the ocean, fails to come up to its usual volume, or if they are late, or if, as has happened in the North Sea but never yet in the Minch, vast tonnages of sandeel are caught for catfood – then the immense bird populations of the Shiants would be threatened with death. That catastrophe has at times in the past twenty years struck in Shetland, Norway and the Americas, where dead birds have littered the sand like feathered surf.

It must happen quite regularly, as a natural event, because sea birds have built into them a set of buffers against it. They can feed on other fish apart from sandeels. Some years on the Shiants, the ornithologists have found the adults bringing mostly sprats and relatively few sandeels. They can also fly further to find other sources of food. But more important for the long-term survival of the Shiant birds is their large-scale life-strategy. Most of them produce few young but live a long time. The puffin only ever has a single chick, and the chick will be five years old before it breeds, but each bird can live up to forty years. If the timing or the food production goes wrong one year, and the chick dies, that is not going to affect the population of the colony. Only failure year after year, and a dearth of chicks coming forward to breed, will begin to shrink the overall numbers.

Mike Brooke, curator of birds at Cambridge University

Zoological Museum, who has twice been to the Shiants to count the puffins, explained the maths to me. About one in four or five puffin fledglings survives to an age when they can breed. On average they then will breed for, say, ten years. Out of a puffin couple's ten fledglings, then, two will survive and so the population remains constant.

These may be the wrong terms, but that sense of robustness, of a marvellously mature and adult approach to risk, with all the elasticity of response that it implies, is, I think, one of the reasons that the spectacle of the summer birds is so stimulating. This life-phenomenon is not sweet, in the way that puffins are often portrayed. Nor is it heroically violent, in the way that nature is often seen. It is a wonderfully sober, serious and ingenious response to the problems and challenges of a sea and island life. What is eternally beautiful about the hundreds of thousands of puffins that come to make the Shiants their summer home is not the individual bird, not the funny little self-satisfied figure in a tail coat and stiff shirt, but this big strong body of genetic intelligence, drawing spectacular life from the hidden abundance of the sea around it.

There is only one clamouring absence. Throughout history the Shiants were the haunt of the white-tailed sea eagle. I have never seen sea eagles on the Shiants but I have seen them in Morvern, on the Sound of Mull, a pair of enormous, tatty creatures, flustered in the breeze, their wing feathers fluttering about them like the rags of an old bag woman, their wings eight feet across and perhaps eighteen inches from the leading to the trailing edge. You can have no doubt, as the shepherds on Mull know, that these creatures can take living, healthy lambs from beside their mothers. They make the greater black-backed gulls look like pigeons.

The Shiants were the famous home of a pair for well over two centuries. In 1690, Martin Martin saw a couple of Eagles here: the Natives told me, that these Eagles would never suffer any of their kind to live there but themselves, and that they drove away their young ones as soon as they were able to fly. And they told me likewise, that those Eagles are so careful of the place of their abode, that they never yet killed any Sheep or Lamb in the Island, tho the Bones of Lambs, of Fawns and Wild-Fowls, are frequently found in and about their Nests; so that they make their Purchase in the opposite islands, the nearest of which is a League distant.

Martin was a modern man, a graduate of Edinburgh University, a friend of Sir Robert Sibbald, the Edinburgh physician and botanist, a doctor qualified at Leyden and a corresponding member of the Royal Society in London. His journeys around the Hebrides were partly, as a good seventeenth-century scientist, in pursuit of vulgar errors. And he makes a modern joke: the Garbh Eilean eagles do their shopping in Eilean Mhuire. But he was also a native of Duntulm in Skye, no more than fourteen miles away, and so a Gaelic speaker, and his description, at least in reporting the Shiant Islanders' view of their native eagles, is filled, I think, with a certain animist respect, an attitude which carries in it a faint echo of those long-distant people in Isbister, who shared their graves with the sea eagles.

The eagles continued to grace these cliffs until the early part of the twentieth century. Even now, empty as it is, the precise location of the eyrie, high up on the north cliffs of Garbh Eilean, is clear: a smallish place about twenty feet across, protected from below by sheer dolerite columns rising from the sea and protected from above by an enormous corbelled roof of dolerite. Lord Teignmouth saw them here in 1828, and forty years later the highly acquisitive birder Captain HJ Elwes saw this eyrie as one of the ultimate challenges. Elwes had lost any respect for the birds. There were sea eagle eyries reported to him in North Uist,

Scalpay, Wiay, Benbecula, above Loch Bhrollúm and several other places in Lewis and Harris. There was even one man, he heard, Dr MacGillivray of Eoligarry in Barra, who had a tame sea eagle for a while 'and this bird used to follow his sons in their rambles over the island.' Virtually every eyrie was on north-facing cliffs but the Shiants' throne was the only one thought to be inaccessible. That is what motivated Captain Elwes.

> May 4 1868
>
> To Shiant Isles in smack – Got there about 1 – on the way 5 eagles were in sight at one time. – 2 golden and 3 white-tailed –.
>
> The eagles' nest was in the highest part of the cliff which is quite perpendicular and positioned as far down that the rope would only just reach it. It was a very nasty place altogether, but Sandy [MacIver, the keeper from Eishken in Pairc] said he thought that he could get it, so we let him down. When he had gone about 23 fathoms he stopped so long that I was afraid something was wrong, so I ran round to see and found that Sandy was so giddy from the twisting of the rope that he could do nothing. He said he could not make out where the nest was even then and that the rock hung over too much to get it. So we pulled him up. I am much annoyed at our failure, and I had made so sure of getting the eggs in the Shiant Isles. – back to Eishken.

This extract from Elwes's journal is preserved, without comment, in Harvie-Brown's notebooks, now in the Library of the Royal Museum in Edinburgh. Elwes was the rule, not the aberration. Harvie-Brown also reproduces nature notes from another near-contemporary called Hogg: '10 April 82. Brollum Hill, Loch Shell. White-tailed sea-eagles. Both birds shot in both places. Very fine old birds.'

It may well have been the invention of the camera which brought this habit to an end. On his visit to the Shiants in 1886,

Harvie-Brown had a photographer with him, William Norrie of Fraserburgh, and in *The Vertebrate Fauna of the Outer Hebrides*, which Harvie-Brown published in 1888, he included a plate taken by Norrie of the northern cliffs of the Shiants just below the sea eagle's eyrie.

It is the earliest photograph of the islands in existence and is peculiarly uninformative: a misty set of columns which look the same today as they did over a century ago. Other photographs which Norrie took of the Campbell family, mentioned by Harvie-Brown in his journal, have disappeared.

But the naturalist, not averse to killing large amounts of wildlife himself (his collected skins were also deposited in the Royal Museum) writes rather differently about the sea eagle:

> In 1887 the Shiant islands pair were still 'to the fore' and gave our party a fine opportunity of watching all the phases of their flight. Long may they continue in their inaccessible retreat; and may the broken overhanging basalt columns, which project far beyond the giant ribs of similar structure down below, resist the tear and wear of time, and prove a sheltering roof to them. So far as we are concerned we are pleased with a feather ('tickled with a straw', if you like) which we picked up on the boulder-strewn beach below the eyrie, ay and a great deal more than if we had shot the bird.

This charming, serious and energetic man was ahead of his time. In about 1905, although the date is uncertain, and the name of the culprit unknown, the last of the Shiant Isles' white-tailed sea eagles was shot. Compton Mackenzie heard that it had been done by 'a clergyman collector' but there is another possibility. The Eishken estate on Pairc was certainly killing 'vermin' on the Shiants' cliffs up until the 1930s and perhaps beyond. When I asked Tommy Macrae, a practised raconteur, loved throughout Pairc, who worked as a keeper on Eishken for a good part of the twentieth century, what was meant by vermin, he had a one-word answer: 'hawks'. His father, a keeper on Eishken in the 1930s, used to go out there to kill them. Elwes had seen a 'Falcon' on the Shiants as well as two sea eagles in the 1860s but there were no hawks on the Shiants in the 1960s, '70s or '80s. Only recently has a pair of peregrines re-established itself on the east cliffs of Eilean an Tighe. The persecution by the gamekeepers from Eishken, intent on eradicating the 'vermin' to protect the grouse, was persistent for decades. It seems as likely as not that the sea eagles were shot in the same cause.

There is a footnote to the story of the Shiant sea eagles. They were seen again over the Minch between the islands and Pairc in the last few years of the 1990s. A pair, descendants of those which since the 1980s the Nature Conservancy and its successors have been reintroducing to Rum and the Inner Hebrides, set up their nest somewhere in Pairc. The present owners of the Eishken estate welcomed and treasured them. Ravens harassed the eagles at their enormous nest but people did not. The officers of Scottish Natural Heritage were considering installing a closed circuit camera so that these precious creatures – there are some twenty-two pairs with territories in Scotland – could be continuously monitored. The nest was littered, just as Martin Martin had described it, with the bones of their victims. Through binoculars you could see on the nest the remains of puffins in the summer-time and fulmars in the winter. These eagles were also making 'their Purchase in the opposite islands.'

Despite all of this and despite the wonderful midsummer glory of the Shiants, there is something troublingly wrong. The modern Minch is an illusion of perfection. The range of pollution in the sea here, even apart from the radioactivity drifting up from Sellafield, makes alarming reading. Some of it is visible. Ships' crew and fishermen throw overboard about three or four pounds of rubbish per person per day. A ship as a whole, it is thought, chucks on average another two hundred and ninety tons of cargo-associated waste into the sea every year. Landlubbers are no better. So-called Sewage Related Debris is increasingly made of plastic. SRD, as it is discreetly termed, includes sanitary towels, tampons, nappies, condoms, bandages, tights and medical waste. Most of the sewage in the Minch area is untreated and so all of this is discharged directly into the sea. I have sailed past much of it in *Freyja*.

The beaches of the Shiants are nowadays lined from end to end in multi-coloured plastic rubbish, and I can walk the length of them finding loo cleaners, soft drink bottles, cans of Coke with Japanese script, dolls' heads, Dettol and Domestos where in the past the shore was scattered with fish boxes on every one of which was the instruction 'Return to Lochinver'.

I don't want to overstate this. The Minch is not a poisoned place. Life here seems more complete than anywhere I know, miraculously uncontaminated considering how near it is to the huge industrial centres of Britain and Europe. But there are signs of something under strain. In addition to the stream of radio-activity pouring into the Minch from the Irish Sea, levels of cadmium and copper were found here in concentrations much higher than expected for coastal waters. These metals probably come from the rivers of industrial England.

The deep health of the sea is the great unaddressed issue of environmental politics. It remains both a toxin-sink and the most egregious example of a property that is over-exploited and mal-treated because it is held in common. No one owns it to protect it. Everyone abuses it because it isn't theirs. The fiendishly compli-cated population dynamics of sea plants and creatures and the birds around them is not properly understood but there is one big, alarming signal: the sea eagles that fly over the Minch are failing to breed. That is as good a sign as any that more attention needs to be paid and more precautions taken. The Shiants' corbelled eagle-throne is still empty and I won't be happy until it is occupied again.

Then, in the house on Eilean an Tighe, I will think of those emperor-birds in residence on Garbh Eilean. Like lairds in their Highland fastness, they will scarcely show themselves to the world at large. The sea eagle is not a self-promoter, does not engage in the sort of daily noisy business of more ordinary bird life. He has his self-regard and his reticence. He is known to be there, a sovereign presence, and there is no need to flaunt it. Eagles colour the country they inhabit, but it is a glimpsed presence not a displayed one. I would not need to see them, but only to enjoy the reverberating knowledge that somewhere on that cliff they were staring out to the north across the Minch, the only truly imperial creature in the British Isles, standing three feet from talon to eye, immensely strong, a creature which, if rarely seen, nevertheless sinks deep into the consciousness, a symbol of grandeur, distance, acuity and imperium.

Occasionally perhaps, inside the house with my daughters, a friend outside would shout, 'Look, look!' We would go out. The sky is a bright blue and on the lip of the hill above us, perhaps four hundred feet above the house and the sea, is the sea eagle. That incredible wing is spread like a floorboard above us. It is a black stroke on the sky made with a fat-bladed pen. There is little you can do when watching an eagle quartering the ground on which you stand but gawp at its leonine presence. Those sprung wings held in a shallow V, a slight flex to them as the air shifts beneath it, the primaries flared at the tips, its quivering, delicate fingers feeling the wind and its own place in it. In the field-glasses, I can see the eagle's head moving, never still, surveying the country, to and fro across us, across the map of house and shore and the abandoned fields. The bird is taking us in, calmly, circlingly, from its ever higher position of distant knowledge. Analyst, examiner, assessor-king.

I know three things about eagles. Their eyes, in whose retinas the rods and cones are packed many times more tightly than our own, have a resolution eight times better than ours. They live in a world of visual intensity whose nature we cannot, quite literally, even dream of. It is said that an eagle can see a shrew twitch in the grass from three thousand feet above it. And, thirdly, if our eyes occupied the same proportion of our skull as the eagle's eyes do of his, they would be the size of oranges.

The bird comes back down on to the cliff-top and sits there, inward and disconsolate. The ravens, which live on the same cliff, whose cliff, in their mind anyway, this really is, flip up out of somewhere and start nagging at the eagle. He sits there being bothered by these birds like gnats around him. His stillness makes the ravens look small. As they dive and pirouette around him, he ducks his head like a half-tolerant old dog, just dropping it down into his neck as the ravens make their pass. You have to love the eagle for that, the old bastard being swatted by the nagging kids. After four or five minutes he has had enough and falls off his throne into flight above the Sound. Then you see the heroic beauty of the bird. He beats his way eastwards along the steepening and darkening cliff, heavy wing-beats, long and laboured, each one giving a visible lift to the body, while the ravens play like Messerschmitts around him. The heaviness of that beat, the grandeur of the creature in his dark and rocky surroundings: I remember Shelley's description of Coleridge as 'a hooded eagle among blinking owls'. The rest of the passage describes the great, impenetrable Coleridge as

> *he who sits obscure*
> *In the exceeding lustre and the pure*
> *Intense irradiation of a mind*
> *Which, with its own internal lightning blind,*
> *Flags wearily through darkness and despair.*

It is those last lines I want to see in flight on the Shiants, that sagacious, unknowable, all-seeing creature, flying to the east along the fissured cliff, while the late sun slides across the rocks beneath him. That is what I want: Coleridge on the Shiants.

10

IN MIDSUMMER, AS THE BIRDS were proliferating around me, and as the cotton grass began to show its white-tufted pennants in the bogs, as the flag irises flowered in the ditches and the meadowsweet bubbled out in the protected corners by the cliffs, the time had come to address the central question of the Shiants. What had happened here? What history was there here? What explained its emptiness now and the remains of buildings distributed across the islands? The old buildings as I walked across them reminded me of a summer beach after the warmth of the day has gone. You can see where each family has been, their scufflings in the sand, the one or two sweet wrappers and scraps of paper left behind, a can or two, the holes where their windbreak had stood, the marks of dug-in toes beside the legs of a deck chair, all the diagnostic signals of life once lived but now finished, waiting for the tide to roll in over it. That, translated into moss and tumbled stone, was the condition of the Shiants.

I wanted to find out more about the islands and that was why I had asked Pat Foster to bring his team of archaeologists with him to the Shiants. He had now done his survey. He had made a few tentative guesses as to the nature of the remains he had identified. Now the time had come to dig. What has emerged from their archaeology, and from the historical documents which I gathered, is a rich and poignant story of a community coming to an end. Its struggles and its ingenuities, the changing circumstances with which it had to deal, its final collapse: all that is revealed. What before had been a contourless silence can now be seen as a tiny island microcosm of Highland history at its most critical juncture, the centuries between 1600 and 1800.

To understand that story, one must go back a little earlier. I asked the leading expert on the history of the Hebridean landscape, Professor Robert Dodgshon, to come to the islands for a couple of days and walk across them with me. The kind of detailed analysis of a single site or building which archaeology can provide needs the broader context of the landscape historian. No island house could make sense without its surrounding fields and sea.

It is one of the repeated pleasures of life to witness an expert presented with a new set of data. Arriving off Malcolm MacLeod's boat from Stornoway one morning, Robert could scarcely sit down for a cup of tea in the house before rushing out to see what the Shiants had to say for themselves. An Atlantic storm was slashing around us like a carwash but it made no difference to the scholarly appetite.

What he impressed on me again and again over the next forty-eight hours was never to think of fixity in a place like this. Human occupation of the Shiants would always have come and gone like the tides, a filling and ebbing, a restless geography. 'Life here,' the professor said to me from the depths of his huddled waterproofs as we stood high on the inland flank of Eilean an Tighe, 'was never some fixed version of the ancient surviving into the modern age.' It would have been a consistently responsive pattern, adapting to its own growth and its own travails, extending its fingers into every part of its natural resource, beaten back at times, only to refill the spaces left by those withdrawals. But that

very pattern of give and take, mimicking a natural popula
is itself a form of permanence, the kind of existence which Fren n
historians have called the *longue durée* – a nearly changeless continuing for century after century.

Of course change did occur. Eight hundred years ago, the
pattern might have been very much what you can see in the Celtic
landscapes of Cornwall or Wales: family farms, each with its own
arable and sweet grazing, with shared rough grazing on the
heights. The Shiants would have been a cluster of privacies, with
a form of communal grout between them. It is not difficult to
imagine them in the five core places: at Annat and the Bagh on
Garbh Eilean, by the shore and in the central valley on Eilean an
Tighe, on the heights of Eilean Mhuire. Amazingly, you can still
see the footings of such a farmstead on the rich ground just
beside the natural arch on Garbh Eilean: a house, a barn, a byre
and a garden enclosure, just uphill from a fresh-running spring.

It is a lovely place. I have camped there in the past and you
see something from these soft green pastures which is hidden
from the house on Eilean an Tighe: dawn over the mainland of
Scotland, the tangerine sun lifting up over the ragged mountains
in Torridon thirty miles to the east with slabs of orange light
daubed across the Minch at your feet. Whoever lived here in the
distant past, while needing to cower from the terrible exposure
here to an easterly gale, must always have loved those wonderful
summer mornings flooding in across the sea.

Elsewhere those early medieval farms have been obscured
by later building but in the larger landscape one can make
out the field walls which must have belonged to those farms,
the careful delineation of private holdings. In their lichened
and crumbling state, their lines infused with a habit of use,
these walls are the most beautiful of ancient marks on the
ground. They can only remain enigmatic, as neither archaeology
nor landscape history has developed a way of dating them.

They are as uninterpretable as the scratches and borings left by generations of schoolboys in a wooden desk; repeated private etchings, their point – beyond the obvious: keep the cattle out of the corn – forgotten.

At some point in the Middle Ages, all of this came to an end. The small farmsteads on Garbh Eilean were abandoned and the system known as run-rig imposed. Each year, narrow strips of arable land were parcelled out among the families of the community, each family receiving different lots every year, as a form of communal fairness. These are the strips you can see all over the Hebrides, often now called 'lazybeds', a term invented by late eighteenth-century 'improvers', perhaps because by this system only half the ground was cultivated, the other half devoted to wide drainage ditches. Robert Dodgshon told me something I had never even considered before: that this strip system, which is so deeply embedded in the visual image of the Hebrides, may well be an alien import. 'Don't the strips remind you of something else?' he asked me as we walked around, muffled in our water-proofs on a bitter, slashing summer day.

'The strip systems in open fields?' I guessed rather wildly, trying to drag an image of huge East Anglian field systems to the islands. That is what he meant. Far from being an indigenous Celtic proto-communism – as everyone likes to imagine – the landscape of cultivated ridges may well be an imposition by feudal landlords in a period of medieval regularisation. The earlier, indigenous, private family farms, were at some point transformed into a shared landscape, a communalisation similar in its way to the collectivisation of farms in Soviet Europe after the war.

There is no saying when it happened here. It may have been after the Black Death in the fourteenth century, which would have devastated the families here, as it did elsewhere in the Hebrides. The older farms may have been abandoned in death and never reoccupied. Or perhaps at an earlier time of sudden and momentous disruption.

This was, after all, the world of the clan. No overarching authority was recognised here for most of the Middle Ages. Each clan, as long as it accepted the fact of vendetta, could attack what it liked and steal what it liked from any other. Violence, and the theft above all of food in the form of cattle, was part of the clan world. The Shiants, at the centre of the Minch, were on the front line of opposing bands based in northern Skye, Lewis, Harris and further south in the Hebrides. The feuds between them continued for century after century and two incidents in particular occurred within sight of these shores.

There was, first of all, the fatal moment, perhaps in the twelfth or thirteenth century, when the glory of the Nicolsons came to a sudden and irrevocable end in the Sound of Shiant. They had owned the whole of Lewis, with a castle probably at Stornoway, and much of Assynt on the mainland opposite. The clan was known for the wealth of its farmlands: 'Clan MacNicol of the porridge and barley bannocks'. John Morison of Bragar in Lewis, writing in about 1680, described the mournful moment: 'Torquill, son of Claudius [a seventeenth-century aggrandisement of the name Macleod] did violently espouse Macknaicle's only daughter, and cutte off Immediatelie the whole race of Macknaicle and possessed himself with the whole Lews [all of Lewis].'

The Nicolsons retreated to Trotternish in northern Skye and things have never been quite the same since. Is the abandonment of the Garbh Eilean farms to be dated to the destruction of the Nicolsons as people to be reckoned with?

More enigmatically, the huge dark bay on the eastern side of Eilean Mhuire, filled in summer with more guillemots than any other part of the islands, crowding there on rock after rock around the whole rim of the mile-long bay, is called Bagh Chlann Neill. It might mean the Bay of the MacNeils but nowhere on the Shiants, nor in Pairc opposite, has ever belonged to the MacNeils. Or perhaps it refers to the family of Nial Macleod, the defender of Lewis against the Fife Adventurers at the beginning of the seventeenth century, whom he once attacked with 'two hundred barbarous bludie wickit Hielandmen'. There is no telling.

There are other bays with the same name in several places in the Hebrides, in Scalpay, Loch Maddy in Uist, between Grimsay and Ronay, and on the north-western side of Berneray in Lewis. There is one in particular in Coll, which is also called Slochd na Dunach or the Pit of Havoc where, it is said, 'a fearful slaughter of the Maclean's enemy is still remembered.' No such story attaches to the Bagh Chlann Neill here, but it is a place where fishing boats do still come in to shelter in a strong southwesterly.

It is not inconceivable that some MacNeils were caught there one day, perhaps by the sudden violence of the Macleods, rounding the corner by Seann Chaisteal in their *birlinns*. The MacNeils would have been trapped in the bay, slashed at by the Macleods, and finally murdered, before the dead were hoisted overboard, leaving only their name on the blood-slicked water. Had the MacNeils been thinking of taking over the riches of Eilean Mhuire? Was it that kind of threat which forced the Shiant Islanders to retreat to Eilean an Tighe?

Those are unanswerable questions and the *longue durée* continues through and past them. Birds, fish, livestock, vegetables and cereals, clay, peat, driftwood, stone: these were the materials out of which life was made. Metal was nearly absent. Roofs, creels and fish-traps, even the strakes of boats, weren't pinned or nailed but woven or bound together with ropes made from heather, hair, grass or roots. There was nothing special about this. Life here would not have been essentially different from life on the shores of the sea lochs in Lewis, Skye or the mainland. An island existence was neither more privileged nor more deprived than anywhere else. In a world without roads, and only long, wet, sludgy paths across moorland, to be on the Shiants was to have the benefit of the good soils, the riches of the birds and fish. It was not to be deprived of anything the mainland could offer. It was a sea room with sea room, a place enlarged by its circumstances, not confined by them. Isolation and insularity were not the same thing.

This constancy and continuity makes an enormous problem for archaeologists. Not only are the materials of one age, even one millennium, barely distinguishable from those of another, but one age consistently uses the materials of another. A modern sheep pen or fank reuses the stones of a nineteenth-century summer shieling, which reuses the stones of a seventeenth-century house which reuses the stones of an Iron Age roundhouse, which has itself reused the remains of a Bronze Age dwelling. An island can only survive by recycling.

It was not quite a closed system. The outside world had its impacts, but the impact was contingent. Things, people and ideas all arrived at the shore, but they scarcely changed the nature of the system they found. In the summer of 1999, on the beach between Eilean an Tighe and Garbh Eilean, a pebble of pumice was washed up, light enough to float. It had come, almost certainly, from the volcano erupting that year in Montserrat in the Caribbean. Others, identical to it, had been found on beaches in Tiree. A few days later, the large, glossy heart-shaped Molucca bean of a plant called *Entada gigas*, always known in the Hebrides as Mary's Nut, washed up, carried here perhaps from the shores of Nicaragua, where it grows above the sandy beaches. Columbus is said to have found these sea-hearts on the coast of the Azores and to have set out westwards in search of the trees that had shed them.

Until about 1600, that near self-sufficiency had defined the Shiants' relationship to the rest of the world. The pumice is added to the beach, the nutrients from the rotting sea-heart are added to the life-system of the islands, which continue on their way, absorbent and indifferent. But between about 1600 and about 1800 that immensity of the *longue durée* comes to an end. This is the period of the Shiants' pivotal crisis. By about 1800, the islands were no longer permanently occupied. No one could be persuaded to stay here and the islands, from having been central to their own existence for millennia, had started to become marginal to a world whose focus was elsewhere. These islands, in other words, had become 'remote' for the first time. Insularity became identified with isolation and that was their death knell. Something fatal had happened to the Shiants: the arrival of the modern.

For the modern world, and for modern consciousness, the Shiants did not have what was necessary: closeness to markets, either for sale and for supply, nor access to the materials of civilisation. This moment of crisis, this shift from one type of world, which had existed, more or less, since the end of the Ice Age, to another which is recognisably like the one we now inhabit, would, I realised, be the most revelatory period in the Shiants' history. It was the period I wanted to investigate in the archaeological excavation we carried out on Eilean an Tighe in the summer of 2000. What happened here? How quick was the change? How sudden the departure? How agonised the experience? Could answers to any of these questions be sifted from the silent evidence which archaeology provides?

When Pat Foster arrived with his team of Czechs in the summer of 2000, we decided what to excavate the first evening. I was already on the islands, having sailed out a few days before, and had swept and tidied the house as if there were no tomorrow. The rat-poisoning campaign in the spring had done its work. There was no sign and no smell of the beasts inside. A couple of poison-desiccated bodies curled up in plastic bags was the only reminder. I burnt them.

The islands were looking their most severe. Cloud was down on the tops and a grin of surf lined the northern shores. The place, when it is like this, can feel like the deck of a trawler. The Czechs looked around them, a little cold and a little disconsolate. Were they really going to be spending two weeks on these grim, sandless, northern rocks? Was this really my apology for a house? Where was the place where we could have a picnic by the shore? But Pat Foster is a richly inspiring person. We walked along the bench of flat land beside the sea looking at bumps and hollows. Anything here that we should excavate? he asked. Anything that I liked the look of? Perhaps not. Too much rubbish in the ruins, too complex a set of overlying structures: modern on eighteenth-century on medieval on prehistoric. Even from the look of the landscape, you could tell that layered complexity was inevitable here. This was the place that had more to offer than any other on the islands. It should not be the site we first addressed.

Petr Limburský, who had been with Pat on Barra, excavating the site of the neolithic house at Allt Chrisal, is a man of precision and gentleness, with a head as massive as Beethoven's and a slightly distant, romantic air. He had gone for a longer, wider walk from which he came back excited. There was a site that seemed ideal, up in the central valley of Eilean an Tighe. It was the largest house, almost forty feet long internally and ten feet wide, with double-skinned walls that were themselves three feet thick. This building was clearly part of a complex.

Small barns had been built next to it, one to the north and one to the south, and all three structures were enclosed within a kind of courtyard within which haystacks would have stood, protected by the surrounding wall from any wandering beasts. It was, in other words, a farmstead. The walls of the main building were still standing three or four feet high. They had not been robbed or reused. It was a fair guess that this building had last been used when the Shiants were last permanently occupied in the 1700s. The shepherds who had come here in the nineteenth century lived down near the shore, almost certainly on the site of the present house. Pieces of Victorian Dundee marmalade jars and the blue nineteenth-century willow-pattern china can be found quite easily on the beach in front of the house where those Victorian Hebrideans threw or dropped them. Up here, though, on a dry platform of ground where the yellow-flowered silverweed grows in thick profusion, was a place not overlaid by the present or the more recent past. This is where we would dig.

The following morning, the weather had changed to a pale iris-blue sky. Bubbled clouds streamed in from Ireland. The Shiants felt Arctic and looked Provençal. The gulls honked and cacked when we entered their breeding grounds. The wind cut across the high plateau site and above it, hardly glimpsed, but heard unbroken for two weeks, a lark sang, rising and falling in the sunshine, its trembling unbroken glissando the ever-present accompaniment to this delving into the Shiants' past.

The work was exhausting and heavy at first, cutting the nettles, slicing off the layer of turf in which they grew, stacking the turf for later reuse, moving the boulders which had clearly fallen from the walls and piling them alongside the house. Once cleared, the slow and meticulous excavation could begin, distinguishing colours of earth, feeling as if in deep snow for the contours of the underlying realities.

As the seven archaeologists scraped away, shaving off successive layers, it soon became clear that the time we had would not be enough to discover everything about the building or its site. It was too big, but we drove on day after day, performing our gradual surgery on the body, exfoliating its past lives one by one. By the end of the allotted fortnight we had not reached anything like its origins. The layers were continuing deep below us. Our final day was spent piling the soil back on to the surfaces we had exposed, and returfing them, to protect the archaeology from the sheep which would wander in here during the winter. Only finally, on the last afternoon, with the sky now grey above us, and spits of rain flecking out of the north-west, with our hoods up, did we light a small peat fire on the spot where one of the hearths had been found. Dry bracken was the kindling and gloved fingers the windbreaks until the fire took and we ate chocolate around its blue, intimate flame. The deeper history of this site, as of many on the Shiants, awaits the excavations of later years.

What we found is enough, with some conjecture and with the help of one or two documents, to re-establish a version of what happened here on that hinge between the ancient and the modern, stretching from the sixteenth to the eighteenth centuries. Of course, archaeology discovers its story back to front. It finds conclusion and ending first. Origins and beginnings are the last

BLACK HOUSE ON EILEAN AN TIGHE

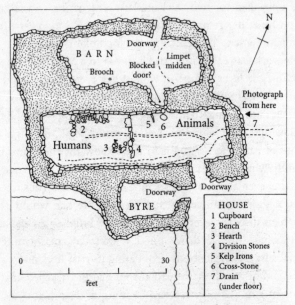

HOUSE
1 Cupboard
2 Bench
3 Hearth
4 Division Stones
5 Kelp Irons
6 Cross-Stone
7 Drain
(under floor)

Plan

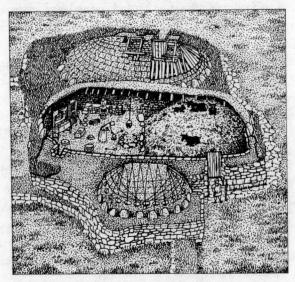

Conjectural reconstruction

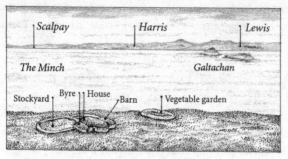

Scalpay Harris Lewis

The Minch Galtachan

Stockyard Byre House Barn Vegetable garden

Setting

N

Looking west during excavation,
summer 2000

to emerge. And so the story here is not the story as it came to us on those beautiful summer days, with the lark decanting its heart twice as high again as the house is above the sea. This is the story of events as I think they might have occurred.

We had no time to look into the south barn or byre at all. It remains covered with its mat of nettles and silverweed, both marks of human and animal occupation and – not to be too delicate about this – defecation. It was always said that women in the Hebrides should relieve themselves with the cattle and the men with the horses. The human manure was added as an equally precious resource to that of their livestock. Much of the disgust of the enlightened eighteenth-century travellers stemmed from this intimacy of everyday life with the substance an urban civilisation thought of as sewage and which was considered here as the source of next year's bread. That wrinkling of the sophisticated nose encompasses the revolution of this period. What one harboured, the other reviled; what one considered an essential part of the closed loop of their lives, the other wished to see disposed of as invisibly as possible. What the Hebrides saw as cyclical, the visitors saw as linear, a one-way process, a model not of the cycle of fertility but of the line of production.

It is a habit that persists with us. Modern visitors to the islands always over-cater in one particular commodity: loo paper. About forty rolls of it clutter the back of the cupboard in the modern house, testament to a modern anxiety. I have taken to using seaweed myself and although I would advise against both laminaria (leathery) and serrated wrack (prickly) or any of the red seaweeds (tendency to disintegrate) I can recommend bladder wrack, a saline swab of the most comfortable and effective kind.

In 2000, we concentrated on two areas: the inside of the house and the north barn.

The earliest layers are the most obscure and in the house itself, they were no more than glimpsed in a single trench – or *sondage*, a sounding, as the archaeologists call it – cut by Linda Čihaková. There are a pair of stone-lined and stone-capped drains in here. Linda removed the dark mud with which they were filled and found a baked clay floor in the bottom of each of them. This level is almost a foot and a half below the eighteenth-century floor and is perhaps the floor of a medieval house. At the same level in the barn, just above some building foundations, a small copper brooch was found, perhaps from the mid- to late-sixteenth century.

It is only an inch and a half across and it is not a rich thing, not in the same class as the torc, a domestic object which would have pinned up a woman's shawl. Others identical to it have been found in Lewis. The ring is incised with what looks, at first glance, like letters but are in fact the worn-away remains of a repeated moulding. Four small crosses are cut crudely into the metal at the cardinal points.

Can a picture be drawn from these enigmatic hints of Shiant life at this earliest of our excavated levels? These are the floors of the Shiants in the very late Middle Ages. There are people living on this island and perhaps on Eilean Mhuire. It is also the moment the islands are first mentioned in a document. In 1549, a man of whom almost nothing is known beyond his name and title, Donald Monro, Archdeacon of the Isles, perhaps Rector of St Columba's Church in Eye, near Stornoway, made the first tour of the Hebrides, perhaps a pastoral inspection. He was coming north from Skye:

> Northwart fra this Ile lyis the Ile callit Ellan Senta, callit in Inglish the saynt Ile, mair nor twa mile lang, verie profitable for corn, store and fisching, perteining to Mccloyd of the Leozus.
>
> Be eist this lyis an Ile callit Senchastell [still the name of the rock off the eastern point of Eilean Mhuire] callit in Inglish the auld castell, ane strength full of corn and girsing,

and wild fowl nests in it, and als fishing, perteining to Mccloyd of the Leozus.

Monro's description of Garbh Eilean and Eilean an Tighe together, and of Eilean Mhuire as a separate possession of the Macleod chieftain of Lewis, hints at a possible history. By the time of Monro's visit, the farmsteads on Garbh Eilean had already been left and that island was now farmed as one unit with Eilean an Tighe. The fertility of Eilean Mhuire, despite its terrible exposure to winter gales, had kept some people living there, with their own farming system of arable fields, hay meadows and grazing.

They are not a poor place, 'verie profitable for corn, store and fisching'. The 'wild fowl nests' here are famous and if a fowl is a bird whose destiny is the pot, these people are eating them. There were some signs of green sticky clay next to the brooch, probably manure, so animals are kept inside over the winter where their manure builds up to be spread on the spring-time fields. It is perhaps a good time, a florescence for the islands.

Those early levels are immediately below the first true floor of what is now called a 'blackhouse', a nineteenth-century term, for what previously would have been called, quite simply, a house. It, too, is of clay, baked hard, reddened by the heat and perhaps by the mixture of peat ash, which is a wonderful soft ochre. The central drain was laid in this floor.

It is of course nearly impossible to assign dates to memories and ghosts of structures such as these. It is like trying to name ripples in the tide. But again one can make a guess. The first blackhouse is an improvement made, perhaps, in the last years of the sixteenth century. Its new floor and its new well-drained accommodation reflect the relative well-being of the period.

Immediately after it, though, comes the first sign of crisis. Quite briefly, perhaps for no more than a decade or so, the house is for some reason unroofed and unoccupied. A thin, dark layer of silt soil, no more than a couple of inches thick, is spread across the well-laid clay that preceded it. Sheep would have trampled in here, the nettles would have grown, died and rotted, people would have been absent. Why? Here, above all, on one of the most favoured places in the islands? The documents provide a possible answer.

Between about 1590 and 1615, anarchy overtook Lewis and its dependent islands. The disaster for the Macleods began with an accident, in all likelihood the worst ever to have occurred within sight of the Shiants. The heir to the Macleod possessions, Torquil Oighre, his second name meaning heir, the son of Rorie, Chief of the Lewis Macleods, when 'sailing from the Lewes to troternes in the Ile of Skye with a hundred men perished with all his companie by ane extraordinarie storme and tempest.' The bodies would have washed up on these beaches and been buried in the cemetery by the shore, without doubt the greatest number of dead ever seen on the Shiants.

The inheritance of the island possessions was now uncertain and a long, complicated and bloody feud followed in which Torquil's younger brothers, three legitimate, by his father's three wives, and three others illegitimate, by other women, plotted against and murdered each other, pulling in allies from the mainland, and slaughtering their followers in the episode known as 'The Evil Trouble of the Lews'. The Macleods were violent heirs to their Viking inheritance. It was said that the Clan MacLeod, 'were like pikes in the water, the oldest of them, if the biggest, eats the youngest of them.' It was a turmoil of mutual destruction.

Is it possible that our thin layer of silt, a mark of abandonment and discontinuity, just above the level of sixteenth-century coherence, is the Shiants' reflection of the Trouble of the Lews? Perhaps. And could it be this period of disruption and change also brought about the withdrawal from Eilean Mhuire, the concentration of people in what may have felt like the collective safety of Eilean an Tighe? That too is a possibility. Certainly by the end of the century, and from then on, the three islands are treated as a single group and the entire population was living on Eilean an Tighe.

The eventual beneficiaries of the chaos were the Mackenzies from Kintail on the mainland. They had tied themselves by marriage to the Macleods, and played a brilliant, many-stranded and double-crossing role in depriving both the Macleods and a band of would-be gentlemen colonists, the so-called Fife Adventurers, of Lewis. They paid over some money (a signal of change: the first time the Shiants were ever bought) and emerged the legalised victors in 1611. *The Genealogie of the Surname of McKenzie since ther coming into Scotland*, complied by John MacKenzie of Applecross in 1667, described how 'The Lord Kintail having now bought ye right of ye Lewes he landed in ye Lewes wt 700 chosen men qr aft. [whereafter] ye taking away of some herschips [plunder] and some little skirmishes manie of ye inhabitants submitted themselves to him and took yr poones [possessions] of him.'

One of those transfers of land, and perhaps some of the *herschips* and maybe some little skirmishes, occurred on the Shiants. Certainly, the islands went from the Macleods to the Mackenzies, who became Earls of Seaforth, in honour of the grandest loch in the grandest landscape of their new island possession. A 1637 charter from the crown, confirming the grant of Lewis and its islands to Seaforth, names these little specks of their new acquisition quite explicitly: 'Iland-Schant'. The Shiants were now Mackenzie country. When, a century later, in 1718, the first surviving rental of the Seaforth's estate comes to 'Shant', the name of the tenant is 'Kennith Mackenzie'. He is the first named occupant of the island, one of twenty-two Mackenzies, tenants-in-chief or tacksmen to the Seaforths, who were occupying the best farms and key properties in Lewis. This Kenneth Mackenzie had been on the islands at least since 1706 (he was one of the few tacksmen unable to attend the hearings in Stornoway in person, presumably because of the weather) and was perhaps the grandson of the Mackenzie who had landed one day in the early seventeenth century on the beach between Eilean an Tighe and Garbh Eilean, his keel sliding onshore, his boots slipping on the slithering cobbles, the large number of Mackenzies he had with him jumping from their boats, coming around the corner, past the wells, past the little church and cemetery and then doing, or perhaps only threatening, the immediate and familiar violence. There is no record here of the casual gore, but that is the story I read in the inch or two of darker soil in Linda Čihaková's meticulous section: blood in the silt.

The abandonment of the house was brief and, over the silt soil created in the troubled interval, another floor was soon laid. It was made precisely like its predecessor: thick clay packed hard. Almost certainly, the clay came from the narrow band of Jurassic mud stones and shales just to the west of the natural arch on Garbh Eilean. That is the only outcrop of clay discovered on the Shiants and the little valley of the stream that runs down there looks as though it might have been artificially dug away. It would be a long, heavy job carrying it in creels down to the little beach there, rowing to the main landing beach and then carrying the loads up the trackway to the site of the house, but not impossible. They would probably have had ponies (there were horse bones in the eighteenth-century archaeological layers) and, besides, unremitting labour is the price of existence in a marginal world.

Contemporary with this floor is the strangest story – it hinges on dearth and the pressures which dearth places on revered customs – ever associated with the Shiants. It carries no date, but probably describes an event in the middle of the seventeenth century. Iain Dubh Chraidig came from Uig on the Atlantic shore of Lewis. Every year, many Uig men used to come over to Pairc, on the east side of Lewis, opposite the Shiants.

John Du used to go in summer to fish for saithe in the
Sound of Shiant. On one of these occasions he took his
mother with him, as there was no food to be got at home
in Uig. Poor John was only there for a few days when his
mother died, which left him at a loss what to do. He wanted
to bury his mother at home in Uig – but he was at the
same time loath to leave the fishing. So this is what he did.
He removed the entrails from the corpse and placed the
body in a cave, where it became mummified. And when he
was done fishing, he took his mother's body home to Uig,
where he buried her alongside her husband.

Evisceration of a loved one was not unheard of in the Hebrides,
particularly if the party was away from home and the corpse
might rot before you got it back to hallowed ground. Some men
from Ness gutted one of their company when they were away on
the Summer Isles, buried the guts there and took the rest of him
home to Lewis. Perhaps only the best of fishing, or the deepest
of hunger, could justify it, but Ian Dubh was not being irreverent.
The opposite in fact. He air-cured his mother because he loved
and honoured her, not through indifference. There is still a cave
on the coast of Pairc opposite the Shiants, just outside the mouth
of Loch Bhrollúm, called Uamha Mhic Iain Duibh, 'the Cave of
the Son of Black John', a name I cannot explain. But is it also
'the Cave of the Eviscerated Mother'?

Just outside the house on the islands, at a level a decade or
two later than this story, the excavators discovered a significant
deposit. Underneath the foundations of the barn – in other words
before the barn existed and, of course, after the medieval building
on this site had disappeared – was a band of limpet shells and a
few animal bones fifteen inches thick. Limpets are not very pleasant eating. I have tried them fried, boiled, with butter, garlic,
parsley. Nothing can really disguise the basic sensation: you are
eating someone else's nose. Limpets are, in other words, famine

food, a desperate recourse, the sort of protein to which you turn if all other options have gone.

This band of limpets, beneath the barn foundations and in use at the same time as the seventeenth-century floor in the house, consisted of about a hundred thousand shells. It is possible to do a little mathematics. Families in houses like this usually had about five members. It is possible to make a reasonably palatable and nutritious limpet broth, in which you can dip your bannocks, if you have them, with about twenty limpets per person. A limpet meal for the whole family in other words needs about a hundred limpets. In the time of birds, between April and August, and in the fair weather of summer when fish could be had, no one would turn to limpets for their protein. They are the famine food of winter and early spring, which in times of crisis might have been relied on for, say, half the meals for six months of the year. That would mean ninety days in which limpets had to feed the family. A famine year, then, might require something like nine thousand limpets. Although limpets were also used as bait, this pile, accumulated at some time in the late seventeenth century, may well represent something like ten years of famine.

That, in the 1680s, is almost exactly what there were. Martin Martin, travelling here in the following decade, refers briefly but conclusively to it. 'They are great lovers of Musick,' he says of the Lewismen, 'and when I was there they gave an Account of eighteen men who could play on the Violin pretty well, without being taught: They are still very hospitable, but the late Years of Scarcity brought them very low, and many of the poor People have died by Famine.'

One can only imagine, from the accounts of other famines in other years, the reality of the horrors which that pile of limpets represents – the drawn faces, the broken tempers, the shortness with each other, the sense of the world being against you, the death of children, the endless, wearing diseases of the old, the temptations to selfishness, the squeezing of tolerances, the exhaustion and the despair. In that vestigial, mirror-image way of archaeology, the evidence of the horror of these years on the Shiants is quite apparent in the section cut through the house floors. After the famine food comes another abandonment. It all became too much. The people who lived in this house either died or left. Once again the roof disintegrated, or more likely in the Hebridean timber shortage, was removed and reused, and a seven-inch thick layer of grey silty soil accumulated over the floor on which the famine had been endured.

The occupied floor is quite different from the layer of abandonment above it. In the floor, astonishingly, you can see some of the smallest details of everyday life. The floor of the entire house is trug-shaped, rising towards the walls on either side and sinking towards the centre of the house, or like an old, thin mattress in a boarding house, slumped towards the middle, steep at the sides.

These are worn, swept places, with the dust broomed away from the hearth, out into the corners and edges. Within the section itself, you can make out the millimetre-thick bandings where a layer of black charcoal or of rusty peat ash has been swept out across the surface. It is a microscopic human landscape of powerful intimacy and unrelieved poignancy. These sweepings, keeping tidy in the face of catastrophe: what deeper sign of dignity is there than that? Above it, the silt layers are inert, a dead and formless accumulation of matter, indicating only absence, silence and the rain falling on forgotten lives.

This is the sequence of the Shiants – as of elsewhere in this marginal world – this coming and going, this suffering and resurgence, this courage in the face of a trying world. How long does that grey silt layer last? Thirty years perhaps? There is no way of telling. But eventually the people return, just as the puffin burrows on the north face of Garbh Eilean, abandoned in years when the population is falling, are eventually reoccupied and rehabilitated. Here, once again, perhaps around 1720, a new floor was made, again on the same principle, and burying the accumulated silt beneath it. It was a new beginning and easily the most sophisticated so far.

There are signs of change. A new stone-capped drain is installed along the south wall of the house. A stone-rimmed hearth is built roughly in the middle of the house and a line of stones makes a 'step' between the east and west end, that is between animals in the byre end and people around the hearth. A large area outside to the south and east is roughly paved and an extension, a barn or byre, is built to the north, on the site of the limpet pile. To a traveller from England or Lowland Scotland, this house might still have looked like a primitive habitation, the sort of thing that men occupied in a cultural backwater, 'a Borneo or a Sumatra', as Dr Johnson described the Hebrides in the 1770s. But compared with what had been here before, this was an improved and rationalised building. The fingertips of the Enlightenment had touched the Shiants.

It was under this floor that we found the inscribed cross stone from the hermit in the seventh century, face down, under the clay of the floor and deeply buried in the grey silt beneath it. The stone's used and pock-marked surface looks like something which far from being tucked away or buried has been in constant, bruising use, dropped and picked up, battered in passing. The stones which most resemble it on Inishmurray in County Sligo (and others which have now been lost on Iona itself) were used even in the nineteenth century in rituals that crossed the borders of Christian and pre-Christian belief. Jerry O'Sullivan, the Irish archaeologist who is currently making a long and careful investigation of the early Christian remains on Inishmurray, guesses that the cross-inscribed stones there may have been used in penance, carried from from one site to another on the island as a form of ritual pilgrimage. The heavier the crime, the heavier the stone. In the nineteenth century, there are also records of them being used as instruments either to bless or to damn. Turned clockwise, or sunwise, they brought goodness; anti-clockwise a curse.

The late seventeenth and early eighteenth century was a time of potent magic in the Hebrides. Stones of almost any kind were used as charms. We found several smooth and beautiful pebbles both in the barn and the byre end of the house, as well as one elongated egg of the same Torridonian sandstone as the cross, all of which might have been used for a kind of magic on animals.

This was also the period, though, when magic was coming under attack from the rationalist ideas of the new Enlightenment. There was an incident off the Shiants at just this time which encapsulates that transition.

According to the late seventeenth-century manuscript chronicle of James Fraser, Minister of Wardlaw, now Kirkhill near Inverness, the accident happened early in 1671, somewhere between Lewis and the northern tip of Skye, perhaps in the tide-rip just south of the southern point of Eilean an Tighe:

> This April, the Earle of Seaforth duelling [?dwelling] in the Lewes, a dreedful accident happened. His lady being brought to bed there, the Earle sent for John Garve M'kleud of rarsay, to witness the christning; and after the treat and solemnity of the feast, rarsay takes leave to go home, and, after a rant of drinking upon the shoare, went aboard off his birling and sailed away with a strong north gale off wind; and whether by giving too much saile and no ballast, or the unskillfulness of the seamen, or that they could not manage the strong Dut[ch] canvas saile, the boat whelmd, and all the men dround in view of the cost. The Laird and 16 of his kinsmen, the prime, perished; non of them ever found; a greyhound or two cast ashoare dead; and pieces of the birling. One Alexander Mackleoid of Lewes the night

before had voice warning him thrice not to goe at [all] with
rarsay, for all would drown in there return; yet he went
with him, being infatuat, and dround [with] the rest. This
account I had from Alexander his brother the summer after,
Drunkness did the mischeife.

That is the rational, reasonable and modern explanation. A
dissolute laird, drinking on shore, loved by his people, displaying
to them, his hounds aboard, the *birlinn* with its new fast rig, no
reef in the heavy canvas sail, so much less pliable and manageable
than the traditional woollen sails, a racing journey home with
the wind on the port quarter, ignorance perhaps of the Stream
of the Blue Men and the holes that can suddenly appear in the
sea there in front of you: these are the accidents with which a
bravado culture always flirts.

But alongside this is another explanation. A raven, the bird of
death, is said to have settled on the gunwale. Iain Garbh Macleod
of Raasay reached for it, to strangle it, missed and drove in the
upper strakes of the *birlinn* and the sea poured in. Why had the
raven settled there? A rival of Iain Garbh's for the lairdship of
Raasay had paid a witch called, perhaps inevitably, Morag, to sit
and watch for his return on the heights of Trotternish in northern
Skye. For days she looked out northwards to the Shiants and the
sea around them, waiting for Raasay's sail. She had her daughters
with her and asked them to fill a tub with well water and on its
surface float an empty eggshell. When Raasay's *birlinn* came into
view, Morag continued to watch but told her daughters to go to
the tub and to swirl the water with their hands as fast as it would
go. They did what she asked and, in the whirlpool they made,
the eggshell filled and sank; just at that moment a squall enveloped
Raasay's *birlinn* and the seventeen men were drowned. It was
always said that on the anniversary of Iain Garbh's death, the
tide boils and stirs at just the place where he and his men went
down.

The two versions of the story mark the beginning of the end of magic in the Hebrides. The burying of the cross stone beneath the blackhouse floor may well be another symptom of the same change. The floor under which it was found, made after about twenty years of abandonment which themselves followed the famine of the 1680s, can perhaps be dated somewhere soon after 1720. A document survives in the National Archives in Edinburgh which suggests a reason for the stone's presence there. In the 1720s a definite and deliberate effort was made by the reformed church, here as elsewhere in the Hebrides, to bring the souls of the islanders more firmly under ecclesiastical control. The Reformation may be dated in Scotland to 1560 but out here, well beyond the reach of central control, what the reformers considered reprehensibly papist practices lurked on. The Edinburgh document is called 'A PREPARED STATE, the Presbytery of SKYE, against the Heritor of the Lews', dated 11 December 1722. The Heritor of the Lews, and the owner of the Shiants, was the Catholic Kenneth Mackenzie, Earl of Seaforth, who as a Jacobite had rebelled against the crown in 1715 and again in 1719, and after the failure of the rebellions had his estates confiscated by the Hanoverian crown. The presbyters from Skye were petitioning the commissioners in charge of the estate to divert some of its revenues to enhance the missionary efforts of the church in the untamed and backward-sliding Hebrides. Lewis, they said was spiritually in a parlous condition: 'This wide and spacious Country, since the Abolition of Popery, was always served by Two Ministers, one at Starnway, the other at Barvas.' That was nothing like good enough and the island should be subdivided, one of the new parishes to be Lochs:

> the Church, Manse and Glebe to be at Keose, and the Minister to go to the South Skirts of the same, as he sees Occasion, there being but few families there who cannot attend the Ordinances at the ordinary place of worship. From the

South-East corner of that Parish lies the Islands of Shant, Six miles from Shore, One of them only inhabited, and in it Five Families, making Twenty Examinable Persons; the Minister should repair thither twice in the Year, to preach and catechise.

The cross stone would have been seen by the new visiting ministers as a primitive totem of Christianity from before 'the abolition of Popery'. In the reformed church's emphasis on the intellectual clarity of the word, the cloud of magical associations clustering around the cross stone would have been anathema. Two sermons a year were preached in the little church by the shore here for the rest of the century. The minister would have been adamant. The stone was to be got rid of. But the Shiant Islanders did not destroy or break it. They buried it. Their precious totem was hidden but still kept, nurtured closely within a yard or two of where they all sat in the evening around the hearth, a secret presence in the substratum – you could say the subconscious – of the house.

This, too, is another version of the hinge of Shiant history. The turning of the stone face-down, the burying of its meanings in the dark, the denigration of an ancient way of thinking and its substitution with a clarified, authoritative Calvinism: all of this has seemed to Gaelic intellectuals, particularly in this century, like the turning-point in the culture of the Hebrides. Among the finds made in the blackhouse was a small folded copper alloy strip, about four inches long and half an inch wide. It may be part of a binding strip used in the eighteenth century to finish the outer edges of a Bible's cover boards. Book replaces stone, word image and intellect the symbolic heart.

The Stornoway-born poet and Celtic scholar, Professor Derick Thomson, has written a poem 'Am Bodach-rocais': 'The Scarecrow', stimulated, he told me, by no particular event but by 'religious antagonism in the Lewis of my youth to secular music, dancing, even secular story-telling', which envisages precisely the kind of moment in which the minister of Lochs walks into this blackhouse. As the biggest building at this end of the Shiants, it might well have been the cèilidh-house, the house in which people met, talked and told stories on the benches around the central hearth, and from which, when the evening came to an end, each would walk back to his own bed, his path lit by a glowing peat taken from this fire:

> That night
> the scarecrow came into the cèilidh-house:
> a tall, thin black-haired man
> wearing black clothes.
> He sat on the bench
> and the cards fell from our hands.
> One man
> was telling a folk-tale about Conall Gulban
> and the words froze on his lips.
> A woman was sitting on a stool,
> singing songs, and he took the goodness out of her music.
> But he did not leave us empty handed:
> he gave us a new song,
> and tales from the Middle East,
> the fragments of the philosophy of Geneva,
> and he swept the fire from the centre of the floor
> and set a searing bonfire in our breasts.

Perhaps that is why the stone has such a strange air to it now. When Linda first found it buried in the floor, and when she first rolled it back to expose its carved face, I was there with her, to hear the shriek and see her look of horror at what she had revealed. All the holiness of the seventh-century hermit who made it is overlaid with the chill behind its burying. That act of joyless denial feels quite unholy and this first phase of the ending of the Shiants' full life left me feeling troubled. I went for a walk that evening high on the east side of Eilean an Tighe, with the pere-grines squawking like farmyard birds in the air beside me, and it came to me then, I think for the first time with the force of reality, that this was not a holiday place; that grim and persistent struggle had been the nature of life here; and that the replacement with a printed Gaelic Bible of a nurtured ancient stone was a symptom not of godliness but of empire, imposition, control and a sort of shrinking of life. The sea room of the Shiants had begun to die by the 1720s.

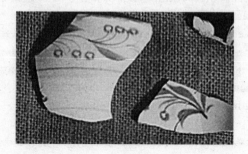

11

EVERY DAY, WE WOKE AT EIGHT, brushed our teeth in the little stream that runs down from the spring to the sea, rubbing the toothbrushes with a sprig of the watermint that grows there in summer, cooked our breakfast and ate it on the rocks outside the house, before dragging ourselves back up the hill to the site of the house and starting to excavate again. The story I can tell you here was not at all clear at the time. The evidence sifted and sorted by archaeologists is fragmentary at best. It is the science of the abandoned, the forgotten and the hidden. All you find is an impression of the life that gave rise to it, like the spoor of a hare in the grass, or the marks left by the wings of a grouse as it takes off from the snow on a bank. It is, in other words, a negative, a mould, from which the thing itself, the shape of life, has to be inferred. Only later when all the evidence is there in front of you and you can arrange it into a form that seems to make sense, can you understand what it was you were finding.

'Record and collect, record and collect': that was Pat Foster's repeated mantra as we squatted with our little scraping trowels on the floor of the abandoned house and in the barn that was built in the 1720s on its northern side. Fragments of anything that might be significant, any flake of stone, bone or china, any shift in the colour of the soil, was picked up, photographed and drawn, with no idea whether it mattered or not. Everything mattered.

Nuance had to be read as carefully as a portraitist would investigate the face of his sitter. But nuance is not enough. Detail has to be set within a larger, overarching picture. I tried to apply what I had gathered of the documentary history to what was emerging from the excavation. It certainly became clear from the carefully preserved papers in the National Archives in Edinburgh that life wasn't easy for the church on the islands and that the ministers had trouble supervising the Shiant flock. 'The Lewis island is the most spacious and most remote of all the western islands', the Skye Presbyters had moaned to the officials of the Society for Propagating Christian Knowledge in Scotland in 1722. Two decades later, in October 1744, Collin Mackenzie, Minister of Lochs, wrote a sad complaint bewailing his circumstances to 'the Very Reverend the Moderator of the Committee for Reformation of the Highlands and Islands'. He wanted extra staff and a raise. Among the most burdensome of his expenses and difficulties were

> the Islands of Shaint (a place well known to seafaring men) at the Distance of Sixteen miles of Sea and Land from the minister's manse lying towards the south. In these islands are thirty examinable persons and the minister can go there in the summer and that at a vast expense being obliged to hire a boat and Crew. Moreover this parish is very discontiguous being divided by three long arms of the sea which renders it difficult for the minister to visit the people and for the people to visit him.

This is, of course, special pleading, but here too is another modern note: the first mention of any idea that the Shiants are difficult to get to. Within a few decades the idea of 'remoteness' would have brought the old life here to an end.

The population had increased between 1722 and 1744 from twenty to thirty 'examinable persons'. These were people who were able to learn and repeat a catechism. Although the second figure only comes from Collin Mackenzie, the Minister of Lochs, and it was in his interest to exaggerate the numbers to justify his demand for more money, it might imply a total population of about forty, including both the younger children and perhaps the simple or the dumb. By the 1760s, the early economist John Walker, in his survey of the Hebrides, recorded twenty-two people on the Shiants, but his figures are often suspect and usually out of date. Almost certainly, that is an underestimate. Then there is a gap until 1796, when the Reverend Alexander Simson, by then minister in Lochs, wrote of the islands in the Statistical Account of the parish: 'There is one family residing on the largest of the islands, for the purpose of attending the cattle.'

The picture is clear: a rising population until the middle years of the century and then a quite sudden collapse. It is here that the Shiant crisis reaches its sharpest point. This is not some slow and gradual sliding into the dark. The number of people increases, the level of work, business and energy has to grow to satisfy their demands, the resources of the islands are stretched and squeezed, the system is pushed to its limits, and then quite suddenly it breaks. After about 1770 – and there is no florid moment in the documents to which one can point as the end itself – life here for a self-sufficient community, for a complex of reasons, becomes unviable. The bulk of people leave and a single family remains, tending the animals, almost certainly not as sub-tenants of the man who rented the islands from the Seaforth estate, but as his employees. The relationship of people to the Shiants had for the first time in some five millennia become commercial, and the islands had entered the modern world.

Could our excavation of the eighteenth-century house, combined with an examination of the surrounding landscape, illuminate this fulcrum of Shiant history? We looked for the signs. When the house was improved in the 1720s, with its new south drain and external paving, the barn was built on its northern side. It was a sign of things going well. The old door that led out that way was blocked and cattle were kept in there. We dug into their manure, transformed over the centuries into a sticky green clay, near the base of the barn walls. Animals were all-important to the way anyone could live on the islands. The small black cows they had were a way of storing nutrients. They reduced people's dependence on the seasons. They flattened out the difference between summer abundance and winter dearth. What the cattle ate on the high summer pastures of Garbh Eilean and Eilean an Tighe could be consumed by people in the form of beef, milk and all the dairy products, almost at will. The little cupboard built into the south-west corner of the house, the dampest and the coldest corner, raised a few inches above the floor, would probably have been the place in which the milk and cheese and butter would have been kept in earthernware pots, sometimes wrapped in moss to keep them cold. It was a tiny, cool room, a larder chilled by the wind. In bad years, when food was short, blood would be drained from a living cow and used to make a blood pudding. Sometimes, at the end of a winter inside, these valuable creatures were so weak that they had to be carried out to the spring pastures by their owners. And they were valuable. Twenty cows would make a very good dowry, but as Samuel Johnson said, 'two cows are a decent fortune for one who pretends to no distinction.' The rates of exchange were clearly established: one cow equalled three ewes equalled a spinning wheel equalled two blankets equalled a small chest or kist.

A cow was portable, or at least drivable, wealth. She also, with her winter manure which built up in the barns and byres, provided fertility for the vegetable gardens and plots of oats and barley. The lower end of the house, as well as the barn, was intended for animals. We found thick deposits of degraded manure there. The east wall of the house was taken down every spring, so that the manure could be shovelled out more easily, and then built back up. That too was obvious in the structure. The neat coursing of most of the house walls was almost completely absent at the east end, the stones haphazardly tumbled back together the last time the wall was reconstructed.

Before things got bad, the people here would also have used ponies to carry their heavy goods up from the beach, the manure to the fields, and maybe to plough the fields. As Robert Dodgshon has shown all over the Highlands and Islands, when a community has plenty of relatively fertile land for its population, and not too many mouths to feed, it makes sense to use a horse where you can. The ground needed to grow hay for its winter sustenance can be spared from growing arable crops. It is reckoned that in the Hebrides, with the traditional varieties of black oats and bere barley – low yielding but necessarily tough in the face of hostile weather – about five acres of cultivated ground were needed to feed a family of five. In the 1720s there were five Shiant families with twenty 'examinable persons' and perhaps another five children. They would have needed twenty-five acres of arable to keep themselves alive.

From walking the islands again and again and by looking carefully at large-scale air photographs, I have measured the amount of ground on the Shiants that was cultivated at some time in the past, or at least for which evidence survives in the form of cultivation ridges. The map shows how it divides.

Apart from the obvious conclusion that the sweetness of Mary was the foundation of all life here, and that Garbh Eilean was mainly for grazing (only 1.7% of the island under cultivation at any time, compared with 21.6% of Eilean Mhuire and 7.0% of

	Island arable	Percent of Shiant arable
Garbh Eilean	4.4 acres	14.3
Eilean an Tighe	9.9 acres	32.3
Eilean Mhuire	16.4 acres	53.4
Total arable	30.7 acres	

18TH CENTURY SETTLEMENTS

Eilean an Tighe), the acreages themselves are significant. Thirty-odd acres of good ground (and one should perhaps reduce that figure because these measurements count all ground ever cultivated, some of it necessarily bad and sour) would be enough for about twenty-five people. As soon as the population started to climb towards forty, then serious difficulties – the prospect of malnutrition, illnesses that could not be shaken off, a loss of morale and eventual abandonment – became likely.

This was different to the crisis of the 1680s. Then, poor crops had failed to sustain a reasonable population. Now, the number of people was outstretching the land's productivity even in a good year. Marginal ground had to be taken into production. The meadows on which the hay was grown to feed the ponies had to be cultivated and so the ponies themselves had to go. The use of the spade, or of the famous cas-chrom, the foot plough or crooked spade, which all visitors in the nineteenth century saw as evidence of a primitive agriculture still at work here, may in fact have been evidence of precisely the opposite: the pressure which the modern growth in population was bringing to bear. With many mouths to feed, a horse and its pasture cannot be afforded. But many mouths also come with many hands and the hand cultivation of enormous areas of ground, back-breaking labour as it is, may have been the only possibility for a Hebridean population under heavy duress from the mid-eighteenth century onwards. Lowland and English visitors, seeing the huge numbers of Hebrideans doing hand work on the fields compared the sight to the labour of Chinese coolies in the paddy fields of Asia.

Almost certainly, that is what happened here. As the century progressed, more and more land was dug. Even today, in some places, the sharp edges of the cultivation ridges show that these were dug by hand. A horse plough would leave a rounded contour, like the ridge and furrow of central England. The entire Shiant population would have been out there every spring, digging, quite literally, for their lives.

High on the windswept side of Eilean an Tighe, above the Norse house, is a field which is quite clearly cut out of rough pasture. It is poorly drained and acid land. Mountains of seaweed would have been brought up here on men's and women's backs to lighten the soil and to create some kind of workable tilth. At some time in the middle of the eighteenth century, the barn next to the blackhouse was abandoned. Roofless, it became the rubbish heap of the household. Among the bones – of puffin, guillemot, shag, pig, whale, all kinds of fish, cattle, both young and old, and dog – we identified the jaw bone of a horse. Perhaps the ponies, when they finally went, provided a welcome meal.

That is all very well, but I want to take this further, to get some kind of real sensation of what life was like in this blackhouse. Could I recreate the atmosphere within these bare, ruined walls? Could I feel my way to the experience of being a Shiant Islander in the mid-eighteenth century, as the pressure came on, as the world seemed to change around them?

There would, first of all, have been no sense of this building being somehow antiquated. The blackhouse was a modern invention. Medieval houses had been shorter and rounder. This beautiful long form, which nineteenth-century travellers always took for an immensely primitive sort of dwelling, first appeared only in the seventeenth century. It is an ingenious structure. Its low, ground-hugging, rounded shape presents no obstacle to the wind and is both a model and symbol of homeliness. It embraced those that entered it. Its narrow width is governed by the shortage of timber in the isles and its length by the need to shelter more than a family from the weather. It is an occupied farm building rather than a house in which agricultural equipment and animals are also stored. It was always built on a slight slope so that the liquors from the manure heap would run out at the far end, rather than pollute the hearth. On occasions, this slope was 'so steep that a cask would have rolled from one end to the other'.

The smoke from the central hearth filled the house's roof and worked as a fungicide to preserve the timbers, which were precious. Meat and fish hung there and were cured in the smoke. Midges, mosquitoes, wood-beetle and other pests were killed off. The sharing of the space with the animals not only provided extra heat in the house, but protected the dung heap and its precious nutrients from the rain, in which its goodness would have been washed away. This arrangement was also healthier than you might think. Lewis had a far lower incidence of tuberculosis than almost anywhere else in the country, a level shared only by dairymaids. It turned out that blackhouses had a sophisticated internal air flow, meaning that heat rising from the cattle and their dung heap carried a weak solution of ammonia (from the urine) across into the human half of the house, where the people breathed it. A weak solution of ammonia, inhaled regularly, is known to prevent TB. Dairymaids were breathing the same air.

If you go into the ruin we have excavated now, the one quality that strikes you above all is its bareness, its lack of detail, the simplicity of structure and form. That is as it should be. These places were never filled or crowded with objects. When the clay floors were first laid, a small flock of a dozen or so sheep were usually folded in there for twelve hours or so to consolidate the floor. The clay is blueish-brown and only turns the red colour we found it when hot ashes are spread across it to warm the floor on which the children sit. There was never much furniture. Alexander Macleod, laird of Harris in the 1780s, 'made a tour around the whole back part of his extensive estate, and even entered the huts of the tenants, and declared openly that the wigwams of the wild Indians of America were equally good and better furnished.'

The Rev. John Buchanan, a missionary contemporary of Macleod's, who eventually had to leave Harris in disgrace after seducing two of the local girls, found that

> The huts of the oppressed tenants are remarkable naked and open, quite destitute of furnishing, except logs of timber collected from the wrecks of the sea, to sit on about the fire, which is placed in the middle of the house, or upon seats of straw, like foot hassocks stuffed with straw or stubble.

Large stones occasionally served the same purpose. Chairs and stools were rare and tables almost unknown. The men sat on a wooden bench or a plank supported on piles of stone or turf against the wall. The foundations of a bench against the north wall, about six feet long, curving out at one end, is exactly what the excavation found, set a little away from the hearth, which in this house was for some reason moved at one point, about a yard to the north. At night, people would simply take a blanket or a plaid and wrap themselves up in it in the corner. The clay of the floor was warm and the atmosphere in these buildings, as the ethnographer Alexander Fenton has described, was a beautiful thick cloud of homeliness, at the centre of which 'a fire of peat smouldered with a steady red glow from which rose, not so much smoke, as a smoky shimmer of heat . . .'. There was no need to shut yourself away from it, at least in the eighteenth century, in a bed. In the morning, the blankets would simply have been folded up. The Reverend Buchanan licked his lips at the prospect of immorality in these conditions: 'Without separate apartments, we need not be surprised to find the virtue of their women too often severely tried,' he wrote, 'and no wonder though the poor unprotected females suffer in such circumstances'. At least, that is what he found.

Although internal walls appeared in the blackhouse during the nineteenth century, at this date there would have been none. The hunger for privacy and for subdivision of living spaces, which had arrived in England in the late Middle Ages, had not yet reached here. This life was shared in almost every detail. The line of big stones that we found across the floor would have been all that separated the upper end of the room from the part preserved for the animals. It was a kerb to the dung heap, nothing more. By early spring, the dung heap would have grown so high that it would have been difficult to get in the door at that end. You would have walked steeply uphill over it before coming downhill again to the hearth. Cows standing in there all winter, along with the goats, sheep, ducks, hens and dogs, would have looked down on the company around the fire with a sweet and beneficent presence. In order to reduce the liquidity of the animal end, the householders 'attended on their cows with large vessels to throw out the wash' – or to keep it as mordant for dyes – 'but still it must be wet and unwholesome.'

A sense of disgust was absent from the intimacy of human and animal in the house. It was lovely to have the cows so nearby. 'And one luxurious old fellow describes the pleasure he found in hearing the sound of the milk as it squirted into the tub.' The cows liked the fire as much as people did 'and particularly the young and tenderest are admitted next to it.' Besides, the warmth was thought to increase the milk yield.

Warm, shared, busy; an animal fug, perhaps a loom in the corner, sheepskin bags or an old chest in which to store the meal, maybe barrels of potatoes, spades, cas-chroms, rakes, blankets, washing tubs, pots, herring nets, the long, many-hooked fishing lines, perhaps the most valuable things here, each worth seven shillings, against four shillings for a bed or chest, and five shillings for the roof of a small house: all these are described in the inventories at the time. This is something of the feeling of a working blackhouse, an organic whole. It was an ingenious adaptation of limited materials to the comforts of home. It would always have been dark. In the evening, rush lights, burning perhaps in seal oil, more probably in fish oil, boiled off from the fish livers, giving a dark viscous liquid 'like port wine', would mean that even on the brightest day, no more than 'a dim religious light' would have filled the place. One or two small holes in the thatch would have admitted the light and let out the smoke, although we did find fragments of a window pane buried in the levels above the floor.

The house itself partook of the cycle of the seasons, blackening through the year, glittering sooty stalactites dangling from the roof trusses, becoming ever fuller with the growing dung heap at the animal end. In the spring-time, as the year begins, all of that is removed. The east wall is demolished, the sty cleared out, the roof covering taken away and a sudden wash of light, as much as now floods across the floor of the ruin, enters the building. It starts the year again, cleaned, freshened and ready, as renewed as a dug-over garden, the new turfs and thatch sweet-smelling, a sense of annual optimism to hand.

That yearly pattern had its daily counterpart. Every evening the fire was smothered, 'smoored' in the Scots word, to reduce its burning in the night but to keep it alive for the following morning. Alexander Carmichael, the scholar and collector of Gaelic culture in the second half of the nineteenth century, witnessed the plain evening ceremony:

> The embers were evenly spread on the hearth ... and formed into a circle. The circle is then divided into three equal sections, a small boss being left in the middle. A peat is laid between each section, each peat touching the boss, which forms a common centre. The first peat is laid down in name of the God of Life, the second in name of the God of Peace, the third in name of the God of Grace. The circle is then covered over with ashes sufficient to subdue but not to extinguish the fire, in name of the Three of Light. The heap slightly raised in the centre is called 'Tula nan Tri', the Hearth of the Three. When the smooring operation is complete the woman closes her eyes, stretches her hand, and softly intones one of the many formulae current for these occasions.

The only peat on the Shiants is on the heights of Garbh Eilean and the marks of peat-cutting are still obvious on the ground there, as well as the remains of a peat-dryer, a rough stone platform that provided a draught under the stack as well as around and over it, where the newly cut blocks would have been left for a year or so before becoming dry enough to burn.

In the house, the women would sit apart from the men on stumps of driftwood grouped around the fire, while the children crouched between them in the warm ashes strewn on the clay floor. There was no oven in Hebridean culture and all cooking was done either on a griddle or in a cauldron suspended over the hearth. At meals the whole family gathered so closely that a single dish could be shared between them resting on their knees, eating from the common dish either with their own horn spoons, or perhaps with a single spoon handed from one to the next. This dish, three to four feet long, eighteen inches wide, called the *clàr*, was made of deal, with straw or grass on the bottom; the straw with crumbs of food in it was afterwards given to the cow. The meals – breakfast at eleven o'clock, supper at nightfall – were the times at which the family drew together and were the only occasions in which the door would be shut. Together they would eat the oat or barley-cakes, the potatoes and herring, and the supper of brochan, a kind of gruel; or boiled mutton if they were lucky, or perhaps cuddies in the autumn, caught from the shore in a tarbh net, or cod, dogfish, saithe, skate, eels, pollack, or halibut – to all or any of which milk or cream could be added and for all of which the Shiants were well known, but only if they had managed to get out in the boat. If not, then it was surely to be the dreaded limpets.

As well as the hearths themselves, some hints of this cooking life emerged from the excavation. Tiny fragments of a cauldron: one of its legs and a piece of an iron griddle, with a curved, raised lip on two sides, were found. Small chips of flint from a strike-a-light to make the spark with which the fire – or tobacco: there was the bowl and stem of a clay pipe – could be lit. The flint chips had been brushed to the side of the house and lost in the shadows. There was half a quernstone, cut from the very coarse-grained syenite, the igneous rock which is found only at the far east end of Eilean Mhuire.

It was tucked against the northern wall. Evening and morning, with this hand quern – it was low quality and would have made extremely gritty flour – the women would have ground as much grain as they needed, sieving the flour through sheepskin sieves, onto wooden or pottery plates.

It is the pottery we found that summons most intimately the old life in the house. Over one thousand, four hundred pottery sherds were found in the excavation, dividing quite clearly into two categories. By far the larger, with over one thousand, two hundred pieces, was the so-called craggan ware, the unglazed earthenware, made by hand without a potter's wheel and fired in the low and variable temperatures of this peat hearth. The Gaelic word *craggan* is related to the English 'crock' and probably comes from the Old Norse *krukka*. The Gaelic for a can of lager is *crogan leanna*.

These home-made pots are an archaeologist's hell. Almost no development can be seen in their style of making, firing or decoration over many millennia. Craggan ware (although the very oldest tends to be finer) has been found on Neolithic sites and it was still being made in Tiree in 1940, although by then only for sale to tourists. The clay for these pots would probably have been dug on Garbh Eilean, as was the clay for the floor, and it was women's work to make these pots. You can see their thumb marks on the clay, pushing at it, folding out the rim, and the places where the unbaked pot was set to rest on the grass, which left its slight impressions on the body. Here and there, very rarely, a piece is decorated with a few slashed lines or with scattered points, where a straw has been jabbed into the clay. Perhaps these are just the work of a bored child, fiddling with the pots her mother was making, playing with the clay when still soft.

There is a symbolic network woven around the craggan, bringing together women, milk, cattle, clay and the hearth. Only women can make the craggan, just as only men can go out in the boat and just as women make butter and cheese in the churn, or in the sheepskin which does for a churn in poorer families. The opening at the craggan's neck, it was said, must be large enough for a woman's hand but too small for the muzzle of a calf. The body of the pot would have been roughly rounded, as high as it was wide, and in various sizes, some big enough to milk into, others little more than a container for butter or curds. Roundedness was important. Although there is one dish, like a sugar dish, probably copied from an import, which is completely flat-bottomed, not a single Shiant craggan pot has a flat base. The pot itself is like a small womb, but made of clay, and so perhaps like a small house.

Unroundedness, even if convenient, would have spoiled it symbolically. Houses too were made with rounded corners. Milk taken straight from the cow into one of these little craggans, which had been warmed by the fire, was called 'milk without wind' and was a cure for consumption. A piece of calfskin or lambskin was used to cover the pot and was tied there with a cord beneath the out-turned rim.

Arthur Mitchell saw a woman making craggans on Lewis in 1863. This would have been the scene in the Shiant house, or perhaps outside its south door, on a bench there, on a warm day in summer, the headscarf down around her neck, her eyes half closed against the sun, her children at her feet and the lark above her, looking out to the distant mountains of Skye.

> The clay she used underwent no careful or special preparation. She chose the best she could get and picked out of it the larger stones, leaving sand and the finer gravel which it contained. With her hands alone she gave the clay its desired shape. She had no aid from anything of the nature of a potter's wheel. In making the smaller craggans, with narrow necks, she used a stick with a curve on it to give form to the inside. All that her fingers could reach was done by them. Having shaped the craggan, she let it stand for a day to let it dry, then took it to the fire in the centre of the floor of her hut, filled it with burning peats, and built

burning peats all around it. When sufficiently baked she withdrew it from the fire, emptied the ashes out, and then poured into it and over it about a pint of milk, in order to make it less porous.

The other ceramic pieces we found might as well have come from the other end of the world. Alongside these Stone Age, hand-made and, to be honest not very well made things (many of the craggan pieces were never fired to a high-enough temperature and crumble at the touch), are a few shards of elegant eighteenth-century tableware, and the moulded white china lion's leg of what might have been a sugar bowl.

I asked the ceramic historian David Barker, Keeper of Archaeology at The Potteries Museum in Stoke-on-Trent, to have a look at the sherds. Did they fit the dates of the documents? Four of them did. There were four diagnostic sherds from the 1760s, moulded creamware; what Dr Barker called 'reasonably upmarket lead-glazed earthenware and white salt-glazed stoneware, including the base sherd of a tea-pot of quite high status.' The pottery almost certainly came from Staffordshire, perhaps from Liverpool. After them, there was nothing in the collection I had given him until the 1820s and '30s, when there were a few pieces of Scottish earthernware from potteries on the Clyde. The house may have been re-occupied for a while by visiting shepherds in the nineteenth century, but the fifty-year gap before them confirmed exactly what the papers had suggested: the old Shiant life came to an end in about 1770.

These pieces are, of course, a sign of the market: tradable objects, the new system of things, of money in circulation, of the world outside the islands. An annual July market was held in Stornoway every year, to which the Shiant Islanders might have gone with their own wares to sell: puffin feathers for pillows, perhaps some cheese, wool dyed with the lichen and woven into tweed, or knitted into socks and jerseys. It is likely that some

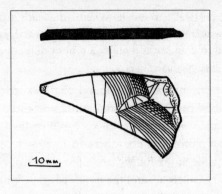

traveller had pieces for sale at the market from the huge factories to the south. It isn't difficult to imagine how beautiful their colours would have seemed to anyone accustomed to the dun and orange-tinged ordinariness of the craggans.

The Stornoway market is a possibility, but one fragment of Shiant ceramic in particular hints at another source. It is a small piece, an inch and a half long by three-quarters wide, of a large dinner plate made in white salt-glazed stoneware.

In the clear glaze, somebody quite carefully has scratched a picture of a sailing ship. No more than one or two bellied-out sails, a couple of shrouds and some ratlines are visible in the fragment, but in the care of the work, and its double expertise – the man knows both the workings of a ship's rigging and how to engrave in a difficult, slippery medium – there are signs here that the Shiants in some way or other had contact with a deep-sea sailor. This, in effect, is scrimshaw work, which the whalers usually carved on bone and tusk, rather than plates, catering for a sophisticated urban market which valued the primitive material. But whalebone was a common material here.

We found a spatula or scraper made out of it in the byre midden, and it would be less attractive for a Shiant Islander than the glamorous, new and expensive kind of china just then becoming available. Is it possible that this plate was brought back to the Shiants, perhaps to a mother, by a son who had left to find work at sea, as life at home seemed to become both constrained and difficult? Is this, in other words, by the hand of a Shiant emigrant, one of the first of the forty-odd inhabitants to leave the world of self-sufficiency for the world of money before the general rush began?

That meeting of porcelain and craggan, of the blue fronds and the thumb-whorls, of the sheeny modern glaze and the chthonic realities of the clay, recurs again and again in the objects we found in the house. There were parts, incredible as it might sound, of a wineglass, as well as many green bottle pieces. There were some scissors and a thimble (machine-made, copper alloy), a leather button and a copper one. Mixed up with them were objects from the other side of the divide: several stone tools and a stone garden hoe, made from Shiant dolerite, polished on most sides, carefully chipped at its point, perhaps from a site halfway between the blackhouse and the landing beach, where there is some evidence of stoneworking on the hillside.

Some tools and wineglasses: these are the sharp edges of a world in transition. The kind of war which that disjunction can generate, between ancient and modern, between local and national or supranational, between the antiquated and the technological, suddenly and momentarily erupted into the Shiant Islanders' lives. Thursday, 29 May 1746 is the only point at which a grander history touched the islands even a passing blow. Bonnie Prince Charlie is on the run and the Minch is thick with naval vessels on the look-out for him. At one point, watchers from the Lewis shore can see fifteen warships spread across the horizon.

One of them is HMS *Triton*, a new frigate, less than a year old, a fast ship, built for observation and pursuit, under the command of William Brett, recently promoted Commander. His log is in the Public Record Office. It was known that the Young

Pretender was looking for a ship back to France and the *Triton*'s cruise, up from Sheerness in Kent, around the northern capes and down into the Hebrides, consisted of one arrest after another: a hoy from Flamborough bound for St Malo, a Danish ketch en route from Stavanger to London, a Norwegian sloop carrying lobsters to the English markets, several Dutch fishermen, a snow (from the Dutch *snaw*, meaning a small vessel like a brig) from Aberdeen carrying hay to the army at Cromarty, a ship from Virginia bringing tobacco to Hull, a schooner bound to Madeira from Rotterdam and another snow from Lancaster heading for Riga. You could scarcely ask for a more vivid demonstration of the surge of new business in the eighteenth-century seas.

Early on the morning of 29 May, with a slight wind coming out of the north, the *Triton* was four miles or so south of the Shiants when she spotted a sail to the north of her in the faintest of dawn light. Brett ordered the *Triton* to give chase. The other ship turned and beat towards the Shiants. Like all naval action in the days of sail, everything happened in slow motion. Only at seven o'clock was the *Triton* near enough to fire warning shots, which they did, several of them, 'but ye chase would not bring to.'

By now the other vessel was in the bay between the three islands and at half past seven that morning Brett from his quarter-deck could see 'a boat full of men go on Shore from her . . . The Boat Return'd with two men which was again filled but our shots now Reaching them they got into ye vessel again.'

Although the ship was attempting to make good its escape to the north, Brett now had them pinned against the Garbh Eilean shore. The puffins would have been wheeling above them, startled into flight by the *Triton*'s warning guns. Clearly, in the islands where the Pretender was undoubtedly still on the run, this was most suspicious behaviour. Had he stumbled on the fugitive himself?

At eight o'clock in the morning the *Triton* came up with its quarry 'and she brought too with her head off Shore and hoisted English Colours. Ditto. Saw their men Rang'd at their Quarters She having fourteen Guns.' It looked for a moment as if a duel was about to take place but the terrifying sight bearing down on them of a fully armed and crewed man-of-war (the *Triton* carried between twenty and thirty guns and a complement of a hundred and thirty) brought a different outcome and a strange story:

> The Mate came on Board and Inform'd us She was a Snow from Dublin bound to Virginia with Bale Goods som Powder and Shot 81 Men & 26 Women Indentured Servants when on ye 13 Instant Being a Hundred Leagues to ye Westward of Ireland ye Servants had rose and Seiz'd the Vessel and order'd her to be Steer'd for ye Ile of Sky in order to make a prize of her & join the Pretender's Son, that 9 of them with 3 women had gone on Shore in the Boats.

Brett took the rest of the mutineers, and the snow's crew, on board the *Triton*. He put his own men on the snow, the *Gordon* as it was called, and took her in tow. He would eventually deliver them to Carrickfergus Jail in Ireland.

But what of the twelve Jacobites who had landed on the Shiants? The next day Brett sent a boat ashore on Scalpay to 'Acquaint the Magistrate of those Rebells which had landed with Arms in order for his Apprehending them.' The naval officer would have been unaware of the irony. Bonnie Prince Charlie had passed this way twice in recent weeks, once only nineteen days earlier, skulking at night in an open boat down the Lewis and Harris shores, running from the hunt that was on for him in the north of the island, and once previously at the very end of April. A shipwrecked Orcadian, giving his name as Sinclair, had landed on Scalpay and had been taken in by the magistrate and tacksman, Donald Campbell. Sinclair rescued a cow from a bog and went fishing in the Minch with Campbell's son before anyone realised he was the Young Pretender. News got out and the pro-government and fearsomely anti-Catholic minister of Harris, the Rev. Aulay MacAulay (the historian's great-grandfather) arrived with a posse to arrest the Prince. Campbell would have none of it and shielded the Prince while he escaped. For many years an inscription on Campbell's house in Scalpay (or at least a later house on the same site) recorded it as the place where Prince Charlie had stayed 'when he was wandering as an exile in his own legitimate Kingdom.' You won't find it there now: the house became a Presbyterian manse and the Jacobite inscription was harled over. One thing is certain: Campbell would not have pursued the Irish Jacobite rebels on the Shiants too hotly. The Shiant population, if they were still Mackenzies, or still attached to the Mackenzies, might well have had Jacobite sympathies themselves. They might have thought, with a Catholic king returned to the throne, that the sterilising Presbyterianism of the Church would have been removed from their necks. The holy stone might have been recovered from beneath the floor. They might have entertained the rebels in this very house, perhaps even able to communicate in Irish and Gaelic, to tell the stories and sing the songs which their shared tradition had preserved. There is no saying: after the *Triton* leaves, the Irish rebels disappear from history and the normality of Shiant life closes back over them like the tide above a rock.

Lying awake one summer night in Compton Mackenzie's house, with the dogs on the bed beside me, and the sky outside already half light, I abruptly realised with middle-of-the-night clarity something about the other house we were so carefully excavating up the hill. The presence of wineglasses, winebottles, sugar bowls, a teapot, a thimble, scissors, a Bible: these were not the belongings of a peasant's house. This was the house of a sophisticated family. I had often in previous years gone to look at it, full of nettles and with a hint of rats in the little cupboard at the corner and in the holes in the walls. I had always seen it as a primitive, roofless shed. Now, though, quite suddenly, I saw it for what it was: this was the tacksman's house. These were his belongings we were finding, broken, brushed to the shadowy corners of the room. This was the house of the last man to live on the Shiants who thought of them as profoundly his, connected to him not by contract but by a deep sense of identity with the land itself. Tacksmen were named after the property they held and this man would have been known as 'Shiant'. Here in our hands were the last flickers of a form of possession which stretched back to the Vikings and which predated any modern understanding of land as a market commodity. We were touching the outer edges of an ancient past at the very moment it was coming to an end.

12

As I walk across the Shiants today, along the path which the black cattle would have taken from the byres by the shore to the high grazings, with the meadow grass and the tiny bilberry bushes brushing at my boots; past the abandoned lazybeds to the cluster of little houses in the central valley; up past the rush-filled kilnhouse, identified by Pat Foster, where the barley and oats sodden in autumn rains might have been half-dried before storage and threshing; and as I stand in the cleared floor of the house we excavated, so radically roofless now, so exposed to the cold and the wet, I feel a vicarious nostalgia for the wholeness which is now absent here.

The walls of a blackhouse are four feet thick. It was always said that if you wanted to build one (a task for the community together) you had to collect the amount of stone you thought necessary and triple it. If it is true to say that you can't remember time, only the places in which time occurred, then I think you could say that the bulk of these enormous walls is a kind of time sponge, deeply absorbent of the moment passing, sucking up lives as they happened, holding events as if in a vast memory bank.

Standing in the house after the archaeologists had left, and listening to the lark still singing above me, I could feel that these stones, and by extension these islands, continue to hold the memories of the life that was lived in them a quarter of a millennium ago.

Perhaps it is more of a desire than a sensation, a wish to feel that the memories remain. Certainly it is an appetite that needs feeding. What was the colour and smell of the ancient Shiant normality? How did the people who lived here behave towards each other, how rich was their life in more than the material sense? How good was existence here in the mid-eighteenth century? One or two memoirs can do something to people the ruins. The Rev. John Buchanan, the lustful missionary, found the people in Harris, as one might expect, divided between courtesy and suspicion. 'They address one another by the title of gentleman or lady and embrace one another most cordially, with bonnets off,' he wrote. 'And they are never known to enter a door without blessing the house and people so loud as to be heard, and embracing every man and woman belonging to the family. They both give and receive news, and are commonly entertained with the best fare their entertainers are able to afford.'

'Neighbour' was the common term of affection and endearment. The essence of life was shared, as much for practical as for moral reasons. The pattern of land-holding, at least below the level of the tacksman, consisted of two concentric circles: the family and its homestead, with its own walled vegetable patch or kailyard, its own animals, its own family tools, a spade, other simple cultivating tools and a distaff for spinning. Outside that, by the eighteenth century anyway, was the joint farm, which would include the neighbouring waters, and for the working of which a jointly owned plough and boat would have been needed. Each of the five Shiant families would have a right to an equal share in the commonly held arable ground and farmed ridges. The operation of both boat and plough would depend on team work. A boat would need five men to launch it, four to row and one to steer and in Gaelic there is a separate system of numbers to describe teams rather than a collection of individuals.

A place like this, where nothing can be given and little risked, where anything eccentric or not done before is likely to be condemned or despised, is the landscape of received wisdom. There is a saying for every occasion, a nodule of deeply conservative and hard-won understanding. And there is a Gaelic proverb for this: 'No one is strong without a threesome / and, with a four-some, at best they'll be limping.'

A plough would need at least three men; one to lead the horse, one to hold the plough and one to turn the sod neatly over after they had passed. But four ponies would be required and each man would have had only one or two. Life was unsustainable alone.

It was far from being a communist system. Private property was fiercely protected, but an equal share of rent, an equal number of stock on the common grazings, an equal quantity of arable land and equal commitment to the work were the essential conditions without which these island communities could not have operated. It would have been impossible to pull up or launch the boat, handle the sheep or dig the ground without your neighbours. I have sweated alone on these islands for hours on these tasks, longing for nothing more than a helping hand, surveying the length of the undug lazybed like a pile of last week's washing up; despairing of the possibility of ever pulling the dinghy above the tide; finally flummoxed by the impossibilities of catching on your own a lamb whose leg had somehow been cut and was bleeding. Work done in common is more than efficient; it is a source of pleasure, stimulation and happiness. When my friends Patrick Holden and Becky Hiscock came around the bay from the house to help me dig the heavy, uncooperative sods of the lazybed which I was attempting to cultivate, it was honestly as if the sun had

come out. Alone nothing, together everything: that is one of the governing facts.

For the Reverend Buchanan, with the idea of individual salvation and private guilt in his mind, all of that community talk seemed to be something of a veneer over a harsher reality. Everyone would keep the head of a sheep he had killed for four or five days after he had done so. The head carried the ears and the ears carried the marks which identified the owner. Only with a head could a man prove a carcass was his own. And the old were given scant respect: 'When a man becomes so frail as not to be in a capacity to look after his flock of sheep in person, he is very rapidly stript of them, and that frequently by his near relations.'

One has to wait for a nineteenth-century account of popular culture in the Isles for life to be seen here in a sympathetic light. Alexander Carmichael, without whose tireless collecting over decades towards the end of the nineteenth century, half the Gaelic cultural landscape would be missing, wrote the following passage in the introduction to his monumental *Carmina Gadelica*, or

'Gaelic Songs', intermittently published between 1899 and the 1970s. It is worth quoting at length because it gives a more affectionate and richer portrait of life in such a house as the Shiant blackhouse than any that has ever been written. The people of the Outer Hebrides, Carmichael wrote,

> are good to the poor, kind to the stranger, and courteous to all. During all the years that I lived and travelled among them, night and day, I never met with incivility, never with rudeness, never with vulgarity, never with aught but courtesy. I never entered a house without the inmates offering me food or apologising for their want of it. I never was asked for charity in the West, a striking contrast to my experience in England, where I was frequently asked for food, for drink, for money, and that by persons whose incomes would have been wealth to the poor men and women of the West.

That is precisely the experience that I continue to have in these islands. Time after time, at the door of Donald and Rachel MacSween in Scalpay, I have turned up filthy and stinking from weeks on the Shiants, and time after time they have housed me, washed me, washed my clothes, fed me, driven me here and there, and looked after me, my boat and my belongings in a way which is scarcely conceivable in any other part of Britain. That much of the old culture remains but Carmichael was travelling early enough to see the blackhouse, and in particular the tigh cèilidh, the party house, still functioning in the way it was intended to:

> The house of the story-teller is already full, and it is difficult to get inside and away from the cold wind and soft sleet without. But with that politeness native to the people, the stranger is pressed to come forward and occupy the seat vacated for him beside the houseman. The house is roomy and clean, if homely, with its bright peat fire in the middle of the floor. There are many present – men and women,

boys and girls. All the women are seated, and most of the men. Girls are crouched between the knees of fathers or brothers or friends, while boys are perched wherever – boy-like – they can climb. The houseman is twisting twigs of heather into ropes to hold down thatch, a neighbour crofter is twining quicken roots into cords to tie cows, while another is plaiting bent grass into baskets to hold meal.

> *Ith aran, sniamh muran,*
> *Is bi thu am bliadhn mar bha thu'n uraidh.*

> Eat bread and twist bent,
> And this year you shall be as you were last.

The housewife is spinning, a daughter is carding, another daughter is teazing, while a third daughter, supposed to be working, is away in the background conversing in low whispers with the son of a neighbouring crofter. Neighbour wives and neighbour daughters are knitting, sewing, or embroidering. The conversation is general: the local news, the weather, the price of cattle, these leading up to higher themes – the clearing of the glens (a sore subject), the war, the parliament, the effects of the sun upon the earth and the moon upon the tides. The speaker is eagerly listened to, and is urged to tell more. But he pleads that he came to hear and not to speak, saying:-

> *A chiad sgial air fear an taighe,*
> *Sgial gu la air an aoidh.*

> The first story from the host,
> Story till day from the guest.

The stranger asks the houseman to tell a story, and after a pause the man complies. The tale is full of incident, action, and pathos. It is told simply yet graphically, and at times dramatically – compelling the undivided attention of the

listener. At the pathetic scenes and distressful events the
bosoms of the women may be seen to heave and their silent
tears to fall. Truth overcomes craft, skill conquers strength,
and bravery is rewarded. Occasionally a momentary excitement occurs when heat and sleep overpower a boy and he
tumbles down among the people below, to be trounced out
and sent home. When the story is ended it is discussed and
commented upon, and the different characters praised or
blamed according to their merits and the views of the critics.

If not late, proverbs, riddles, conundrums, and songs
follow. Some of the tales, however, are long, occupying a
night or even several nights in recital. 'Sgeul Coise Cein',
the story of the foot of Cian, for example, was in twenty-four
parts, each part occupying a night in telling.

That beautiful nineteenth-century account of a disappearing
culture, its warmth and coherence, its sense of shared life, of a
vital communality, is of course what many Victorians longed for
and pined after, from Disraeli to Ruskin and Marx. But if Carmichael describes it with love, he does so in a way that animates
the Shiants. If anyone ever visits the ruined blackhouse here,
those are the words he should have in mind.

The air of approaching crisis steepens after the middle of the
century. The Seaforths, like many Highland landlords, were short
of money. Rents had not been keeping pace with expenditure
and the tacksmen, to whom the best parts of the estate were let
out, were not attuned to the realities of the new financial world.
In the middle of the eighteenth century, the old Seaforth tacks,
the Shiants among them, were relet for higher rents to new men.
The islands were now let to the highest bidder. In 1766, the Shiants
were let out to Donald MacNeill for £7 10s (a steep increase from
about £4 9s in the 1720s). In 1773 they were let to George Gillanders, Seaforth's own Chamberlain of Lewis, for £9 and in 1776 to
a Kenneth Morrison for £10 15s. Just how this increased rent –

more than double in fifty years – was raised from the Shiants is not clear, nor is it known what happened to the departing tacksman himself. Many left for the New World, and the tacksman here, named like all of them after the territory he held, a man known as 'Shiant', might have been among them.

In the wake of his departure, there are signs of real strain and breakdown of long-established customs. It was a process witnessed by Dr Johnson in Skye in 1773, and to his romantic Jacobite Tory sympathies, it looked like a social and cultural disaster. 'If the Tacksmen be banished,' Johnson asked,

> who will be left to impart knowledge, or impress civility? Hope and emulation will be utterly extinguished; and as all must obey the call of immediate necessity, nothing that requires extensive views, or provides for distant consequences will ever be performed. As the mind must govern the hands, so in every society the man of intelligence must direct the man of labour. If the Tacksmen be taken away, the Hebrides must in their present state be given up to grossness and ignorance.

Signs of that cultural breakdown became apparent on the Shiants. On 26 September 1769, Dr John Mackenzie, Seaforth's commissioner at Brahan Castle near Dingwall on the east coast, wrote to George Gillanders, the estate chamberlain on Lewis. They were friends. Mackenzie's brother had been Gillanders's predecessor and Mackenzie had got Gillanders the job:

> D[ea]r George,
>
> It is now some time since I wrote to you or heard from you and I dare say you'le very soon be thinking of coming to the main land and I hope with the rents in your possession which I can assure you are much wanted by the owner and all his conections.
>
> Immediately upon receiving yours about the wreck of a ship upon the rocks of Shant I wrote to Lord Stonefield

and Mr Davidson [Edinburgh judge and lawyer respectively] requiring their advice for your direction in prosecuting those guilty of plundering the ship but unluckily they were both out of Town at some distance so that it must be some time before we can get any advice of theirs on the subject. I doubt not however that you have taken all the care possible in taking a precognition [a series of witness statements] so as to fix guilt upon the barbarous actors of the Robbery and if you have got that done I dare say your commission as substitute admiral [a power to act on behalf of the crown in anything to do with the sea] will enable you to prosecute the delinquents either on the spot or by sending them prisoners to be tryed by some other Court of Justice, in short no pains must be spared in bringing them to punishment and I beg you may come sufficiently prepared for that purpose.

Here the letter is torn, but it resumes:

... as we never had more need of Cash. my Compts to Peggy and to the rest of your family. I hope she keeps her health

I am your etc
John Mackenzie

Unfortunately neither Gillanders's earlier letter to Mackenzie nor anything describing the outcome of the case seems to have survived, but evidence of stress crowds in. The growing population and the shortage of land was leading to breakdown of family relations. On Lewis, children were turning their parents out of the shared home, setting them 'loose upon the world and a begging, and will not give them any sort of subsistence', as Gillanders described it in March 1768. His solution – and he is a sympathetic figure: a modern manager trying to deal with an intractable situation – was not to allow any tenant of the estate to take in their son and daughter when married nor to subdivide their properties in any way, on pain of eviction.

Gillanders was busy with the kelp business. Since the late seventeenth century it had been known that the seaweed, whose alkalinity had always been used to sweeten the islands' acid soils, could be burnt and the sticky soup that resulted would solidify into a solid mass which was easily transported, and from which both soda and potash could be extracted. As these chemicals were vital in the making of soap and glass, and were needed to bleach linen, there was a prospect here, for the landlords, of good money.

The long, dirty and exhausting extraction process would be undertaken in June and August. The kelp was piled into large, often stone-lined trenches. Pat Foster identified one on the north shore of Garbh Eilean, a slightly ramshackle arrangement of stones almost indistinguishable from the mass of other fallen rock in the area.

It is next to the bay where the kelp still grows thick and dense, with tiny beadlet anemones clinging to the dark brown blades and where, at low water springs on a sunny day, the mass of weed winks and glitters like a plate of eels in the stirring of the swell. Just here, in William Daniell's prints, from sketches made as late as 1815, a skein of smoke drifts from the kiln towards the horizon, and small boats are gathered to take the burnt residue to the Lewis shore.

The kelp was burned for four to eight hours, the fire kept going with heather and hay. The women would often have the job of watching it, adjusting the heat to keep it alive all day without wasting the precious fuel. The men with long-handled iron spikes or hooks would stir the heavy mass to ensure an even burning of the weed. Not a single one of these 'kelp irons' had ever been discovered, but we found a pair in the excavation of the blackhouse.

One is a heavy iron spike, two feet long, with a socket at one end into which the shaft of a long wooden handle could be fitted. The other is sharply hooked, pointed at one end and with mineralised wood clinging to it, remnants of a handle which would once have been much longer. A ring is rusted to the spike, but no one yet has been able to explain its purpose. After the

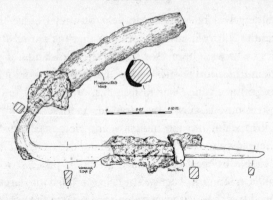

MINERALISED
WOOD

0   0.05   0.10 m.

WORKING
EDGE ?

SOCKET RING

mass of kelp had been thoroughly melted, the pyre would be covered with turf and stones to prevent it getting wet and then left overnight. The following morning the spikes could be used again to break the glassy agglomeration into lumps that could be carried to the boats.

Why these useful tools should have been left here is a curiosity. And I have been unable to find any documents relating to Shiant kelp. Thick lumps of paper survive in the Seaforth records detailing the arrangements which Gillanders was making for his proprietor, sending surveyors out to estimate the volume of the seaweed in different parts of the Lewis shore, arranging for ships to be piloted into the tricky sea-lochs on both east and west coasts of the island, sending Lewis kelpers to work on the Seaforth estates in Kintail, paying for the kelp which was to be sold in Liverpool, Whitby and Dublin with oatmeal, bearmeal (the flour of bere barley) and by remission of rent.

Huge amounts were made – 89 tons 9½ cwt from the parish of Lochs alone, baked and delivered to the waiting ships in the summer of 1770. There are receipts from the captains preserved in the Edinburgh records, still tied together with a piece of brown wool and thumb marks on the paper from what must have been a filthy cargo. But no mention of the Shiants. The only possibility is the strangely large quantity of kelp collected from Donald McKenzie at Valamus just across the Sound in Pairc, 6 tons 12 cwt for 1770 alone. Other shoreside settlements rarely produced more than a ton each. The Valamus return may include kelp transshipped from the Shiants.

The kelp business is another note in the Shiants' death knell. As the kelp went into the heritable proprietor's kilns, it could not be applied to the fields. A desperate shortage of fertility was inevitable; hunger accompanied the work. James Hunter, the historian of crofting, quotes William MacGillivray from the 1830s. The conditions would have been similar here half a century earlier:

> If one figures to himself a man, and one or more of his children, engaged from morning to night in cutting, drying, and otherwise preparing the sea weeds ... in a remote island; often for hours together wet to his knees and elbows; living upon oatmeal and water with occasionally fish, limpets, and crabs; sleeping on the damp floor of a wretched hut; and with no other fuel than twigs or heath; he will perceive that this manufacture is none of the most agreeable.

'The meagre looks and feeble bodies of the belaboured creatures,' the Reverend Buchanan wrote, 'without the necessary hours of sleep, and all over in dirty ragged clothes, would melt any but a tyrant into compassion.' It is from MacGillivray's account that one word glares out: limpets. They are here by the Eilean an Tighe house in abundance. Limpets, about a quarter of a million of them, are piled in and over the walls of the ruined barn. There must have piles like this all over the Hebrides. Dr Johnson saw them: 'They heap sea shells upon the dunghill, which in time moulder into a fertilising substance.' We dug at them for day after day. Using the same maths as before, but imagining a bigger family, perhaps eight of them, this second limpet deposit represents about fifteen hundred limpet meals, or fifteen years of hunger. The figures can only be approximate, but the size of the limpet pile is articulate enough, fifteen feet long, six wide and four high, a ziggurat of strain and sorrow.

As we excavated the limpet midden, you would come across clusters of shells that had clearly been dumped there in a single throw, the shells still nested into each other, chucked from the pot onto the heap. The thickness of the pile diminished from east to west: whoever had taken the meat out of the limpets had done so in the house, had walked out of the door, around the east end on the roughly paved platform, and chucked the contents over the ruined barn wall. Here and there was a clot of fishbones, or in one place five puffin heads still lumped together from a single stew. Elsewhere, the heap was widely and deeply disturbed: dogs, chickens and perhaps children had picked it over and stirred it up even as it accumulated. Many of the bones seem to have been drilled for the marrow and others look chewed, either by men or by dogs. Drilling for marrow is a sign of hunger, of squeezing out every last drop. The archaeologists could find no layering, no diagnostic stratigraphy, in the heap. The limpets were muddled together with every other bone. But the meaning was clear: life on the edge.

The picture is graphic enough: the landlord requires a higher return from his estate as a whole; at the same time the number of people on the Shiants rises; the islands are let to new men at higher rents and the place is squeezed agriculturally, both to pay that rent and to feed those people; it is a desperate time and from the 1760s onwards the population drops through emigration; kelp manufacture turns the islands towards the production of a global commodity; that lasts for a few years and then the population collapses, leaving a single family tending the cattle. The map-makers working for the Ordnance Survey in 1851 noted a few ruins and heard from their informant Neil Nicolson of Stemreway that 'the islands were formerly occupied by Five families (about Eighty years ago) who it is said procured a comfortable subsistence by their produce, and the fish which is found in great abundance around their Coasts.' That gives a date of about 1770 for the crucial departure. Why do they leave? Because kelpers can be brought in seasonally and the rent is more easily paid by abandoning any attempt at arable farming here and turning the place into a giant pasture. A single employed family is needed where a community had existed before.

By the last quarter of the eighteenth century, the entire way of life which places like the Shiants had supported was looking out of date, unenlightened and doomed. The economist, James Anderson, follower of Adam Smith, friend of Pitt's, in his *An Account of the present state of the Hebrides*, published in 1785, voiced the Establishment view.

> In the Hebrides, unless it be at Stornoway in Lewis, and Bowmore in Islay, there is not perhaps a place without the Mull of Cantire, where there are a dozen of houses together: – very few indeed are found but in scattered hamlets only.
>
> We ought not to be surprised at the poverty of the people in those regions, nor at the indolence imputed to them. They are indeed industrious; but that industry is unavailing. – They make great exertions, but these exertions tend not to remove their poverty. Is it a wonder if, in these circum- stances, they should sometimes think of moving to happier abodes?
>
> In consequence of this general system of dispersion that prevails in all those regions, the proprietors find their lands overstocked with people who are mere cumberers of the soil, eat up its produce, and prevent its improvement, with- out being able to afford a rent nearly adequate to that which should be afforded for the same produce, were their fields under proper management.

All the strain that is evident in the Shiants, the cutting of new fields out of the unproductive moor, the pressure of the increasing rents, the crowding of people in the houses, the desperation of those who had to survive on limpets, the robbing of the wreck, the back-breaking strain of gathering and burning the kelp for benefits which seemed to accrue more to the landlord than to those who were doing the work, all of that is reduced to the grim phrase: 'mere cumberers of the soil'. Even now, at this distance, can anyone not feel indignant at the description? I feel like taking the shade of James Anderson (living in Edinburgh, dying in Essex, existing, I guess, somewhere in Purgatory), showing him the limpet pile and asking him what he might make of that. Did he not grasp the reality of what that pile represented, nor imagine what that life might have been like?

No one now would tolerate living on the Shiants. People had come to understand the virtues of concentration, of agglomeration, of the division of labour, and none of those things were possible stuck out on the Shiants, where a man was forced to be his own ploughman, labourer, tanner, mason, shipmaster and butcher. The emptying of places like the Shiants was the product of a profound change in the nature of economic life, in which the local is subsumed in a much larger system. Nowadays, it would be called globalisation.

The Shiants died. There are the faintest traces in people's memories of who these departing Shiant Islanders might have been. Hughie MacSween, who had heard it from his uncle Malcolm or Calum MacSween, thought a man called Hector, Eachann, had lived at the south end of Eilean an Tighe. And, even more remotely, a whisper on the ether, a woman in Toronto, Allana Maclean, has posted on the Internet her own family tradition that her great-great-grandparents, Donald MacDonald and Janet McKinnon, or more possibly the parents of one or other of these, at some time in the last decades of the eighteenth century left the Shiants for Skye. But that tells you little. They are nothing more than names attached to absences.

The Shiantachs left not because people like James Anderson willed it – there is no evidence of a Shiant clearance in the classic sense – but because life was no longer tenable there, largely because the expectations of land and its productivity had risen. Human life on the Shiants had been founded on cyclicality, a kind of stasis in which each year, with luck, would be no worse than the one before. That is the meaning of the saying recorded by Alexander Carmichael: 'Eat bread and twist bent, / And this year you shall be as you were last.'

But the idea of working capital, trade, expansion of markets; above all of growth, and an expectation of growth, of increasing demands, increasing expenditure, increasing comfort and increasing wealth, cannot be accommodated in such a system. For the capitalist, every year is a failure unless it is an improvement on the one before. For a while, places like the Shiants reacted. The population increased, the attempts were made to get a commercial crop of kelp, but the ceiling was soon reached and the new life could not be sustained here. The Shiants now became, for the first time, a back room, a place in which animals could be grazed, and where people were perhaps needed to look after them, but not really a scene for human habitation. The new society had to retreat from places in which the old had felt at home. Insularity was now a symptom of backwardness and isolation a kind of failure.

It was not a new process. People had been draining out of the farthest Hebrides for generations. In 1549, there were forty-two inhabited islands attached to Harris and Lewis. By 1764 that had sunk to sixteen. In 1841 there were still sixteen (although not the same ones: some fertile islands such as Pabbay in the Sound of Harris had been cleared; others, much less suitable, reoccupied by the land-hungry). More than a hundred Hebridean islands have been abandoned since 1549, but most of them were deserted between 1549 and 1764. It is a sign of how rich a place the Shiants were that, despite their distance from any other shore, and despite the ferocity and difficulty of the seas around them, the people should have gone only after most other islands had been left.

There is a chance, although I think it unlikely, that the people were evicted from here. In the spring of 1796, the Seaforth estate cleared a large number of people off many townships across Lewis, a total of five hundred and seven tenants and thirty-one tacksmen. The sheriff officers were paid fivepence a mile (measured one way only from Stornoway); their assistants fourpence a mile, to travel out to the townships and give the news. It was considered important that 'the subtenants should also receive a verbal notice each from the Ground Officer.' The documents are sobering enough, name after name written out in the clerk's slightly shaky copperplate hand, all of them, as the writ for 22 March 1796 puts it,

> to hear and see themselves decerned & ordained by Decrees and Sentence of Court to flit and remove themselves their Wives Bairns Familys Servants Subtenants Coaters & dependants and all and sundry their Goods and Gear forth & from their pretended Possessions above mentioned and to leave the same void Redd and patent at the term of Whitsunday being the fifteenth of May next to come, to the end the Pursuer by himself or servants may enter thereto Sett use and dispose thereof at pleasure in all time coming.

One of the tacksmen named in these 1796 Summons of Removing is 'Murdoch Macleod, shipmaster in Stornoway, Tacksman of Limerbay and Shant Isles'. Is it possible, then, to think of the Ground Officers arriving here with their written summons, bringing them into house after house, first by the shore, then up to the middle valley, following the cow path between them, ducking into the low doors of the houses, showing the people the names of 'Murdoch Macleod' and of 'Shant Isles' (everyday Gaelic in the 1790s already had a leavening of English and the inhabitants of the Shiants were not necessarily illiterate: remember the Bible binding on the house floor) and giving them the verbal notice, eight weeks, until Whitsun, to leave, just as the puffins were coming in, just as the manure was to be spread on the fields, just as the year was to begin again?

It is possible, but I don't think anything so dramatic happened here. When also in 1796 the Reverend Simson describes this most outlying part of his parish, he implies that there has been only one family here for a while. That cannot mean the place had just been cleared. The Summons of Removing, or Warning Away Notice, can be explained as a bureaucratic mechanism by which the terms of Macleod's lease were changed, or by which the landlord gave it to someone else at a higher rent. It was a sign of something already being at an end, not the instrument by which it was ended.

The roofs of the abandoned houses fell in. The archaeologists found, just beneath the modern turf, the thick residue of the collapsed roof lying directly on the ash and charcoal of the abandoned floor, an earthy layer, rummaged about in by the rats. In amongst the rotted turf and thatch were thirty-four iron boat strake rivets. The house must have had a piece of a boat patching the roof. (*Freyja* would produce thirty-four rivets from a section of her hull three feet deep and seven long.) Inevitably, in a place where timber was so short, a washed-up boat, perhaps part of the wreck they had been plundering in 1769, would have been put to good use.

It was this hunger for timber – a constant in the Hebrides, but everything is heightened at this time – which lay behind the most shocking of all the stories associated with Shiants. I took *Freyja* across to the scene of the Pairc Murders one evening, a calm and beautiful journey, with the mountains of the mainland opalescent in the evening sun, and lenticular clouds, as smooth as sucked sweets, hanging over the hills of Lewis. The sea at the mouth of Loch Claìdh lay as still as marble next to the shore. I could look down into its green depths twenty feet to the cobbled bed and see the starfish sprawled across them. On shore, with the sheep nosing among the stones, was the ruined and abandoned hamlet of Bàgh Ciarach, 'Gloomy Bay', where the murders of 1785 were committed. The buildings lay in shade, plastic flotsam clogged the beach and I had no desire to land. This is known as the most haunted place in Lewis and I was happy to stay offshore in *Freyja*, looking at the sour abandoned township from the comfort of her thwarts.

As Donald Macdonald, the historian of Lewis, has described, and as Dan MacLeod of Lemreway told me the story, the people from the village of Mealasta in Uig had gone to Gairloch on the mainland for wood to build some new houses. When in the Sound of Shiant on their return, a terrible storm out of the north-east overtook them. In a blizzard, they were forced to seek shelter here in Bàgh Ciarach, where two or three houses were occupied by poor people called Mackay: 'The natives of these parts, seeing the weakened condition of the crew, frost-bitten and unable to defend themselves, and envious of their boatload of tree-trunks, killed each in turn by hitting him on the head with a large stone contained in the foot of a stocking.'

As Dan Macleod told me, 'the bodies were buried in a bog and an unusual kind of weed has been growing there ever since.'

The women of Mealasta thought their men had drowned but one night the ghost of one of them appeared to his sweetheart and sang her the song called 'Bàgh Ciarach':

The girl of my love is the young brown-haired one.
If I were beside her, I would not suffer harm.

This year my family are seeking and searching for me,
while I lie in Gloomy Bay at the foot of a pool.

The men of Pairc threatened us with axes,
But our utter exhaustion left them unharmed.

Duncan, the mountain man, attended to me:
the world is deceitful and gold beguiles.

While climbing the hillside I lost my strength.
By the crags of the headland the blond-haired boy was murdered.

The young woman woke with the words of the song and its tune on her lips. The next July she was at the yearly cattle market in Stornoway. A huge crowd of people was there. Among the crowd, as Dan Macleod said, 'the Uig girl saw a jersey she had knitted herself, for her dead lover, on the shoulders of a man from Pairc. She recognised the pattern of her stitches and she grabbed the wool, pulled at the man, but he broke away from her and disappeared into the crowd. No one knows if he was ever brought to justice.' Another version, told by Donald Macdonald, says instead that the girl was looking through a pile of blankets for sale at the fair. As she picked through them, she saw, on one of them, in its corners, the small pieces of tartan she had sewn in there herself. It was Nicolson tartan and the men from Mealasta were Nicolsons.

It was late on a summer night, after eleven o'clock. I turned *Freyja* southwards, raised the sail and started back along the Lewis shore to Scalpay and the MacSweens. A light northeasterly blew in over my left shoulder. The motion through the still water at the mouth of Loch Seaforth was as easy as those first days' sailing in *Freyja* in Flodabay. The water rattled against the boards of the hull like a ruler against the railings of a fence. For all the melancholy of the eighteenth-century history here, I felt happy, at home on the summer night sea. The dogs slept on the boards at my feet. The moon rose as the Shiants sank into the dark and at one in the morning, as *Freyja* and I slipped in between the arms of Kyles Scalpay, I watched its reflected light around me, scattered and broken on the bubbling of the tide.

13

ONE DAY LATE IN THE SUMMER – it was 13 August in 2000, the 19th in 1999 – the puffins leave. In the morning, the place is as full as it has ever been and the sky at the colony quivers and flickers with the hundreds of thousands of bodies in flight. The rocks on the boulder screes around Garbh Eilean are incandescent with the yellow of the lichen and the air is thick with the tang of guano. You then turn your back to some other task. The boat needs fixing, the rushes around the well should be cut away. Look again, in the afternoon, and the birds have gone. The place is empty. The rocks glow as they ever did, but nothing lives among them. Acre after acre of the colonies is empty; silence clings to them. The sudden stillness is haunting, *sianta* is the Gaelic word, and these are now the Shiant Isles. The guano fug still wafts around you. The rocks are still spattered with it, the kittiwake droppings white where they have fallen straight down the cliff from each rock-ledge nest, the guillemots' brown on the ledges where the birds have stamped and shuffled across it for the summer months. But the party is over. What the Shiants could offer – a place for an egg, near a sea full of fish, away from predatory enemies – is no longer needed. For the rest of the year, dispersal across the ocean is the better option.

Not everything has yet gone. The skuas are still here and they are teaching their young to fly, the giant juveniles clumsying after their parents, shadowing and modelling their behaviour on the skill and expertise on display in front of them. The baby shags, now just waterborne, cheep like budgerigars in clusters next to the natural arch. There is a mass of snipe in the marsh, fluting at night over their territories, and a short-eared owl, the only daytime owl, cruises low over the rushes for the voles that are its only prey.

At this turning point of the year, at least in a good summer, the islands have turned Cretan with drought and the grass is so dry that as you walk through it the stems rustle against you. Where the sheep cannot reach, the long bluish threads of the ungrazed grass hang like wigs. Over the stone foundations of the medieval farmstead at the bay, the turf has turned brown, mapping the structures beneath it.

This is also the moment for the arrival of the most mysterious of all Shiant creatures. In thirty-five years, I have seen it only once. From Stocanish, at the north-west point of Garbh Eilean, I had been watching with my children the north-going stream of the tide as it swept past the Galtas. It was running hard and fast through the big gap between Galta Mor and the other stacks, tailing like a mill race of roily water. Galta Beag was throwing a big curve away to the east, as though the flow were meeting a coffer-dam there. Downstream of all the rocks, the currents were blotched with balloons of upwelling water. Each was as heavy as a pond of olive oil and they were dotted across the stream like the spots on the flanks of trout. This pattern of rough and smooth was spread across an area a mile wide and at least one and a half miles long, the glitter of the turbulence coating a thousand acres of the sea.

Gannets pay attention to the tide. As it floods, they fish here by the Galtas; as it ebbs they move to the riffles off Seann Chaisteal and Sgeir Mianish. If you want some fish, it's a good idea to follow them. We launched the boat and dropped our weighted lines just where the running water breaks and shivers over the

hidden rock ridges. You haul the fish in, no skill here, the metalled bodies lying on the boards beside your feet, the big coppery pollack, the saithe steely blue, the occasional small, fat mackerel, and sometimes a little red gurnard slipping out of the mouth of the bigger fish, caught just as the prey was in its gullet.

It was, in that way, an ordinary late-summer day, a taking of the fish which the Shiants have always provided. I baited some creels with the heads of some of them, a fleet of six, no more, and set them – or 'shot' them, as the word goes, but that is too dynamic a term for the gentle lowering of these cage-traps into the waters of the Minch – and left them there for the night, when the lobsters would emerge from their rocks to feed.

I had my sons, my sister Rebecca and my first wife Olivia with me in the boat that day. We were right in the middle of the three islands, the Shiants' navel, and the tide must have been at dead water. The evening was calm and the Minch was wearing its sleek summer skin, with that oily, rich viscosity which is merely the thickness of plankton in the water, the favoured pasture of the sharks.

We were in a big wooden dinghy and there were five or six of us in there, floating about between the half-enclosing arms of the islands. Looking up, away to the south, where the sky was daubed by the swell into patches across the water, I saw a fin. 'Is that a shark?' I said. The boys thought I was joking. But we looked harder and saw the fin moving through those slack colour-islands of sea and sky. It was a fin and I turned the boat towards it, perhaps two or three hundred yards away. Within seconds Rebecca said quietly, 'There's another, there are two of them.' The fins were trailing each other, one pursuing the other through the soup, perhaps fifteen feet apart. A few seconds more as we edged towards them, the outboard gurgling down into its lowest register, and then we realised, simultaneously I think, the whole boat coming to the same idea: not two sharks but two fins, the dorsal and the tail of the same animal, fifteen feet apart.

Lovers on St Kilda sang to each other:

> *He*: You are my turtle-dove, my song-thrush,
>   You are my sweet-sounding harp in the sweet morning.
> *She*: You are my hero, my basking shark.

I've tried the lines out on a variety of people and they laugh, but for me that is as good as a North Atlantic haiku, at least in its sudden, final turn from everything that is sweet and coherent to the huge masculine simplicity of that other creature, *cearrabhan* in Gaelic, the unmeasured, the unsugared, unsinging presence of the giant wild.

It was like that the evening we met our shark. The beautiful surface ease of the sea, its time-lapsed slopping from one state to another and the way it looked like a bed in which you could loll and roll for hours: all that concealed another place. Those two fins were the blades of one world cutting up into the air of another. I stopped the engine, the boat drifted and the grazing shark was moving across our bows. I wasn't frightened as it turned, a little below the surface now, and circled us, its head as wide as a table, its body the length of two dinghies, its dredger-bucket mouth agape for the food-rich water streaming through it, the skin a mottled grey and a manner as casually proprietorial as a landlord behind his bar, as a Macleod in his Minch. It circled us, one full circum-navigation of the boat, and then moved away, still underwater, its outline breaking up as the coloured sea closed over.

That was twelve years ago and I have never seen one since. Numbers have certainly dropped catastrophically since the 1940s, and no one knows why. Dan Macleod at Lemreway blames 'the Norwegians'. Others the rampaging depredations of shark hunters such as Tex Geddes and Gavin Maxwell in the Forties and early Fifties. And there is some evidence to suggest that the shark population goes through boom-bust cycles with a period of about half a century.

I hope and pray it does because I know that the way to see these animals is not in that rare single sighting, which is rather a twitcher's view, the precious conservationist with his awe in his pocket, but in the grandeur of the shoals among which Maxwell and Geddes played such havoc. Maxwell had, I think, an admirably complex attitude. He felt no, or little, compunction about shooting these enormous animals. In *Harpoon at a Venture*, he maintained that to kill a basking shark is no more or less cruel than to kill a herring. But his sense of wonder remained intact. Only from him do I know a description of the basking shark en masse: 'Down there in the clear water,' he wrote of one summer day in 1946 off the southern coast of Skye,

> they were packed as tight as sardines, layer upon layer of them, huge grey shapes like a herd of submerged elephants, the furthest down dim and indistinct in the sea's dusk. A memory came back to me from childhood – Mowgli and the elephants' dance, and the drawing of the great heaving mass of backs in the jungle clearing.

That's what I want: a vastness of vast presences, ranks of them stepping down into the green dark of the sea.

* * *

A couple of weeks later, in early September, the shepherds arrive 'to take the lambs home'. That is a euphemism: the real destination is Stornoway market, and then the butcher or, if they are not quite fat, some lush southern pastures where they can be finished. In 1999, Shiant lambs from Eilean an Tighe and Garbh Eilean (those from Eilean Mhuire were, as John Murdo Matheson the shepherd says, 'ready fit for the hook') went to a buyer from Lancaster, who sold them on to a farm near Dover, where they spent the winter, fattening a little more, and from where they finally went to the butcher the following spring. There is nothing new in this: upland and island stock have been fattened and finished on richer farms further south, nearer the urban markets, for centuries. The whole of Scotland was laced with the drove-roads along which they travelled.

Ever since the departure of the old Shiant population in the 1770s, the islands have been a stock-raising place. At first, it was a mixture of the old black cattle and sheep. But improvers soon cast their eye over the potentialities of the place. 'The Schant Isles are certainly the greatest curiosities I ever contemplated,' Rev. James Headrick, a geologist who had been invited to Lewis in 1800 by Lord Seaforth, remarked: 'Were they known, men fond of viewing all that is grand and uncommon in the productions of nature would come from the remotest corners of the world to see them.'

But Headrick was employed more for an economic than a picturesque survey:

> These islands are better adapted for sheep and a few goats than for cows, which cannot be kept from falling over the rocks, – an accident that happened while I was there. I should think the fine woolled Cheviot breed would thrive well on them. I mentioned this to the tacksman: but he said that sheep were to apt to get fat there; and then they became lazy, and fell over the rocks, like cows. But this objection is easily obviated by stocking more fully, which would prevent them from

getting more fat than necessary. Cows cannot get at half the grass. I am also apt to think that these Isles might form a commodious fishing station. The seas around swarm with fishes of various sorts, and there is a commodious landing place for boats between Garve and Y-Kill.

The fishing station was not a good idea – no anchorage and no market – but since Headrick's report, the Shiants have been a sheep place. Sheep get fatter there quicker than on the mainland of Lewis (Hughie MacSween said that in some years he had fat lambs from Eilean Mhuire by June, whereas in Scaladale or on Seaforth Island, where he also had his stock, they would never be fat before the end of August) and they also have more lambs. Because the Shiant sheep tend to have – and are able to rear – more twins than elsewhere, the average lamb survival rate is about one lamb per ewe, or a ratio of a hundred per cent, whereas on Lewis, even in a good year, they are pleased to get seventy per cent. It is said by Tommy Macrae and other Lewismen that Shiant lamb has yellow fat, which only a few weeks' grazing on Lewis can turn white, and it is the 'sea birds manuring the grass' that is to blame. And at Dingwall Market outside Inverness, the wild and springy stock from these islands had a reputation before the war as the 'Shiant Isle Jumpers'.

It is the relative riches of the Shiants which has kept the shepherding tradition alive here, despite the costs and difficulty. The islands are a step up, not down, for Lewis or Harris sheep men, which is what makes coming out with them here such unalloyed pleasure.

The grazing tenancy has been handed down in this century in an unbroken chain. Calum MacSween, the Tarbert baker, was Lord Leverhulme's tenant, then Compton Mackenzie's and my father's. He left it to his son Johnnie, and it then went to his cousin Donald 'DB' Macleod of Scalpay, a butcher, poet and romanticist. When he died, it went to Hughie MacSween, Calum's nephew, and from him to another cousin, Donald MacSween, the Scalpay fisherman. When Donald had some trouble with his heart, he was forced to give up the Shiants, but there was a man waiting in the wings. John Murdo Matheson of Gravir in Lewis, who is now twenty-nine, had left school at sixteen ('I didn't have the academic brain to go on') and had started work part-time at Stornoway Mart and part-time on a farm north of the town. He wanted more than that and the man who owned both mart and farm encouraged him to have a go at taking on the Shiants. He knew Hughie MacSween from his visits to the market and when, in 1989, John Murdo heard that Hughie was thinking of giving up the Shiants through illness, he 'clicked into gear'.

John Murdo's father had a nickname for him: 'Friends of the Earth', because of his unrequitable hunger for land. The family already had two crofts, one at Gravir above the lochside and another a few miles away at Calbost, and now he wanted to add the Shiants to the collection. He has a way with animals and a natural authority. Mackenzie, Nicolson and Matheson blood all flow in his veins. I once remarked on this to him. 'Oh yes,' he said, 'I think we've got it all covered.' But he was only seventeen and that was too young. Besides, he couldn't raise the money to buy the stock from Hughie. The islands went to Donald Mac-Sween and only in 1996 did he transfer them to John Murdo. By then, he was working both at the mart and as a slaughterman at Heather Isle Meats in Stornoway. Few of these arrangements have anything to do with the nominal proprietor; he is the lucky recipient of the grace, courtesy, charm, energy, loyalty and gener-osity that pours out from one Hebridean tenant after another. No rent is paid nowadays, but we share the costs of maintaining the house.

The pattern of the shepherding year is immutable. The tups are put on in November, about eight or nine of them for the three hundred-odd ewes, and are taken off in February, 'knackered' as John Murdo says. If the weather prevents them being collected and given cake and nurture at home in Calbost, as happened in the dreadful storms of early 2000, with winds in Stornoway recorded at a hundred and six miles an hour, the exhausted and expensive animals can die on the islands. Lambs are born in late April or early May, deliberately unsupervised. If anyone lands on the islands and disturbs the ewes at this time, the likely outcome is that the sheep will desert their lambs. At the end of May the lambs are marked – male a red spot, female blue – and the ram lambs castrated. The flock is shorn in July, an exhausting, hot few days, as the wool is clipped entirely by hand. In early September, the sheep are gathered again, the best ewes and ewe lambs kept back for stock on the islands and the cull ewes and marketable lambs taken to Stornoway. In November, finally, the tups are put out there again for the winter.

Each trip also has its pattern. You arrive usually on a Saturday and as Hughie MacSween says, 'there may be a dram or two in the provisions. And the first night we arrive, whether it was a Friday or a Saturday – now DB didn't approve of this – we'd have a dram. And that first night the whole lot would be perished. The whole lot.'

The perishing of the dram is a wonderful chute to oblivion, an increasingly sentimental slither into the night. John Murdo has brought his uncle Kennie Mackenzie, a joiner from Leurbost in Lochs, and 'two boys from the mart' with him. Kenneth Angus MacIver – Toby – is a shepherd and stockman. Nona, whose real and unused name is Donald Smith, is a shepherd and ex-butcher. The tilly lamp hisses over us. John Murdo has cooked us a leg of lamb from his own sheep at Calbost, which he slaughtered and butchered himself, and some of the potatoes I have grown in the lazybed at the far end of the bay.

Toby: There is nothing like a good potato. And that is a good potato.

John: You don't want too much seaweed on it. Seaweed makes the potato wet.

Kennie: I hope you didn't plant those on a Sunday, Adam.

Adam: No, I'm sure it was a weekday, Kennie.

Kennie: Because nothing planted on a Sunday ever grows.

Adam: No, and fish mustn't be landed on a Sunday.

Kennie: It's better that they rot on the shore.

Adam: Even if they're caught on the Saturday and you are late coming in?

Kennie: You would benefit more by throwing the lot than eating even a morsel of one of them.

The coal fire glows so hot that we are all in shirt sleeves and sweat pours down John Murdo's face.

Toby: You think it's hot in here, Adam? You should see us at the clipping. Fifteen ewes and it's in the sea to cool off. Especially on Mary Island, where the sun shines off the rocks by the fank there. Lambs jumping all over you. It's hot work then. It's fast work. You might think it's hot now. I can tell you it's hot then.

The rats scuffle behind the boarding around the room.

Nona: Ah, there we are. That's a sound I like the sound of. It's always nice to know you've got some neighbours handy.

John Murdo is king here. Only a slight gesture is needed from him, nothing more than moving to untie a knot or shift a coal on the fire, for the others to jump to, looking to him.

The dogs, which have been tied up outside, are brought in: John Murdo's Sheba, a delicate little thing, Toby's Queenie, hyperactive, with darting eyes and quivering ears, Kennie's Roy, one eye brown, the other eye blue, and Nona's Spot, a sweet-natured, big clown of a creature, named after a spot on his ear, and who refuses ever to go to his left. They curl up at their respective masters' feet and their ears are stroked.

John: When Sheba gets home she'll be on the tips of her toes for a few days. It's hard-going for the dogs here. Her feet get so sore and her pads are soft. She needs a bit of looking after.

Nona: Not like this one. The first year we were here, wasn't it, over by the salt pool above the cliffs next to the natural arch, that was Spot's day wasn't it?

Kennie: Wasn't it?

Adam: What happened?

Nona: We were gathering them down there and I sent Spot off on a run over to his left to get behind the sheep, out, you know, in a curve like that. As soon as I'd given the whistle I knew I had made a mistake. It wasn't even worth looking. Phut. He's gone straight over. I told John it wasn't worth looking over. He's dead. So we went to the cliff edge and there he was, wet through, on a rock down at the edge of the sea barking up at us. It must be sixty, seventy feet down there.

Adam: What had happened?

Nona: It was his speed that saved him. He must have leaped out right out wide like that above and over the rocks and into the sea eighty or ninety feet below him and then somehow climbed to the rocks at the shore.

John: It was a terrible swell that day. We got round there in the boat but if he hadn't jumped for the boat, we'd never have got him. But he jumped for the boat.

Nona: And I had to keep him going not to let him stiffen up. He would have stiffened up if he'd laid down. And when we got home he was sore for days afterwards. He must have smacked into the sea, his belly. But it didn't change him. He's a good dog.

John: I had a dog die here. Meg. She'd been poorly at the beginning of the year, a liver complaint, and then we were out here in March and she wasn't right. She wouldn't come out of the house. And then that night she was lying there next to me at night on the other bed and in the morning she was as flat as a pancake.

Nona: A good dog she was, always on the go, a good soul, wasn't she?

We all stare at the fire for a while as the dram continues its perishing around us.

Toby: What about the boy who got a Russian one out of those catalogues?

Nona: A dog?

Toby: No, it was a wife, Nona. There are a few tasty bits in there.

Nona: What was his like?

Toby: A hefty number.

Nona: I don't think she's arrived yet.

Toby: She's a lawyer, isn't she?

Nona: Well, she'll have him if she is.

Kennie: But that's no way to get married.

Toby: He only knew her a week or two.

John: He had one before. She didn't last long.

Toby: Women are best left out of it. I've got more daughters than I can count and none of them can boil an egg. They should be let out once a year to cook the Christmas dinner.

The five of us disintegrate into whisky-sodden hysterics and John puts another coal or two on the fire.

John: How many people would give their eye teeth to be here now?

Kennie: Aye, away from the cares of the world.

Adam: Hughie told me once that his uncle Calum, sitting on the beach here waiting for the boat, always used to say, without anyone ever prompting him, 'There is no place outside Heaven's Gates where I would prefer to be sitting than the place I am sitting in now.'

Nona: On a day like this you would never want to leave, would you?

The next day, being Sunday, nothing is done here. We go for a walk, we sit in the sunshine, we read the newspapers that we brought with us yesterday. We listen to the radio. It is a holiday away from the world. But come Monday, after a sober tea and coffee evening the night before, the work begins. In the drenching rain, we gather the sheep island by island. First on Eilean Mhuire, easily gathering them in a smooth and continuous sweep around the island and down on to the shore. There with the washed-up kelp on the floor of the fank, and wool and dung mingled on the cobbles, the bodies of the wet sheep pressing against the hurdles and the seals wailing on the offshore skerries, it is easily and quickly done. All the sheep are dosed with the worming drench, the fifteen best ewe lambs are marked for collection on Wednesday and then released back up to the pasture again.

Toby, in his yellow jacket and orange trousers, keeps muttering at Queenie, 'Come into heel, will you,' and Nona stands there with Spot beside him. 'That's the lambs, or some of them. They'll look better when they're dry.' I asked him why he had given up butchery. 'I couldn't stand it on a good day, stepping out the back door and looking at the sky.'

In the dripping, drenching rain, Garbh Eilean is a different proposition altogether. The shags have gone now. There's just nest after nest of fulmars crowded with grown chicks. The cloud is down low on the islands like a lid. It clings like smoke around the cliffs. The colour of the screes has been dulled in this early autumn rain and the corpses of sea birds, a kittiwake, a puffin, have already dissolved away – or perhaps the rats have had them – leaving just the feathers on the rain-glazed grass.

Garbh Eilean is a big, stocky brute of an island to shepherd. It is high and steep. Different parts of the flock are hefted to different areas and resist being herded. In particular, those which spend their lives down on the sweet rich grass at the Bagh don't like coming up on to the sour acid moor of the high ground. One of them in particular, an old ewe that John Murdo calls 'the old ski champion', goads the rest. For year after year she has niftily dodged the gathering, allowing herself to be led almost to the top and then, when they think they have done it, suddenly turning round and skiing past men and dogs back down to the bottom, taking her sisters and granddaughters and enormous extended family down with her. There are ewes down there, with three unshorn fleeces one on top of another, which look like abandoned sofas.

In a mile-wide line, the five of us, each with a crook, and the four dogs, set about clearing Garbh Eilean. 'Get on, come on, get up, goo on, goo on, shsssh, sssh, whistle, heaaunk, heank,' – a grunted pushing with the back of the voice – and then to the dogs, 'That'll do. That'll do. THAT'LL DO!'

John Murdo strides easily around the island, jumping down into a cleft to collect a ewe and a lamb that have squeezed themselves in there, Sheba endlessly tearing here and there to his whistles. 'Just get up over, come up over. Sheba!'

He had asked me to drive the sheep the length of the south-west shore, down towards Annat and then on to Stocanish, and not to let any of them past me. It was a struggle in the broken ground, steep slippery places, some gooed over with shag muck, and with the sleeting rain slicking the surfaces of the rocks, as I sweated in my waterproofs, much too aware of the need to keep up with the others spread out across the hill above me. It is not exactly the dynamism of these men that is so impressive, more the habit of exertion, the muscle and resilience learned in a lifetime of work. I felt like a stick of asparagus next to them.

I emerged on to the high ground, thinking and hoping that I had kept all the sheep in front of me. I could see John Murdo in his green waterproofs, half a mile away, gesticulating to me and shouting.

'What?'

His words were torn and broken by the wind.

Again and again, he was waving his stick in the direction I had come. I couldn't hear but I guessed what he meant. Some sheep had doubled past me. I should go back to gather them, and so I did, half a mile back and half a mile back again, driving a couple of ewes and their lambs firmly in front of me. It worked this time, and I finally joined up with John Murdo and the others. 'There were some ewes and lambs behind you,' he said quietly, smiling.

'I know,' I said.

Now the difficult part: driving this gathered flock of some hundred and thirty ewes and the same number of lambs, along with the four tups which had survived the spring, down the steep south side, the Sron Lionta, of Garbh Eilean. 'Don't get below a sheep on that hillside,' John Murdo said, 'or if it falls or tumbles down on to you, that's you.'

Slowly we edge them towards the lip. They seep across the hillside. This is not a way they usually come and there is a hesitation in the movement, a stickiness which means that as they come to the edge of the steep slope, which is at a gradient of perhaps two in one ('There's no point in describing it,' Kennie says. 'Just call it the Eiger.'), they stop. The sheep tremble on the brink. It is something like those films of wildebeest crossing the river in the Serengeti, with the steam coming off the exhausted and bleating animals, many of them crammed on to little rock ledges, uncertain where to turn. A lamb suddenly slips and we watch it falling and rolling like a doll towards the sea, over and over, jerking and jumping over each new rock, all the way down to the little cove at the bottom, breaking its neck as it goes, dead before it is halfway there. It is left for the gulls and the rats because its flesh is bruised and no good for anything. 'You can't eat them,' John Murdo says to me straightforwardly. 'They are just wrecked. It would be all right if it fell into the sea. It would be all right if you could slit its throat and bleed it then,

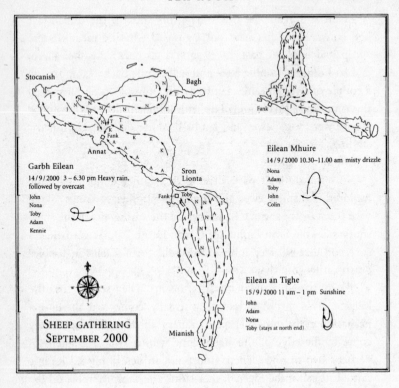

Stocanish

Bagh

Fank

Eilean Mhuire
14/9/2000 10.30–11.00 am misty drizzle
Nona
Adam
Toby
John
Colin

Garbh Eilean

Garbh Eilean
14/9/2000 3 – 6.30 pm Heavy rain,
followed by overcast
John
Nona
Toby
Adam
Kennie

Annat

Fank

Sron
Lionta

Fank   Toby

Eilean an Tighe
15/9/2000 11 am – 1 pm Sunshine
John
Adam
Nona
Toby (stays at north end)

SHEEP GATHERING
SEPTEMBER 2000

Mianish

but with the bruising, the bloods's clotting and it's no good.'

Something in the quivering, bunched queue of sheep finally gives and they begin to trail carefully down the rocky path to the shore, the exhausted shepherds gently pushing them down in front of them. They trail across the isthmus and into the fank on the other side. Everything is in, including the champion skier. 'There she is,' Toby says, 'the bastard from the Bagh, the bastard from hell, the bitch.' The best twenty-five ewe lambs are marked to go back to Garbh Eilean and the rest are kept in, 'to go home'.

The next day on Eilean an Tighe is easy by comparison. A steady sweep down to Mianish and back up again, with the big

stocky body of a peregrine flying over the driven animals, draws the Eilean an Tighe flock into the fank by the house.

Only afterwards did I realise something which may or may not be significant. Every one of the islands had been gathered in a clockwise direction.

This might seem coincidental were it not for the fact that well into the historical period, recorded from Martin Martin in the 1690s to Margaret Fay Shaw in the 1930s in South Uist, the habit of doing things clockwise, which is also the direction the sun travels, from east to west, was in the past regarded as a form of blessing. Boats on leaving the shore, supplicants at holy wells, hosts greeting strangers, those resanctifying women after child-bearing, anyone visiting an ancient and holy cairn: all these would involve a clockwise or sunwise turn, *deiseil* in Gaelic, as a form of charm. And here, even the way in which the sheep were turned from one holding pen to another within the fank was sunwise.

I am not suggesting that John Murdo or any of the others is indulging in heathen practices. Nothing could be further from his mind. It is just the way it has always been done here. And it fits the place. If this is an inherited pattern, it is entirely unconscious.

The sun had come out and we were looking over the lambs gathered in the fank beside the house. The lambs were not quite as good as everyone had hoped.

Nona: It was the wet spring that did it.
Toby: That was what kept them back.
Nona: Aye, and the dry summer.
Toby: Aye, that would have kept them back too.
Nona: And it's been cold these last few weeks.
Toby: That wouldn't have helped.
Nona: No, they're not as good as they might have been.
Toby: But there are some big ones in here.
Nona: Monsters some of them.
Toby: There's some good lambs in there.
Nona: Look at that horned ewe with her twins.
Toby: There's some very heavy lambs here.
Kennie: It'll be heavy work getting them into the dory.
Toby: Come into heel, will you.
Nona: Once you get a good year, you expect a good year every year. It must have been '98, was it? That was a corker. But you're not going to get that quality every time.
Toby: No, not every time, that's right.

As the shepherds looked the animals over, we had some visitors. The grey-hulled, thirty-eight-foot ocean-going twin-diesel estate boat from Eishken on Lewis, the *Incorrigible*, pulled into the bay and off-loaded its passengers, about eight handsome men and women, in their late teens or early twenties, in fleeces and sunglasses.

John glanced up from his work. 'Oh, they're from Eishken,' he said. 'They've been here before with their black labradors when we were trying to get the sheep down off the big island. They had their dogs on the beach and I had to shout at them to get out of the way because the sheep wouldn't come down. You'd think they might have guessed.'

In the sunny afternoon, as we worked at lifting and drenching the sheep, the people from the boat came and sat on the grassy bank a hundred yards or so from us and watched. None of them moved towards us, nor did the shepherds greet them. Instead, we spoke quietly amongst ourselves.

> *John*: Look at them. Look at them lying there like that. There's no reality in their lives. You slog your guts out on a day's work and then you see them there and you realise you don't have the first idea how the other half lives.
>
> *Nona*: Toby, you're the one for the girls. You go and talk to them. You're the one who nearly cut that head off that sheep at the clipping when that girl in a miniskirt came along with some eighty-year-old husband or other and you very nearly slit its throat open.
>
> *Toby leans against the side of the fank with his bum outstretched in the direction of the Eishken party.*
>
> *John*: Each of those sunglasses probably costs more than I get for a day's wages.
>
> *Nona*: At least they could come and say hello and have a look at what we are doing.
>
> *Toby*: Yes, but they probably think we are going to rape and murder them.
>
> *Nona*: We could hold them to ransom.

Toby: How much do you think? It's diamond money, isn't it, at Eishken?

Adam: No, I think it's nightclubs, tenpin bowling and Burger Kings in the north of England.

Suddenly landed in this piece of class drama, I thought I should go over to them.

'What are you up to at Eishken?' I asked the ranks of silvered wraparounds.

'Probably drinking too much,' one of the boys said. A girl said she felt like climbing a hill and so I pointed out the way up the side of Garbh Eilean. She thanked me but didn't move. Was it shyness that was hobbling their behaviour? God knows what we looked like, covered in sweat and sheep shit. I later heard from someone at Eishken that the party had been told that shepherds were working on the Shiants and they weren't to interfere with them. And so they lay back and enjoyed the sun. This is the kind of accident by which moneyed gaucheness becomes intolerable arrogance to those who are exposed to it.

John, Toby, Nona, Kennie and I put the holding pen up on the beach while the Eishken boys and girls watched from just above us. Eventually, having visited ten yards or so of the islands, they sloped back down to their dinghy, which had been brought into the beach by one of the Eishken estate staff. 'I'll think I'll climb a smaller bump tomorrow,' the girl said as she walked past me.

Christopher Macrae, the head keeper at Eishken and a good friend of John Murdo's – his brother, the fisherman Ruaraidh Macrae often brings John out to the Shiants in his boat, the *Astronaut* – appeared and they waved and said hello to each other warmly. But that warmth did not extend to the passengers. Macrae's assistant in waders was holding the dinghy in the shallows. One by one the girls and boys climbed in and sat down, so that with their weight the dinghy grounded on the cobbles. The employee had to push like a Number Eight in a scrum to

get them off. John Murdo watched in silence. 'Even if they had been properly stuck,' he said to me quietly, 'they would have sat there and let him struggle.'

We went back to the house. The Bitch from the Bagh was causing a rumpus in the holding pen and in the excitement of sorting it out, Spot nipped Nona in the bottom.

We got up at five the next morning. It was still night and you could just see the breakers in the sea outside, creaming in from the south-west. The fishing boat from Ness was expected at seven and we scraped around getting ready in the darkness. Most of us ate a breakfast by candlelight of black pudding, sausages, bacon, bread and butter but John Murdo was too nervous. The wind had got up in the night and he was worried we weren't going to get off. He was taking two hundred-odd lambs to market, four thousand pounds-worth if the prices came good. That was the reason for no breakfast.

In the first light, we drove the sheep down on to the beach. The wind was wet and frozen. The boat from Ness arrived and its aluminium Russian dory, with hurdles on both sides, came into the beach. Its shallow draught bow just nosed against the shingle. We made a human chain from fank to boat and handed the heavy lambs down one by one. A man stood in the bow of the dory and we lifted the animals in to him. He held them tight against the hurdles with his knees. It was hot work and even in the cold of the wind we were down to our shirts in it, with the braces of the waterproof trousers up over them and sweat rolling down our faces. The lambs struggled and kicked but we held them at the hips and under the chin, exhausting and relentless work, tons of lamb transferred from shore to dory. They were taken out ten at a time the couple of hundred yards to the fishing boat standing off in the rising wind. There they were lifted up again, over the gunwales and on to the deck. Some of them kicked to get away. 'Ah, you bitch,' Toby would say as they flung out at him and the stones of the beach clattered around us. The tiredness grips your whole body but particularly in the ends of the fingers, which ache with exhaustion. Each of the tups needed four of us to carry it, one at each corner. 'The angry bitch, he'll have your knees if you don't watch it,' Nona said.

'Look at the size of that lamb,' Toby said. 'You could go to sea on that lamb.'

'That's one for the freezer,' Kennie said.

'Get your hands out of your pockets,' John said to me at one moment, as we were waiting for the dory to return for another load. This is not a luxury life.

At last, they were all on. The big fifty-eight-foot fishing boat was down at the bow with the weight of animals on its deck and in its hold. The shepherds lay collapsed on the piled nets in the stern, smoking roll-ups. Someone produced some cans of lager. 'Nectar,' Nona said.

'I don't know we've had this many passengers on her before,' the skipper of the boat said in his wheelhouse. Next to the ruddiness of the shepherds the complexions of the fishermen looked grim and industrialised. 'I wouldn't dream of having anything to do with sheep myself,' the fisherman said to me, smoking on his chair behind the wheel, his feet up on the desk beside it. 'It's all manual labour, isn't it?'

The deck was getting slithery with the muck of two hundred lambs. The ones from Eilean Mhuire were to blame. We had picked them up directly from the island where they had been grazing all night. The others had been kept in the fank and were dry. As the big fishing boat, drawing six feet at the stern, headed out into the still Minch, the skipper looked at his cargo with some distaste. He had seen waves out here, he told me – we were now in the Stream of the Blue Men, looking this morning as neat as Hyde Park – as high as the mast out of the wheelhouse. 'We had to crouch down to see the crests out of the windows,' he said, 'and it was coming in, great lumps of water coming down below.'

John Murdo was painstakingly picking his way through the lambs, checking that none of them had slipped and fallen, suffocating under the others. He had lost three or four a year or so ago like that, and found them dead under the others' bodies. They were chucked overboard. I scrutinised the other shepherds and myself. We looked as if we had returned from another world: all the wool caught in the velcro of our jackets; our hands brown and greasy from the wool and the shit; our faces creased and tired; our bodies smelling of sheep, sheep sheep, sheep; and, hanging over it all, a certain air of triumph.

14

IN THE WATERY LIGHT of autumn the abandoned buildings on Eilean an Tighe, which in the mid-eighteenth century had housed the forty-odd inhabitants of the Shiants, are softened. Drops of rain hang on the blades of grass sprouting from their walls. One of them is flooded. Rushes and flag irises grow inside its single room like a salad in a bowl. In the spring-time, frog spawn thickens the water in the shadows. Now it is dark and dank. Other ruined houses, on higher ground, are drier and the sheep graze up and over them, along the tops of their wide walls and inside on the turf-covered floor, mowing them as carefully and tightly as a barber with his clippers, but the walls bow and stones fall out of them and the buildings are sinking back into the place.

It would have been different in the early nineteenth century. The old island community had disappeared in about 1770 and time would have had little opportunity to muffle and subdue the deserted houses. They would have looked raw and cold, empty eye-sockets in a bony skull, with the nettles on the muck heaps and the silverweed coating the derelict gardens. The islands would have been littered with reminders of the old ways of doing things.

A single family had been left behind to look after the stock. They probably lived down on the shore, near the present house, the beach and the sweet water of the well. To them, the islands must have felt empty and diminished. Evening after evening, talk must have turned to life as it once was 'when we were young', 'when the others were here'. It isn't difficult to imagine the circumstances. Life was arduous without friends or neighbours. The women and children had to struggle with the boat on the beach, with the spades in the ditches and ridges of the lazybeds, with anything going wrong and with the limitations of their own company, with no contact or friendship outside the constrictions of the family circle. Life on the Shiants, which for centuries might have felt like a blessing, would now have been like a prison. It was like a cloud closing over the sun.

In those early decades of the nineteenth century, the Shiants were exposed to a regime of callousness and stony-hearted brutality which is still remembered in Lewis and Harris. It is the first time in the islands' long history that individuals with identifiable characters emerge on to the Shiants' stage and the drama they act out is one of harsh economic facts, deprivation and cruelty. But the period is drenched in irony. Just as isolation and loneliness were making the Shiants a kind of hell, the first dreamy-eyed travellers from the south were coming to see the islands as a vision of earthly beauty. As the place became difficult and empty for the Hebrideans, it became beautiful and empty for outsiders. In the summer of 1803, James Hogg, the Ettrick Shepherd, a poetic autodidact from the Scottish borders, wrote to his patron, Walter Scott, from a ship lolling in the Minch:

> I remained on deck all night. The light of the moon at length prevailed. She hovered low above the Shant Isles, and shed a stream of light on the glassy surface of the sea, in the form of a tall crescent, of such lustre that it dazzled the sight. The whole scene tended to inspire the mind with

serenity and awe, and in contemplation of it I composed a few verses addressed to the Deity . . .

> *While viewing this scene with amazement and wonder,*
> *I see Thee in yonder moon's watery gleam.*

Even Hogg admitted these lines were 'sea-sick'. He got no closer to the realities but in about 1815, John Macculloch, the geologist, landed on them. At first he fell in love:

> They are verdant, being entirely covered with long rich grass; offering a delicious solitude, if suns would always shine and seas were always calm. If the Highland sea-fairies had been desirous of a maritime kingdom for themselves, I know not where they could have chosen a better.

But then he visited the one shepherd family on Eilean an Tighe, saw people clearly in crisis, and was revolted.

> We paid a visit to the shepherd, whose house we found, like that of all his countrymen, little calculated for elegant retirement at least; his arrangements, as usual, being such as neither to allow him to enjoy the advantages in his reach, nor to ward off the evils to which he was exposed. We turn with disgust from filth and darkness, and the more so when they are not necessary, when they might be avoided or remedied: nor is it easy to feel, argue as we may, that happiness, that any other happiness at least than that of a hog, can be found in the midst of privations and inconveniences, which the slightest exertion would remove. Turning from the loveliness of nature, from the bright sand and the fair rock, the enamelled green turf, and the sweetness of the summer breeze, it is difficult to view these things without a feeling of somewhat like anger at the barbarism which is placed amidst bounties and beauties that it will not enjoy.
>
> Cleanliness and order cost nothing. His floor need not be of mud; it need not, at least, be a collection of hill and dale. Nor need the outside be a collection of pools, and

rubbish, and dirt, through which he can scarcely gain access to his door. His windows may admit more light, and light is a standing enemy to disorder and squalidity.

The lease of the Shiants, and of Pairc with which they were included, had been taken by a group of new men from outside Lewis, led by Lachlan Mackinnon of Corrie near Broadford in Skye. One of Mackinnon's partners was his brother-in-law, the Reverend Alexander Downie, the minister in Lochalsh. James Hogg had in fact stayed with Downie on his tour, lapping up his 'excellent board, and plenty of the best foreign spirits . . . Besides the good stipend and glebe of Loch Alsh, [Downie] hath a chaplaincy in a regiment, and extensive concerns in farming, both on the mainland and in the isles, and is a great improver in the breeds both of cattle and sheep.'

He was, in other words, the sort of fat, laird-friendly minister against whom the church radicals would rebel in the middle of the nineteenth century. Three of the isles to which Mackinnon and Downie's improvements were to be applied were the Shiants. Their manager there and in Pairc was Donald Stewart from Perthshire, who in 1816 became tenant himself, and after him his two brothers, Alexander and Archibald.

The Stewart brothers are remembered throughout Lochs and Harris as horrible villains, handsome, arrogant, said to be descended from the royal Stewarts of Scotland. As Angus Smith of Lemreway heard it from Donald Mackay of Kershader, who had heard it from Uilleam Maol Donhnaich, known as Lodie, of Caverstay, who died in the 1950s, aged ninety, 'They were strong people and always wore the kilt. If they heard of anyone who had a reputation for being strong and tough, they had to see them, because they thought that they themselves were the strongest and toughest.'

'No, they weren't of the best, a bad, bad crowd,' Hughie

MacSween said when I asked him. That response to their name is shared all over the islands, a retraction in horror from their memory. 'You would not believe what was done here,' Mary Ann Matheson, John Murdo's mother said to me at supper one day. 'You would never believe what they said and what they did.' There is no sense here of wallowing in a picturesque history; only revulsion at wickedness.

The brothers and their servants lived in a fine stone house at Valamus, on the south-east coast of Pairc, nine miles or so from the Shiants, a beautiful place on the Eishken estate. I have been over there in *Freyja* and the ruins of the Stewarts' house, barn and quay, tucked in at the head of its own small loch filled with seals and otters, sit among their lawns and gardens in a vision of completeness and comfort. On a summer evening, you can hear a cuckoo in the surrounding crags and daisies grow on the deer-nibbled grass. It was from here that they dominated their world, keeping the lease of the islands and Pairc until 1842. Under their aegis most of the townships of Pairc were cleared and the people driven out to the villages of North Lochs and Balallan. The cleared area is now the Eishken estate. Its emptiness was the work of the Stewarts and their successors as tenants of the Pairc Farm.

'Valamus was the first to be cleared in Pairc,' Dan Macleod, the weaver and merchant seaman from Lemreway told me. 'It was the most fertile township in Pairc and once they had that, they began shifting people here, there and everywhere.' The Stewarts were big men and, Dan says, telling me this two centuries after it happened, as though it happened yesterday, his brows opening and closing with each turn of the story, a light coming into his eyes as he reaches the climax,

> if they saw a well-built man, they would challenge him.
> One time, they had a strong bull, a very wild Highland bull.
> They were evil people. They invited a strong man to come
> and see them from the local village. 'You better go and see

the new bull,' they told him. They got him into the building where the bull was kept and when they had got him in there, they shut the door. They heard the rumbling going on. And of course inside the bull was going for him. But he got a spade and with the spade he managed to get up on to the rafters. Then everything went quiet and they thought he was dead. They left it for a moment, to be sure, and then opened the door to see where his body was. As they opened the door, he walked straight out. 'Well,' he said to them, 'if you want to make any use of that bull, you better bleed him first.' No, they were very evil.

The people were driven out of many of the Pairc townships by the Stewarts. At the end of the century the sons of the cleared crofters, by then old men, still burned with resentment at their treatment. In June 1883, John Smith, from Balallan, giving evidence to the Royal Commission under Lord Napier, said that the people of Pairc had been 'dealt with as a herd of sheep driven by dogs into a fank.' He thought a hundred and eight families had been cleared from thirty-four townships, something approaching seven hundred people.

Nine years later, the Gaelic monoglot Alexander Maclennan,

from Marvig in Lochs, gave evidence to a second Royal Commission, examined through an interpreter.

> Chairman: Do you yourself remember when any part of the land [in Pairc] was occupied?
> Maclennan: I recollect seeing the men coming from there with their furniture. When they were flitting.
> Chairman: Do you know what was the occasion of their being removed from Park?
> Maclennan: In order to make it waste for sheep.
> Chairman: Was there a house erected for the Stewarts?
> Maclennan: They had a white house at Valamus, which was the principal house in Park at that time. Eishken is the principal house now.

These Royal Commissions were some of the most admirable instruments of liberal social policy in the nineteenth century, but they were formal and alarming occasions. The full loathing of the Stewarts survives more in the court records and the remembered slights.

Hughie MacSween told me a story, which, he said, 'still makes my blood go cold'. What he didn't say, but what I know to be true, is that the experience of uprooting, of being subject to the deep uncertainty of placelessness, and the power of the landlord to decide your fate, remains close beneath the surface. He and his wife Joyce and son Iain live at the foot of the huge glaciated valley of Scaladale on the borders of Lewis and Harris. Iain is one of the great sheep men of the islands, quicker than anyone in Harris or Lewis to identify which lamb belongs to which ewe at the summer gathering, and at the same time Head of Mathematics at the Nicolson Institute in Stornoway. The Shiants were his for the asking when Hughie retired. His father tried to encourage him. I have heard Hughie saying to him: 'I enjoyed every moment I was there.' It was no good. Iain doesn't like boats or the sea. He can just about cross Loch Seaforth to the island in the middle, but the Minch is another question. He ruled himself out.

Their house is on the shores of Loch Seaforth, opposite the rounded heights of Seaforth Island. Hugh's grandfather arrived in Scaladale from Scalpay in 1885 (the family had already been cleared once from the west side of Harris) 'because there was no room on Scalpay. He had to leave.' Scaladale, given the option, would be one of the last places anyone might choose. On a winter's day, it can feel like the end of the world. Cold winds funnel up Loch Seaforth and down from the cragged hills around them. The steep sides of those hills block out all sunshine from November to February, 'although,' as Joyce told me, 'we do see the sun over there on Seaforth Island.' By 1901, Hugh's grandfather had built them a big house, with byres behind it and they had claimed the place as their own.

It is this near-personal experience of uprooting and struggle which animates the stories of the Stewarts. Hughie tells them with the rolled cigarette between his fingers, the smile just beneath the surface of his long, expressive face and that half-questioning manner of talking, as if always waiting for the other to interject.

The pack of sheepdogs growls and grumbles around us and all three of the MacSweens growl and grumble back at them.

Hugh: Go on now.
Iain: Get down now.
Hugh: Get down with you.
Joyce: Out with you.
Iain: Get on out.
Hugh: Be quiet now.

The dogs are as much part of the family as the human beings: Meg and Gail who are both working; Phil who will work for Hugh but won't work for Iain; Barry who will only work with the sheep in the immediate area of the house and Penny who won't go on the hill at all; and Young Fly, who had a hysterectomy a year or two ago and now won't shed her coat. Joyce says 'she stinks as she's got two or three fleeces on her and she always will.' Young Fly is twelve or thirteen now, past anything. 'We don't like to put her to anything.' It was another Fly that went over to the Shiants, in DB Macleod's day, and jumped off the fishing boat to save some sheep stuck on rocks off Eilean Mhuire. This Fly's mother was Lassie Brown, who would work in the Shiants but not in Scaladale. They also had a Lassie Black at the time. She would work in Scaladale but not in the Shiants. 'We've never really trained the young ones properly,' Hughie says, looking at them like his children around him.

'The Stewarts are still remembered,' he says,

> for their cruelty and their shocking inhumanity. They were Skye men. They had a shepherd out in the Shiants and they didn't get on. They had quarrelled. I don't remember what it was. And I don't think I ever knew the name of the man. Eventually, there was a ram trapped at the back of the big island, at Tobaichean Caola, at the point near Stocanish. They set out, the shepherd and themselves, to go and pick it up. The shepherd went down on the rope, a long way down, on the rocks there, where they are cut into by the sea, and when he was well down they threw the rope away. They thought that was the end of him and they took to their heels. They thought that was it.

'So he died?' I asked.

'No, he didn't. He got back up, and they had shipped out. He would have killed them. They had tried to kill him and he wanted to kill them.'

. The story ends with a deep indraw of breath from Hughie. Disgust mingles with disbelief at the treachery two centuries old.

This was the world the tourists were gawping at, unaware of the criminal realities among which they were passing. William

Daniell, here in 1815 to make the sketches for his aquatints, found the place intriguingly gloomy. 'It is said that this cheerless spot is still the constant abode of a family;' he wrote insouciantly,

> but the only inhabitant we perceived on this visit was a shepherd tending some flocks. The isle, though to all appearances barren, produces exceedingly good pasture, and sheep thrive on it better than might be expected. It must be a lonely life for a man to dwell here for months together, with no other companion than his dog, and to be never enlivened by the 'cheerful hum of men', except at the periodical visitations of the kelp burners, who collect a very fair proportion of that commodity from these seemingly unproductive rocks.

In July 1823, someone finally dared take the bullies to court. Kenneth McIver of Kirkibost made his deposition:

> Archibald Stewart residing at Vallamus did wickedly attack Bett and brusd the pursuer to the effusions of his Blood kill his dog and disabled his boat by taking away the rigging for having landed with his boat to take shelter in one of the Chant Islands, till the storm would abate that he might proceed on his intended voyage to the mainland and altho the pursuer has often desired and required the said Archibald Defender to make him proper reparation for his outrageous conduct upon him yet he refuses at least postpones.

As in *Freyja*, the mast, sail, halyard and stays can all be taken from a boat very simply, by detaching a couple of hooks and removing them. Archibald Stewart wrote in his defence to James Adam, Chamberlain of Lewis:

> Valamus 23 July 1823
>
> Dear Sir –
>
> Kenneth McIver states that I have bett & bruised him in the Shant isles, but I have only defended myself he maintains

that I have disabled his Boat by taking away the Rigging. I did not deprive him of his Rigging but all such time as he would [not] give me his name in order to get him presented [at the court] for trespassing. I hard the dog barking through the Island before I could observe the Boat.

Also he states that there was a Storm at the time that is a falsehood it was calm I desired him to come to Valamus with me and that I would give him anything he wanted or to go the herds house in the Island which I can prove.

It is no defence. He does not deny beating up McIver, nor killing his dog, nor stealing the rigging. He was forced to pay fifty pounds' damages and twenty pounds' costs. In the same month, he had to pay the same again to Murdoch Macleod and Norman Macmillan, both of Eishken, for claiming that they had drowned one of his animals.

This is the degraded and brutalised world into which the Shiants had now entered: lies, violence, braggadoccio, attempted murder, cheating, bullying and an all-pervasive air of inhumanity. Donald Stewart had been accused of smuggling tobacco, when a boat of his containing a cask of it with no permit was seized by the Customs officers at Stornoway. Characteristically, he claimed 'the Tobacco had been taken on board without his consent or knowledge by a woman who happened to take a short passage in the Boat.' It was a forty-pound cask, not exactly a handbag-full; the Customs men at Stornoway didn't believe him and kept his boat 'with her Oars and Sail and the Tobacco'.

Conditions on the Stewarts' Shiants were dire. Macculloch had seen the poverty and isolation in which the shepherd and his family – so casually patronised by William Daniell – were actually living. In the late 1820s, the isolation proved literally fatal. There was only one family living here, in the summer months, but the evidence of who they were is contradictory. A family called Munro was here as the Stewarts' shepherds in the 1820s. Donald and his wife, Mary Mackinnon, had a son, Murdo Munro, born on the Shiants in 1829. He is the first islander born on the Shiants to have his name recorded.

Apparently overlapping with the Munros (an impossibility) are another family, the MacAulays. The shepherd despised by Macculloch may well have been Murdo Macaulay, *Murchadh Ban*, 'Blond Murdo'. He and his wife and family came to the Shiants from Bernera on the Atlantic side of Lewis. On arrival, at least according to a story remembered in North Lochs, Murdo made himself a coffin. Throughout their time there, it sat in the corner of the house by the shore. When asked why, MacAulay said that if he died, there was no one to make one for him 'as there was only his wife and young family with him.' Isolation distorts existence.

When Murdo eventually left the Shiants in 1827, his brother, whose name is not remembered, took his place there.

> Murdo's brother was in the habit of lowering his wife down the cliffs on a rope to gather sea fowls. She killed the birds and hooked them by their necks, into the rope around her waist. One day, whilst harvesting the birds in this manner, the rope broke, and his wife fell into the sea, where, because of the number of fowls hanging from the rope around her waist, she did not sink, but floated out to sea watched by her husband, who could do nothing to help her. And in this awful manner Murdo MacAulay's sister-in-law met her demise.

Seen by the Shiant Islanders themselves, these are, of course, desperate conditions. The single family here is debilitatingly alone. There is no one on whom they can call to help. When the horse-hair rope frays on the stepped rocks at Tobaichean Caola at the north-western corner of Garbh Eilean, where the Stewarts had attempted their murder, and where Mrs MacAulay has gone down to collect the guillemots that still cluster there in their uncountable thousands, there is no one who can help the husband out with the dinghy to save her. The children have been left behind in the house. They are too small to push the heavy boat down the beach. He can only watch as his floating wife is swept away on the flood tide into the Sound of Shiant, the two of them shouting to each other and the voices growing fainter until the wind tears the words away.

Few things on the Shiants have seemed more pitiful to me than the suffering of these stories, with families stuck right out on the edge of a viable existence. They are symptoms of modernity and of the death of community. These are aspects not of a profoundly ancient culture on which the modern world is at last throwing some light, but of a system drastically distorted by the change of the preceding decades.

In 1828, for an instant, the two Shiant worlds merge: an English traveller comes out to the Shiants in the company of one of the Stewarts. Lord Teignmouth was no ordinary tourist. As Sir John Shore, he had been Governor-General of India in the 1790s and for many years had been a leading member of the Clapham Sect, the group of powerful, cultivated, evangelical Christians, all of whom had chosen to live near each other in the small village of Clapham south of London. They were clustered around the central figure of William Wilberforce, and for decades they campaigned not only for the abolition of slavery but to ban bull fighting and bear baiting, to make gambling on lotteries illegal and to reform prisons. They were the first to advocate Factory Acts to improve working conditions for the poor and, at their instigation, Sierra Leone was founded to provide a home for refugee slaves. Its first governor, one of the Claphamites, was Zachary Macaulay, grandson of the Reverend Aulay MacAulay, the Minister of Harris, who had tried to arrest Bonnie Prince Charlie on Scalpay, and father of TB Macaulay, the Whig historian.

It may have been that Macaulay connection which drew Teignmouth north on the journeys he described in *Sketches of the Coast and Islands of Scotland*, published in 1836. When he came to the Shiants in the summer of 1828, he was seventy-seven and perhaps a little more gullible than he had been when younger. One has to look a little carefully through his mandarin prose to detect the truth behind it. Teignmouth and his companion, 'a gentleman of Ross-shire' had walked overland from Stornoway, an exhausting journey over 'one vast moor', before coming down to the house at Valamus, then occupied by Archibald Stewart.

Stewart sailed the ancient peer out to the Shiants and landed him on the beach where Kenneth McIver had been so brutally beaten and his dog killed five years earlier. Around the corner, they came to the shepherd's house. Here, uniquely in the history of the Shiants, Teignmouth gives an account of people at work:

> The shore of Akilly presents a striking contrast to the precipitous cliff of Garvailon: protected from the northern blasts by that island, it yields a considerable crop of good hay, which we found a large party of men and women busily employed in gathering in. The animating scene was exhilarated by the rays of a brilliant sun.

Can one really believe this bucolic picture? It is like a Stubbs in the sunshine, more Arcadia than Shiant. But there was a darker side to it:

> The industry of the workmen was stimulated by their desire to quit the island, as during their stay they have no better lodging than that afforded by a single cottage and an adjoining shed, the women occupying the former, and the farmer and his men the latter. The cottage is the residence of a shepherd and his family during the summer months, but they were preparing for departure, and no consideration could induce them to remain there longer.

Teignmouth, who had no Gaelic, heard this from Stewart. Was it true? Knowing what is known about the Stewarts, it is easy to see this situation in another light. Without doubt, the accommodation for the 'large party of men and women' was atrocious. Photographs taken by Robert Atkinson in the 1930s show the modern house on the site of the cottage which Teignmouth mentions. Behind it, still just standing, is the shed in which the farmer and his men stayed, half-underground, trogloditic, looking more like a yak than anything else, with a makeshift chimney and a fishing net thrown over the thatch to hold it down in the gales.

The women are crammed in with the shepherd and his family and the men – how many? five? – in the shed behind. But these are conditions which it is in Stewart's hands to improve. He could easily have roofed one of the other ruins here, but he chooses not to, presumably to save money and because he does not think his work-force deserve it. The people want to leave because Stewart is housing them in just the sort of cramped and verminous conditions which the newly industrialised work-force all over Britain was then enduring.

And what about the remark that 'no consideration could induce [the shepherd family] to remain there longer'? You can hear Stewart saying it, confidentially to Lord Teignmouth in his ear, one man of the world to another, how difficult it was to find good staff nowadays. It scarcely rings true. No consideration? When Teignmouth landed back on the Lewis mainland at Loch Sealg that evening, hoping for a meal from the inn there, he 'found, save a bowl of excessively sour milk, the negative catalogue complete.' They had to walk several hours to the manse at Keose to get any food. Famine was never far from the grotesquely over-crowded and under-resourced people in nineteenth-century Lewis and that has been true even within living memory. I know a woman living on the shores of Loch Seaforth whose mother used to say to her, 'At least you never went to bed without the next morning's breakfast in the cupboard.' Her father was a fishermen and for fishing families in these islands a literally empty cupboard was never an impossibility. There are Scalpay families alive today of which the mother has picked winkles from the shore to feed the children. It is is inconceivable in the 1820s that any man offered a paid job shepherding on the Shiants during the winter would not have taken it.

There was another reason for the autumn departure of the shepherds and, as Teignmouth sailed away that afternoon (Stewart himself stayed with the harvesters but his boatmen took the guest to Loch Sealg), he encountered it: 'We met on returning to the coast, a large wherry, proceeding to the island, to convey the shepherd and his family away after the harvest. No one can be prevailed on to reside permanently upon them.'

The large wherry was there to collect more than the shepherd. He and his family could have gone in a small Norwegian boat like Stewart's. The wherry was coming to take back the hay harvest itself to the beautiful stone-floored and stone-walled barn at Val-amus, which is still roofed and standing on the hillside above the loch. And why should the shepherd go back with the harvest? Because once the long summer grass has been cut, and the hay stacked and removed from the islands, there is no need for a shepherd. The shepherd's principal role is to keep the sheep from entering the hay. He is a human fence. Once the hay is cut, he is redundant and that is why he leaves. The truth is precisely the opposite of what Teignmouth had been told. It is not that shepherds refuse to stay on the islands during the winter. The Stewarts will not pay them to remain there. It is a seasonal hiring. The sheep that die over the winter, or as Stewart told Teignmouth, 'are lost, offering, as it is conjectured, an irresistible temptation to the crews of vessels passing', are nugatory by comparison. They will only return when the grass begins to grow in the spring-time. Meanwhile, they may or may not find employment over the winter on the Lewis mainland, where they will have to shift for themselves.

Sometimes on an early autumn evening in the Shiants, when the Minch can be as perfect and still as it was on the day of Teignmouth's visit, I think of that wherry making its slow and beautiful passage to Valamus. The hay is stacked high amidships and the big dun sail boomed out to one side. From a distance, it looks charming, absurd, like a pregnant heifer stepping slowly across the sea towards her byre. On board, the party of men and women and the shepherd's family are all lying on and around the hay, fiddling with the stubs of the sweet vernal grass between their teeth, joking, chatting, stretching with the exhaustion of their work, while in the stern, Archibald Stewart in his Highland dress, sitting there next to the helmsman, notebook in hand, is calculating future prices – the rent for Pairc and the Shiants that year is three hundred and twenty-six pounds – and all the other costs of dominance.

The Stewarts gave up their tenancy in 1842. They had moved on to richer pickings on the beautiful west side of south Harris, clearing people out of the township of Scarista, where the rich and flowery grazing of the machair stretches for miles along the Atlantic shore. The people left, either for Cape Breton in Canada or over to the acid exigencies of the Bays on the east side of Harris, where, cramped and hungry, they turned to fishing for the semblance of a livelihood.

On the Shiants, the new tenant was a grazier from the parish of Hawick in Roxburghshire on the Scottish borders, with the resonant name of Walter Scott, but no relation I think of the novelist. Scott did not bother with hay or any other crop on the islands. He was a sheep man and he would turn the place over to sheep. He left them there to graze unsupervised all year long. With no crops to protect, there was no need of a summer shepherd and for twenty years the Shiants were empty, visited occasionally for the sheep and called on by yachtsmen. In 1859 the antiquarian, TS Muir, looking for signs of early Christianity on the islands, found himself wandering over an abandoned landscape. He identified the church and chapel on Eilean an Tighe but on Garbh Eilean all he saw was 'a ruined hut here and there on its undulating surface ... indicative of a former population – shepherds only, perhaps, as there are no traces of cultivation.'

15

On a calm day, when the swell is not running too high, you can stand at the door of the Shiant house, and in the binoculars see the nearest roofed buildings. There are two of them, one above the other, stepping up the hillside away from a beach of big, white stones. The place, called Molinginish, is twelve miles to the west on the Harris shore. The entire settlement of about eight houses, the others still ruined, now belongs to a Stornoway lawyer, Simon Fraser. There is no road there and he uses it as a weekend and holiday place, walking in from the small village of Rhenigadale a couple of miles away. He is now the Shiants' nearest neighbour.

One lovely quiet evening, with the Minch as still as a metal plate, I took *Freyja* over there, motoring on the outboard and with a pod of dolphins part of the way for company. Simon Fraser had seen me coming, met me in his own boat just out from the shore, tethered *Freyja* on his mooring and invited me into the huge empty barn of a house, perhaps four times bigger than the house on the Shiants, for a glass of whisky. He is a tall, powerful, successful and confident man, an influential figure in the Western Isles, involved in many dimensions of its political and commercial life. In the half-dark by the fire, surrounded by his handsome sons and their beautiful, silent girlfriends, and walking around the crumbly paths of the settlement, scratching past the thorn trees that have sprouted between them, we talked – it felt a little strange, as if we were men in a club, although I was still in my survival suit from the boat and we were here, so far away from the world – about the others who had lived in our two places before us.

They were intimately connected. The family of Campbells who lived on the Shiants from 1862 until 1901 originally came from Molinginish and eventually returned there. For four decades, the journey I had just made would have been one of the central threads of the Shiants' life and it was through those Molinginish Campbells that the Shiants had one last, full and intensely female flowering before they were finally abandoned.

In 1857, the islands had a new tenant, a man called Mitchell Scobie. It may have been Scobie who wanted to reintroduce a shepherd to the islands. Fishermen had long been in the habit of stealing sheep from the Shiants. The Stewarts had told Teignmouth about it; there are stories from the late nineteenth century of guilty fishermen leaving a few pennies inside the skin of a stolen sheep on the beach between Eilean an Tighe and Garbh Eilean; Malcolm MacSween would later complain to Compton Mackenzie about it; and Hughie MacSween once saw a fishing boat put a dinghy out and head for the shore – 'I'm sure they were intending to grab something' – before catching sight of him and rapidly turning tail. Scobie may have wanted simply to protect his stock and reduce his losses. But there might, I think, have been another reason. Donald Campbell of Molinginish and his wife Catherine Morrison may have been desperate to go out to the islands.

Early in the nineteenth century, the Campbells had been cleared off the township of Telishnish, on the shores of West

Loch Tarbert on the Atlantic side of Harris. They drove their flocks overland while others of the family sailed their boats round by the Sound of Harris, and up to this stony place on a harsh shore. It was neither worse nor better than any number of places to which the cleared families moved on the shores of the Minch. 'They have a terrible sea to fish on,' James Hogg had said of the Hebrideans, 'and a terrible shore to land on.' That is true of Molinginish, where the ebb tide and contrary wind whip up a white mass of disturbed water in the bay and where arable soil is as scarce as on Mars. Here the women and children were sheltered by the shore while the men fished Loch Seaforth for herring.

The Campbells were a dynamic and fertile family. Donald had six brothers and four sisters. One of those brothers, Blond Norman, had eight children with whom he emigrated to Manitoba; one of the sisters, Little Mary, married a Morrison, had ten children and left for Quebec. The size of the Campbell flocks were famous throughout the island, and they kept goats and cattle too. Any girl marrying into this hotbed of fertility and energy might well have been in danger of submergence.

In the mid-1850s, Donald was about thirty and Catherine Morrison, from somewhere in Lochs, in her early twenties. They were married in about 1857. Two years later, their first children, Roderick and Marion, were born. They were twins and within a year they were dead.

In the autumn of 2000, on a long walk through the glens of Pairc, thinking about the Campbells, wondering why they should have come to live on the islands, when the current at the time was running so strongly against remote island life, I met, by chance, a woman whose life had also been dominated by the death of her son, when a baby, several decades before. She was old now, living on a croft from which no other light could be seen. Would I help her? she asked from the doorway as I was walking past. There was a tup in the far field, she said, and he was 'always after the ladies'. Could I move it into another field where it wouldn't be bothering them the whole time? She gave me a bucket full of sheep nuts to entice the animal into another enclosure.

I found the tup looking excitedly over his fence at the ladies, shook the bucket at him and he trotted after me. I then had tea in the scoured and empty kitchen of the croft.

'Where do you stay?' she said. '*Coit do'n bein sibh?*', 'Where do you belong to?'

'In England.'

'Where there is no God,' she said, with resignation.

'How do you know?'

'I hear it on the radio.'

Her husband had died. He was a tall man, as tall as me, and he died ten years before. At his peak he weighed eighteen stone, but that went down to twelve before he died. So was she alone now?

'No, I've got a daughter. I lost a son when I was eight months pregnant. She's asleep through there.'

'I'm sorry,' I said.

'You may be sorry,' she said, 'but you're not listening.'

'What do you mean?' The question opened the door to a monologue filled with the language of the pulpit.

'You're not listening to God. I knew God for the first time when I was just married. God was speaking to me and I wasn't listening. I wouldn't know him. I would not know him. God was saying, "The little man, he's not yours, he's mine, and I'm going to take him to me because he doesn't belong to you." And everything He was telling me, everything He said, that is what happened. The little man, Norman we called him, he lived just two hours and then he died. And that was right. Everyone needs to learn that God is high and you are low and that's God's way of teaching. That is what He did for me.'

I scarcely knew what to say. 'That's a cruel way of doing it,' I said.

'It's not cruel. Because that's what taught me. And still there is a place for him, for Norman, in this house now. If he'd lived, he'd be forty-six now and I wouldn't have had to send you for that tup.'

The family had endured a hard life. The husband had worked on the roads and she had done the farm. 'I was milking two cows for the house. There wasn't anything else. It was what we needed. He'd be doing the sheep and the lambs.'

She returned to her subject. 'You don't know God,' she said again. 'You don't know that He is high and you are low. And I will tell you this. The little man came back to me, little Norman came back to me, in a white raiment held in front of Him and I am going there to join him. All I must remember is to put nothing below me. Humility. I am low and He is high. That is what I must remember and I will join him there in Heaven. That is what God taught me. He taught me that by taking the little man. How old are you now?'

'Forty-three.'

'Ah well, by the time you're fifty, you'll be starting to think about it. Our minds are too small to understand, to know what the air is made of or what water is made of. We don't know because our minds are too small to comprehend it. And everywhere the Lord – you know what I mean by the Lord? – the Lord is a silent listener at every conversation. You can't understand that. You can't understand how the Lord can be everywhere at the same time. Our minds are too small to comprehend it.'

It is usual for outsiders to ridicule the fundamentalist Presbyterianism of Lewis and Harris and it is sometimes difficult not to laugh, out of surprise and embarrassment, if nothing else. I have attended a sermon in Lewis which began: 'Some of you here might think you are on this earth to enjoy yourselves. You are not. You are here to suffer . . .' Almost the only possible reaction is to shift a little in your seat and smile awkwardly beneath the unequivocal glare of the Almighty.

That is scarcely enough. This deeply conservative religion, with its sharp delineations between good and evil, its unequivocal sense of the reality of Hell and the goodness of God, whatever hurt and injury the world He created might impose on His followers, emerged as the people of the Hebrides and the Highlands went through the catastrophic social and economic crises of the eighteenth and nineteenth centuries. At a time when nearly all worldly sustenance was either stripped from them or was falling away under the influence of huge economic and political forces, the radical ministers of the Church were among the very few who stood by the people. As God's world killed the children, through famine, poverty or disease, God Himself, mysteriously and unknowably good, remained all-powerful, the only refuge and guarantee against a lost eternity.

The churches here, in other words, are a bastion against erosion. They are defensive structures, a form of retreat from the modern and an insulation against the wickedness of the new. However much they have argued and divided over the years, the churches hold on to their congregations because they give a kind of nourishment and support which the material world has often failed to provide.

After speaking to the lonely and troubled widow in her croft, and thinking of Catherine and Donald Campbell at Molinginish after the death of their twins in 1860, I wondered if the Campbells' move to the Shiants two years later was not also motivated by some desire for a retreat, to the insulation of island life, away from the damage which the world could work and incidentally away from the crowding presence of the other Campbells. The Shiants may have seemed to Catherine Morrison like a refuge.

For whatever reason, they went to the Shiants and for forty

years the family became identified with the islands. Donald was known as *Domhnall Mor nan Eilean*, 'Big Donald of the Islands'. He was said to have been 'a big strong man, hard-working and a thorough gentleman.' Catherine was the more austere and dominant figure, controlling the lives of her children. Soon enough, and certainly within five or six years of their coming to the Shiants, three of them had been born: John or Iain, who turned into a blond, powerfully built giant, a tremendous worker, who was also deaf and dumb. Hughie MacSween thinks it was John who cut the steps up the rocks from the beach on to Garbh Eilean. He had two sisters, Mòr or Marion, and Catriona or Catherine. And they were to become famous throughout Lewis and Harris.

The house they were occupying was, I think, not on the site of the present one, but just to the north of it and just south of the old graveyard.

It was later used by lobstermen from Scalpay and remained roofed at least until 1928 when, at the invitation of Hilda Matheson, Compton Mackenzie gave a slightly woozy-eyed talk about the islands on the BBC:

> You see that diminutive hut thatched with reeds, mind your head, the door is only four feet high. You had better sit down at once, or the smoke will make your eyes smart. It's rather dark inside because the only light comes from the hole in the thatch which is letting out the smoke. Gradually, however, your eyes get used to the dimness and you find yourself in a dwelling place that has grown as it were out of the island like one of its flowers. It is as genuine a product of environment as Robinson Crusoe's residence. It makes you a little impatient even of a tent. Every bit of wood used in the construction has been washed ashore on the island beaches – even the planks covered with rushes on which you are going to sleep. You might disdain your quarters at

first, but after you've climbed all over the islands you will be glad enough to lie down and sleep with the firelight flickering on the sooty thatch, watching the blue cloud of smoke above your head and pearl-grey Hebridean night through the only aperture.

There, for the first ten years or so of their Shiant life, the Campbells lived. They grew 'potatoes, barley and oats, cabbages and etc.' as Calum MacSween told Compton Mackenzie, and cut peats on the heights of Garbh Eilean 'but as to how he managed to come down from Garbh Eilean to House Island with a bag of peats on his back is a conundrum.'

Life soon improved. In 1870, the tenancy of Pairc and the Shiants changed again. The new tenant was Patrick Sellar, son of the infamous Patrick Sellar who was tried (and acquitted) for his cruelties in the Sutherland Clearances. This Sellar, who had mainland farms as well, would be pilloried by a string of witnesses from Pairc in front of the Napier Commission in 1883, but at least he did something good for the Campbells. He built them a new house, with two rooms and two garrets, a fireplace in each end and two large windows looking out to the Galtas and Molinginish on the Harris shore. It was in this house and its predecessor nearby that the Campbells sheltered the crew of the *Neda* when it was wrecked on the south-west tip of Eilean an Tighe in February 1876. All visitors to the Campbells speak of Donald's charm and courtesy. With generosity and warmth, he and Catherine looked after the shipwrecked sailors, and in particular the child that had been swept into the surf.

In June 1879, the naturalist John Harvie-Brown came out to the Shiants, hitching a lift on HMS *Vigilant*, a fisheries protection vessel. Harvie-Brown, thirty-five, enormously rich, charming, bearded, a bachelor, slightly asthmatic and a little fat, profoundly and invigoratingly fascinated by all aspects of the natural world, gives a sudden sight of the Campbells at home. With him was his friend, Matthew Heddle, Professor of Chemistry at St Andrews, the pioneer of mineralogy in Scotland, who was now fifty-one. Donald Campbell was now about fifty-three, Catherine forty-six, their son John nineteen and daughters Mòr and Catriona seventeen and fifteen respectively. On board the *Vigilant*, the two gentlemen, as Harvie-Brown wrote in his diary:

> reached the bay below the shepherd's house & landed. None of the Shepherds' family spoke English except the two daughters who spoke a little. The family consists of two daughters both uncommonly handsome girls. My fancy was the younger & I think sweeter-tempered and merrier of the two – Bella – Profr. Heddles fancy was the tall graceful dark haired black-eyed Spanish looking belle who would have graced any ball room. She certainly is one of the very loveliest women I ever beheld. Then there is a deaf & dumb son who afterwards assisted us and acted as our guide – a fine looking, strong fair haired giant, a little bonny girl – a younger sister – and the father & mother.

The little girl was in fact Donald's niece, Mary Campbell, daughter of Donald's brother Kenneth. She was here, extraordinary as this has always seemed to me, as servant to her uncle and cousins. She was about six years old. There is no need to imagine any sort of Dickensian cruelty but the idea of a maidservant on the Shiants in the 1870s – and she remained with them here until the 1890s – suddenly reorientates any primitivist picture you might have had. These beautiful girls, in a well-run household, in a modern house, with extensive vegetable plots around the bay, a professional father – he was away 'at the clipping' on one of Sellar's mainland farms at the time of Harvie-Brown's visit – with a capable and consistent concern for the well-being of others: this is not at all like Compton Mackenzie's peat-smoked vision of naturalness. This was modern civilisation alive and healthy on the Shiants. Life here was better than in the cramped and highly stressed conditions of either Molinginish or Scalpay, where by the 1870s five hundred people, cleared off good land in the north-west of Harris and the island of Pabbay, had been crushed on to an island which before the 1840s had supported two families.

The deaf-and-dumb boy guided Harvie-Brown on his ecstatic trip around the islands. 'Puffins breeding here and filling the air and covering the sea with their hosts. Compared with other rock stations of the Puffin I would fancy that the Shiants far surpass any other,' he wrote excitedly.

The gentlemen left the next day, 'after bestowing our little presents all round, and were rewarded by the bright smiles and thanks of this most interesting and kind family. Before leaving the Shore, I received a small collection of eggs of the various birds which are found breeding here, originally collected by the shepherds family for food.'

The beautiful Mòr and Catriona were, increasingly, trouble for their mother. Among the attractions for the Lemreway boys who drowned here in 1881 may well have been the prospect of spending an evening with the two uncommonly handsome Shiant daughters. Three years later, another yacht, the *Stella*, owned by Mr J T Marsden of Lancaster, called in at the Shiants. There must have been many other visiting yachtsmen but Marsden was known to Harvie-Brown, and a page from the *Stella*'s log is preserved among Harvie-Brown's papers. Marsden had a party of sporting London doctors on board: AK Gale, a surgeon from Fulham, Dr Atkinson from Kensington (known as 'Professor') and Dr RJ Reece from Bart's Hospital in Smithfield.

July 23rd 1884

Shooting and fishing is now the order of the day – puffins, Guillemots, razorbills, Kittiwakes &c falling to the gun ... Not waiting until the anchor was dropped, [an] eager party consisting of Reece, Gale, Professor, Skipper, and

Bobby [cabin boy] lowered the dinghy and rowed ashore, intent upon slaying many wild fowl and armed with guns, rifles, & revolver in a most formidable manner.

From information received from the book of sailing directions, we were under the impression that the islands (3 in number, but one is inaccessible), were not inhabited except by sheep: what then was our surprise to come upon first, a boat hauled high and dry upon the narrow neck of gravel connecting the two most southerly islands. It was much cracked and dried by the sun, and perfectly unsea-worthy and bore the appearance of having been out of the water a considerable time. Leaving this, and turning a corner of the rocks, we came upon a calf and a cottage and proved it to be used exclusively for cattle. Further on we came upon yet another cottage, and approaching it, we were met on the threshold by a colly dog who showed his teeth in anything but a friendly manner. The dog was followed by an ancient Gael [Donald was about fifty-eight] who kept us in conversation of a limited description (owing to his ignorance of English and ours of Gaelic). Evidently this delay was to enable his family to put their interior in order, for presently we were invited to enter by the Gael's wife [now about fifty-one] and two blooming daughters [twenty-one and nineteen] (the latter, by the way, the best looking lassies we have yet seen in Scotland). Milk was set before us. After a short chat of rather limited description, the party separated . . .

The ancient Gael was taken on board by the Skipper and treated to whisky and various cakes of tobacco, which made him almost dance for joy. Professor afterwards came on board and after rummaging several silk handkerchiefs from his locker went ashore again and presented them to one of the damsels aforesaid. She seemed inclined to hug him but was evidently controlled by the presence of her mother who never for a moment left her.

Nothing could be clearer: fierce attraction between the young English doctors on the hunt and these extraordinary island girls, their father's universal good will and good cheer, and in the background Catherine's anxious, overseeing, patrolling severity. One can only imagine the scene after the doctors have left, the silk handkerchiefs the object of Catherine's contempt and of the unfavoured sister's silent envy.

Harvie-Brown returned a couple of years later, this time on his own yacht, which he had called the *Shiantelle*, and with a photographer, William Norrie of 28 Cross St, Fraserburgh. They had come, Harvie-Brown wrote in his journal, 'in order to get a photo taken'. On 24 June, there is this note: 'Fog, fog, fog as we lay at anchor at the Shiants. With line caught Dab, landed and Mr Norrie took several photos of the Campbell family – the shepherds on the Shiants. Mr & Mrs C, their deaf and dumb son and daughters, a nice group.'

I have searched the world for those photographs. Harvie-Brown deposited his collection with what are now the National Museums of Scotland. Norrie's glass plates are likely to have been among the papers given to the museum but the curators cannot find them. There is some confusion between departments and accounts of a few 'clearings-out' of their holdings in the Thirties and Fifties. The Shiants photographs may have been thrown away then. There are some Norrie photographs in the Geological Museum in London, but any picture of the last Shiant Islanders is not among them. William Norrie himself died in South Africa, pursuing minerals, but there seems to be no trace there. The family then moved to America and William Norrie does have a grandson alive in Idaho, but the Idahoan Norrie has been ill and no one with an interest in the photographer has yet had access to what he holds. It seems as if those precious images, captured on a foggy June day in 1887, have disappeared.

Before Norrie and Harvie-Brown left, they gave the Campbells some presents and received others in return: '2 pairs of lovely stockings, a basket of eggs and a bottle of fine milk.' Those are the objects by which to judge the Campbell's life: knitting by the fire, chickens on the midden, the house cow, milk in a bottle, an exchange of presents, a sense of generosity, civility, beauty, industry and grace.

By then, though, the catastrophe which Catherine Campbell must have been dreading for years had already struck. Every winter, lobstermen came over to the Shiants from Scalpay to set their creels in the incomparably rich waters around the islands. Even into the twentieth century, there were so many lobsters around the Shiants that one boat from Scalpay in the 1920s caught sixty dozen in the space of a single week. I have spoken to a member of its crew, Bullet Cunningham. ('Why is he called Bullet?' I asked a neighbour. 'Because standing in his way was never thought to be that good an idea.') He can remember hauling up a creel at the Shiants with six fully grown marketable lobsters inside. 'Six of them snapping like there was no tomorrow.'

The nineteenth-century Scalpaymen were here for income and food. They took their lives in their hands in search of it. Only two years before the visit, a boatload of four young Scalpay fishermen, two of them Morrisons, had disappeared at the mouth of Loch Bhrollúm. Their eighteen-foot open boat had been overwhelmed in a sudden surge. Donald MacSween told me about it when describing the 'bad corners' of the Minch:

> There's a rock there, not so wide a channel as between Mianish and Sgeir Mianish on the Shiants, and the rock is not so high but you can just squeeze yourself in there and the theory is that they went in there, that day, a rough day, a bad day, and the backwash just caught them. There was another boat that got in that day ahead of them but they didn't get in and they only found the pieces of the boat, nothing more, not the men. That was a Morrison boat and

there was another boat disappeared not long after. They
didn't known where because they had gone for a week's
fishing and they didn't come back, and no one knew where
it was they were drowned but they think it might have been
there, because that is a bad place, a bad corner.

The mother of the Morrison boys searched the shore for weeks,
looking for their bodies, but found only a cap and the tiller of
the boat. Glamorous, charming, brave, healthy, strong, witty, sexy
men: is it any wonder that Mòr and Catriona Campbell fell for
them?

When William Norrie was photographing his 'nice group' by
the house, Mòr, the elder, then about twenty-three, was already
pregnant with a child, a girl, called Catherine or Kate, who was
born later that year. The father was a young fisherman, John
Morrison of Scalpay. Two years later, her younger sister Catriona
followed suit and gave birth to a boy, Donald. Her lover, unrelated
to the other, was another young Scalpay Morrison, Donald, a
fisherman. Neither man married his girl.

You can still hear a faint echo of the talk in Scalpay at the
boys' conquests. It's ribald enough. High on the south-east side
of Eilean an Tighe, at the top of the sea cliffs, not far from the
peregrines' nest, there is a rock formation, of the sort to which
people like to give names. A couple of boulders have fallen and
jammed into a cleft. From the sea, as you come round the point
of Mianish, it looks like the silhouette of a man with his head
slightly bowed and his penis stuck out in front of him. I have
heard that Malcolm Macleod, the Stornoway boatman, likes to
call it 'Adam Nicolson finding relief'. The name for it on Scalpay
remains, a little chillingly: *Iomall Tòn Catriona*, 'Catriona's arse'.

Not that Mòr or Catriona would have been that unwilling.
Songs collected by Margaret Fay Shaw in South Uist in the 1930s
are quite clear that a kind of excited sexual naughtiness was
common currency among Hebridean girls. 'Brown John,' one

love song begins, 'catch me, Brown John, hug me, / Brown John, catch me, before I make for the wood. / If you do not catch me, someone else will.'

Another is more explicit still, an invitation to rape, sung to Margaret Fay Shaw by Màiri MacRae of Glendale, then perhaps in her sixties. It might well have been a song the Campbell girls knew.

> *Did you see the modest maiden*
> *whom young Neil ravished*
> *on the top of a mountain on a sunny day . . .*
>
> *Alas, oh King! that I was not his.*
> *I would not shout out*
> *or cry out loud,*
> *though the bosom of my dress were torn.*

Mòr and Catriona kept their little children with them on the Shiants and the Morrison boys never married them. The Campbell girls, who would have graced any ballroom, remained spinsters all their lives. Illegitimacy was not unheard of but it was a source of shame. I have spoken to an old woman on Lewis about her own illegitimacy. She knows of her own half-sister, a teacher on Lewis, and has seen her and even spoken to her, but the teacher doesn't know that they share a father, and the illegitimate daughter 'will not trouble her with it.' She had never talked to her own mother about it either. 'I didn't want to drag it up again, not just to hear the story. What was the point of that?' And at the end of every sentence, as I asked her about this, she would say 'That's it', with a closing sigh.

Those, I guess, might have been Catherine Campbell's words too, an exhausted resignation, perhaps accompanied by an intensifying of control, perhaps a deepening of the anger. The women themselves were considered at fault. I have heard a story in Scalpay, scarcely repeatable, and certainly not with names attached, of a married man who was in the bar in Tarbert, being ribbed about his inability to father any children. 'It's not me,' he said. 'It's the wife.' The others doubted him and he walked out of the bar to prove it. He went to his wife's sister, a woman 'of easy virtue'. She duly became pregnant, had the child, his honour was saved and she was banished for the rest of her life to a house on the edge of the moor, away from the heart and warmth of the village, 'a terrible fate', as it is rightly considered on Scalpay today.

Not that the Morrisons disowned their children. Both Mòr's daughter Kate and Catriona's son Donald were accepted as Morrisons by their families and treated as such, although again I have heard people say on Scalpay that Kate, when she was an older and still beautiful woman, known as Kate of the Island (she had never left the Shiants until she was fourteen), would always be coming around to see her Morrison relatives, insisting, too much it was felt, on their blood relation, as if her island conception and birth somehow cut her off from a sense of belonging.

These beautiful and sexy girls out in the middle of the Minch, surrounded and besieged by the man's world of boats and danger at sea, exercised a powerful pull on the male imagination of Harris and Lewis. Stories still circulate there – and I don't give them much credence myself, in the light of Donald's character – of incest in the family, and of Kate and Donald as the products of incestuous union. Others tell with some relish of the girls rowing themselves across the Minch to visit their boyfriends on the opposite shore. It was what, I suppose, every man there longed for. Tommy Macrae, the keeper at Eishken, even told me that one of the Shiant Islanders, no name, had a lover in Crossbost, fifteen miles from the islands. It was, he said, just near enough for the boat to be carried up there on one tide, for a single kiss to be snatched from the girl, before the Shiant Islander, whoever he was, had to turn again for home on the ebb. Tommy Macrae also told me, with a face as straight as a die, that a sea monster had landed on the Shiants when the Campbells were there and had impregnated one of their cows, that a calf had been born, that it had 'been carried ashore' at Lemreway in Lewis and that every cow now to be found in Lemreway is a descendant of that calf.

My father, in one of those cross-generational meetings that seem to collapse the passage of time, met Mòr Campbell in Tarbert in July 1946. Calum MacSween introduced them. 'She is eighty-six years old, can neither read nor write, and speaks no English,' my father's diary says. There was not much beauty now. 'She lives in a one-roomed poor-house, crouching over a peat fire, or sitting at a distaff.' Her mother, she told him through MacSween, had not allowed her to visit Harris until she was nineteen, in the early 1880s. When there, 'she was very homesick for the Shiants and cried all day until she was taken back. When we got up to go, she laid a skinny hand on my knee and tears came into her bleary old eyes. She clearly loves the Shiants very much.'

One small object survives from the Campbell life of the 1890s. It was found by the naturalist and historian Mary Harman, author of a classic work on St Kilda, who was on the Shiants researching a book on other smaller, outlying Hebrides. Tucked into the stones of the kailyard next to the eighteenth-century house on Eilean an Tighe, she found the wooden hull of a small boat model.

It is a finely carved and subtly formed thing, cut out of a single block of deal, and beneath its lichened surface are the remains of one or two coats of paint, a fleck here and there, the black boot-strap at the water-line, the green hull above it, red below. I took the boat to Simon Stephens, the Curator of Ship Models at the National Maritime Museum. He knew immediately:

It's a Zulu, vertical stem, raking stern, double-ended. That is a classic Scottish Fishing Zulu. Invented on the east coast,

1878, something like that. When was the Anglo-Zulu war?
1879 was it? And what did Zulu mean? Something classy,
modern and outlandish I suppose. This one's been through
the wars. 'Weathered' shall we say? But you can see what
it is. It's the work of a fisherman or whatever, someone
who understood the boat.

This is the last of the Shiants' list of tutelary objects: the torc,
the hermit's pillow stone, the medieval brooch, the decorated
cragganware, the stone tools, the scrimshawed plate, the kelp
irons, the boat nails from the house roof and now this. Who
made it? It might well have been one of the Scalpay lobstermen.
Donald Morrison himself, Catriona's lover, may have carved it
for their son Donald. All the Scalpay boys used to have their toy
boats and all except this one have now disappeared. But there is
another possibility. The deaf and dumb John, in his thirties by
the 1890s, was well known for his skill in woodworking. It is
possible that the Zulu was made by the silent and indulgent uncle
for his small nephew, to play with on winter evenings or in the
summer when the family was up at the grazings on Eilean an
Tighe, keeping the flock from wandering down to the vegetable
patch and arable rigs around the bay, filling his boring hours
with this wonderful modern toy. Perhaps that was why it ended

up in the wall of the kailyard. Young Donald just pushed it one day between the stones, leaving it there – he was twelve in 1901 – and never came back.

At Easter that year, his grandmother Catherine died. She was about sixty-eight, by all accounts exhausted and saddened by the turn her life had taken, with her family – a disabled son, still referred to on Lewis as the *balabhan*, the dummy, two fallen daughters and their bastard children – held in a vice around her. Schooling had been compulsory for all five- to thirteen-year-olds since the passing of the Education (Scotland) Act in 1872 but no Shiant Islander had been near a school. They were not allowed away. Nevertheless, Catherine was undoubtedly loved and revered by her son John. He made a coffin for her out of driftwood, so perfectly, I was told by DR Morrison, historian and poet on Scalpay, that 'when the undertaker from Tarbert, Robert Morrison the joiner, was asked to prepare her for burial, all that was necessary was what they call the braid, the cloth for the body, and the handles for the coffin. Everything else, even just with the driftwood he had, John had made flawlessly.'

There are other signs, though, that Catherine's death was a form of release. As soon as she died, the family lit a fire on the beach next to the house, a place in which a flame is clearly visible from Molinginish, where their Campbell cousins were still living. Catriona's grandson, Donald Morrison lives in Tarbert. His father Donald was the owner of the toy boat and I have now returned it to him. He knew little of the life on the Shiants but had heard from his father about the urgency of their departure from the islands.

> The timing could not have been worse. It was Easter – it must have been Good Friday – and all the people were away from Molinginish and Rhenigadale at Tarbert, at the Easter Communion. They were there for several days and there was no one on the shore in Molinginish to see the fire they were making on the beach. And so for days they had to

wait there on the islands keeping the fire burning. It was only when they were coming back from the communion, walking on the path that comes over the hill to Rhenigadale and Molinginish, that they saw the light in the Shiants. It was then that they roused people on the shore and took a boat from Rhenigadale out to the islands and found that the lady had died.

Catherine's family left with her body in the perfect driftwood coffin and never returned. The urgency of their departure is strange. Donald Morrison did not hear any explanation for it from his father. Why should they have been in such a hurry to get away? Why did all of them leave on Catherine's death, when none of them had left in the previous forty years? The only explanation I can give is that she had been keeping them there. She had refused to go back to the Campbell enclave at Molinginish and had wanted to preserve the moat of the Minch between her family and the world. Her death released them and they returned to the other Campbells at Molinginish. There are buildings on the hillside there, pointed out to me by Simon Fraser, still known as the houses of Donald, John and Kate of the Islands. Donald died in Molinginish in 1910. John, the deaf and dumb giant, died there in 1937. Catriona had another illegitimate son Roderick and died in Tarbert in 1945. Young Kate worked for a gamekeeper on the Eishken estate at Mulhagery, just opposite on the Pairc shore. Every evening as she gazed out at the islands, which she had not left until she was fourteen, she is said to have wept at the loss of her home. Later on, as Mòr told my father in 1946, she went to keep house for 'an old gentleman in Edinburgh'. Young Donald became a merchant seaman. Mary Campbell, old Donald's niece, is said on Scalpay to have run away with a gamekeeper in Pairc. The memories of the Shiants slowly faded away and since Easter 1901, no one has lived there.

Catherine's body was taken by boat and then along the rough

moorland road to the graveyard at Luskentyre on the Atlantic shore. It would be difficult to think of a more beautiful place in which to be buried. The bodies of the cleared reclaim some of the good land in death. The bay is the colour of the Bahamas and the rollers curl in off the Atlantic. The sand blown in by the winter storms is spread between the graves like a covering of snow and the fine machair grasses poke their tips above it. The stones of the most recent graves are big, black slabs, with the names of people from the villages of the east side, Rhenigadale, Scalpay, Urgha, Tarbert, Geocrab, Flodabay, carved on them, but the most poignant of all these memorials are the earliest, scattered around a low hummock to one side of the cemetery. They are poverty itself, a flake or two of pink-veined gneiss, picked from the surrounding moor, neither polished nor engraved, but marks of a kind, articulate for their inarticulateness. Nowadays a thicket of roses is encroaching on this oldest part of the Luskentyre burying ground. Somewhere within it, where the wrens jump from one thorny stem to another, landing from time to time on the little stones, the body of Catherine Campbell is concealed.

16

I WAS ALONE ON THE ISLANDS again in the very last of the autumn. It was the beginning of October and winter was in the offing. I was waiting for the geese to return from Greenland. Every day, I would go up to the cliffs of Garbh Eilean with the binoculars, lie down on the grass there by the Viking grave, and look out to the north, hoping to see the moment when they would come back in, the flock wheeling out of the northern sky, fresh from Iceland and the Faeroes. It was cold and wet. The days had shrunk and I could feel the year closing down around me. The summer birds had gone and all the people had left. There were no yachts on the winter Minch. All the business of the year, the comings and goings of the experts and scientists, historians and archaeologists, shepherds and fishermen, was done with and at last a kind of silence had descended. The islands were empty now, in a state of suspension, and a powerful absence hung over them.

Back in the house, I sat over the fire and warmed my hands, while the dogs nuzzled their bodies next to me. A party of three shags flew low across the sea towards the beach and a family of eiders, all now grown, bobbed in the chop beside the black rocks. I looked out of the door at the cardboard-grey of the sky, felt the rain spitting at my face, went back in and switched on the radio. In a studio in Portland Place, a man I knew, an art historian, was speaking about EM Forster in Tuscany, the colour of apricots and the feeling of sun-warmed terracotta on the palms of his hands. Apricots would never have been eaten in the Shiants. Cherries would have been unknown. There was an orchard on Eilean Chaluim Chille in the mouth of Loch Erisort and apples might have come over from there. No plums, though, nor peaches or nectarines: only the unyielding substance of Shiant life.

I turned to the fire and scraped the chair a little nearer across the lino. In Gaelic, you can only say you are 'in the islands' not 'on the islands' and 'in' is the right word. The Shiants on days like this surround and envelop you. You are embedded in them, not perched on top, not the tourist but the occupant, as secret here as a puffin in its burrow or a man in his bed. I could pull the islands around me like a coat against the wind.

It was too late in the year for *Freyja*. I had taken her back to Scalpay a few weeks earlier. The weather on the evening before I left had been threatening, a cold southwesterly, driving the waves on to the beach. It had been a high spring tide and the sea had broken through the isthmus, as it does from time to time, so that the surf tailed out into the bay, where the gulls picked at it, looking for the little shrimps, I suppose, that had been washed out of the old weed on the shingle. I had my mobile phone with me – an innovation, as during 2000 a series of masts were erected in Lewis and Harris – and rang Rachel MacSween in Scalpay. 'Is that Adam?' she asked. 'In a muddle as usual?' It was. I asked her whether Donald, if he was around, could look out for me the next day. And perhaps take *Freyja* in tow if I was having difficulties on a lumpy sea? She said she would ask him. And she would see me that afternoon, 'with your dirty washing as usual. And you dirtier than it.'

As it was, the day was easy, and *Freyja* took a straight run in from the islands to the mouth of the Sound of Scalpay. When I was still a good way off, I saw a boat coming out towards me. It was Donald in the *Jura*. I had waited for the tide and it was now early in the afternoon. He been been fishing for prawns since four o'clock that morning and instead of going home to wash, eat and sleep, had come out to see that I was all right. 'That's you, Adam,' he said on the radio.

'Yes, Donald,' I said, 'I don't know how to thank you.'

'Ach, no bother,' he said, 'no bother, no bother at all.' With that, he swung the wheel and I saw the *Jura* ahead of me taking a wide sweep around on her own wake. We were soon alongside.

'How's it been?' I shouted up at him. He was looking out through the window of his wheelhouse, a tired face, with his crewman Donald MacDermaid standing outside on the deck.

'A desperate week,' he said. 'The prawns aren't there. You're all right though? Have you had a good time?'

'A wonderful time,' I said.

'Well, that's all that matters then. See you later.' He leant on the throttle and the *Jura* surged towards the Sound and the North Harbour in Scalpay, leaving me in her wake, wondering if anywhere else in the world a man would come out for you like that.

The twentieth century on the Shiants became increasingly a history of men at play. It was the holiday century where southerners with southern money came to entertain themselves in a romantic and deserted island. To begin with, a faint echo of productive use hung on. Lord Leverhulme, the Lancashire soap magnate, who bought the Shiants as part of Lewis in 1917, visited them three times. According to Neil Mackay, one of Leverhulme's employees who accompanied him, the Lord of the Isles first arrived at this remote speck of his island kingdom under a terrible misapprehension:

His Harris factor had told him that the islands were overrun by rabbits. 'Right,' said Leverhulme. 'I'll breed silver foxes there. Foxes eat rabbits and rabbits eat grass, so it will cost me nothing.' As they were approaching the island, I told him that he had been misinformed. There were no rabbits on the Shiants but large numbers of rats. Leverhulme was furious and on that occasion didn't even land but turned back for a dance in Tarbert.

All the same, despite these horrible inhabitants, there is a hint that Leverhulme might have loved the place too. After his death, very nearly the entire Leverhulme estate in the Western Isles was put up for sale, broken into lots. The auction was held on 22 October 1925 in Knight, Frank and Rutley's Estate Room at 20 Hanover Square, London. The Shiants were Lot 13. It was the first time they had ever been sold separately from the other 355,000 acres of Lewis also up for sale that afternoon. 'These interesting and rugged Islands,' the catalogue began a little waftingly, 'extending to an area of about 475 acres, upon which there are no buildings, but which are the haunt of numerous sea birds, are let as a farm to Mr Malcolm Macsween on a lease expiring Martinmas 1928, producing an annual rental of £60.' If that didn't sound very inviting, there was this specious worm dangled off the end: 'The rights of netting salmon in the sea *ex adverso* of this Lot are included in the sale.'

Both then and now, salmon are seen leaping in the bays of the Shiants about as often as a Blue Man invites himself aboard the Uig-to-Tarbert ferry. 'These islands are the breeding ground of hundreds of seals,' Malcolm MacSween later told Compton Mackenzie, 'and you know how salmon and seals agree to share a coast. "The former are always devoured by the latter."'

Perhaps the Shiants were made to sound deliberately boring because Lord Leverhulme's son had told the auctioneer, Sir Howard Frank, 'to see that he obtained this Lot. He desired for sentimental reasons to reserve this small portion as a memento of his father's interest and also because he was now Viscount Leverhulme of the Western Isles.'

Sir Howard, thank God, was incompetent. He recognised a man among the throng in the auction room and for some reason assumed he was bidding on behalf of the Viscount. He wasn't. He was a professional valuer, a fan of Compton Mackenzie, the novelist, and had instructions from him to bid up to five hundred pounds for the Shiants and no more, half of a book advance which had unexpectedly come Mackenzie's way. Five hundred pounds was little for an island producing sixty pounds a year rent, never mind the other benefits. 'The bids went in quick succession and I put in my top figure, and Sir Howard knocked it down to me.' There was a row but the sale had been made and Compton Mackenzie was now the owner.

Perhaps it is true of any island, but over the decades, from generation to generation, anyone who has known the Shiants has come to love them.

Malcolm MacSween to Compton Mackenzie

October 1925

Sir,

I write this note to introduce myself as I understand you are now my proprietor . . . I became tenant 4 years ago and I myself had a small offer on them, but was not extra keen on account of recent reasons I need not touch on at present. I have about 200 ewes on the three islands. But they are capable of grazing another 200; if I could afford to get them . . . I do not keep a shepherd. It is too lonely a spot for a shepherd. I couldn't get anyone to go. There was a shepherd on some time and the stone wall of the house is still as good as the day when he left . . . Only that one of the gables fell off a bit . . . I will await your further consignment of queries which I will be always pleased to answer. I am quite sure of this that you will really enjoy a trip to these ancient islands and any time you come I will make it my business that you will get out to them as comfortably as possible.

Compton Mackenzie eventually married two of MacSween's daughters, Chrissie, the elder, and, after her death, Lily, whom he had first met in Tarbert in 1925 when she was eight years old. He was a fervent Scottish nationalist and, as his biographer Andro Linklater has said, the Shiants were for him 'a talisman of Scotland'. As Compton Mackenzie wrote in an article soon after buying them,

> To most people, the Shiant Islands mean nothing. To some they mean the most acute bout of sea-sickness between Kyle and Stornoway as the MacBrayne steamer wallows in the fierce overfalls that guard them. To a very few they mean a wild corner of the world, the memory of which remains for ever in the minds of those who have visited their spell-bound cliffs and caves . . .

In the incomparable beauty of their sea, their rock and their grass – 'the bottle-green water at the base of this cliff, the greenish-black glaze of these columns, that lustrous green of the braes and summits . . .' – they were a link to his Mackenzie ancestors. He reroofed the house which the Campbells had left in 1901, putting corrugated tin over it, panelled the inside and used it for a day or two at a time to write. The Shiants is the setting for his two-volume novel, *The North Wind of Love*, published during the war, in which they are called the Shiel Islands. The hero, a Mackenzie-like playwright, John Ogilvie, builds a house (with a Tuscan loggia!) on Eilean Mhuire, called Castle Island in the book, from which he dreams of and plots for an independent Scotland.

At one point, Ogilvie/Mackenzie, suffering from acute Shiant-love, takes his daughter Corinna to a favourite place at the far end of the island from the house:

> There was one cave in which a great emerald of sea-water blazed in what seemed the heart of it, and from the roof enamelled with rose and mauve a slim silver freshet spurted forth to meet the sea-water in a perfect curve. And then as the boat penetrated deeper the air in the cave lightened and the sides danced with reflected ripples until presently it was seen that the cave was an arch leading to a beach so nearly hidden by great basaltic columns on either side that they had passed it in the boat unperceived.
>
> 'I don't think there can be anything so lovely as this anywhere, do you?' Corinna asked her father.

In his ginger suede shoes, his green check suit, his pipe, his posed stance in front of the fireplace, with the writing room in his house in Barra wallpapered in gold and his dazzling ability to write a novel while listening to a record he was reviewing for the magazine *Gramophone*, Mackenzie bewitched the Hebrideans. The Shiants have never known a man like him. But it was this theatrical egotism, allied to the obsessive habit of moving from one island to another, from Capri to Herm and Jethou in the Channel Islands, on to the Shiants (via an unsuccessful attempt to buy Flora Macdonald's house at Flodigarry on Skye) and then Barra, which lay behind an attack made on him in 1926 by DH Lawrence. The Nottinghamshire apostle of candour and intimacy would never have condoned the play-acting, self-aggrandisement and self-regarding island-love to which Compton Mackenzie was prone. 'The Man Who Loved Islands' was a scarcely veiled attack on Mackenzie for which Mackenzie never forgave Lawrence. The story is the only moment a writer of world standing comes any-where near the Shiants: 'There was a man who loved islands. He was born on one but it didn't suit him, as there were too many other people on it beside himself. He wanted an island all of his own: not necessarily to be alone on it, but to make it a world of his own.'

The love of islands, the story maintains, is a neurotic condition. They are not so much islands as I-lands, where the inflated self smothers and obliterates all other forms of life. The story ends with the Mackenzie-like figure contemplating what had once been his beautiful private landscape now dead and sterile under drifts of egotistical snow. The place had died at the hands of an imposed personality.

It is not a great story, too much the working out of a theoretical type, but it is a symbolic moment in the history of the Shiants and it marks a change in the history of attitudes towards islands. In the early eighteenth century, to Robinson Crusoe, for example, an island was in some ways a prison, a symbol of his suffering, divorced from the company of men, full of hostilities which his own energy and enterprise must struggle to overcome. An island was a reduced form of what the world could offer.

By the middle of the eighteenth century, that view had begun to change, largely at the hands of one man. The grandfather of the modern love of islands, of all those visitors to the Hebrides, of Robert Louis Stevenson and Gauguin, is Jean-Jacques Rousseau. It was Rousseau who invented the idea that islands were not some-how less than what the world could give you, but the most perfect of places in which the solitary self could flower.

In the autumn of 1765, Rousseau went to live on the tiny Ile St Pierre, set in the Lac de Bienne in northern Switzerland. He had recently been stoned by religious conservatives in the Swiss village of Môtiers, and on the tiny island, where there was a farmhouse, his paranoias and fears were calmed. He felt secure within those visible shores. He botanised with patience and care and had a plan to write a book about this most precious and protected place. People might mock, he thought, but love of place could only attend to minute particulars. 'They say a German once composed a book about a lemon-skin,' he later wrote. 'I could have written one about every grass in the meadows, every moss in the woods, every lichen covering the rocks.' The Ile St Pierre was the Eden away from society that he sought:

> I was able to spend scarcely two months on that island, but I would have spent two years, two centuries and the whole of eternity without becoming bored with it for a moment. Those two months were the happiest of my life, so happy that they would be enough for me, even if they had lasted the whole of my life.

That was probably Compton Mackenzie's view of the Shiants too. But Lawrence's point is the modern and post-Freudian one: the healthy state is social; isolation is aberrant; and islands represent a withdrawal from the mainstream where in some ways it is our duty to remain. This is a return to the early-eighteenth-century view that uninhabited islands, and other stretches of empty country, are places which would be better off occupied, used and made social. In Scotland, because of the continuing resonance of the Clearances, this remains a power-fully held position: the cleared is the wronged; empty land is an insult to society; privacy is an indulgence of the powerful; there is no distinction between 'land' – the acres – and 'Land' – the nation; and in that coalescence the land clearly should belong to all. It is inconceivable nowadays that a Scottish Nationalist would proclaim his private ownership of the Shiants in the way Mac-kenzie did. He would have transferred it to the community many years ago.

Eventually, Compton Mackenzie had to get rid of the Shiants for more mundane reasons. His finances had been chaotic for years and finally, in 1936, to assuage the bank manager and the Inland Revenue, he had to sell the islands. Malcolm MacSween was in (slightly befuddled) mourning when Colonel MacDonald, DSO, of Tote in Skye offered himself as a purchaser.

Malcolm MacSween to Colonel Macdonald, May 1937

> Mr. Mackenzie never charged me for rent. But of course Mr. Mackenzie's equal is not to be found in Scotland. No more than is better than his island's grazing is to be found. He is and was the best friend I ever had.

Mackenzie squeezed fifteen hundred pounds out of Macdonald, whose elaborate scheme involved the intermittent transfer of horses, sheep and cattle between the Shiants and a farm on Skye. It was never realistic and within a matter of months he readvertised them. My grandmother, Vita Sackville-West, wrote to her husband Harold Nicolson:

> I've got another activity in view: three tiny Hebridean islands for sale, advertised in the *Daily Telegraph* today, 600 acres in all. 'Very early lambs. Cliffs of columnar basalt. Wonderful caves. Probably the largest bird colony in the British Isles. Two-roomed cottage.' Do you wonder? I have written to the agents for full particulars and photographs. They cost only £1,750.

She sent those details to my father, Nigel Nicolson, who was then at Balliol aged twenty, having just inherited some money from his grandmother. He was as drawn to them as Vita had been and that summer he visited them for the first time. His mother would not let him stay the night, frightened that he would be trapped there by storms, and so he had a single day in which to make his decision. He fell in love with them on the spot. As he wrote in his autobiography, *Long Life*:

> I loved their remoteness, isolation, grandeur. Was it romanticism or melancholy? Both, added to an atavistic desire to own land in the Hebrides (the Nicolsons were originally

robber-barons in the Minch), to have an escape-hole, to enjoy nature in the wild . . . On me the difficulties of access to the Shiants acted as a magnet, on others as a deterrent. There would be some danger in total isolation – cliffs, tides, illness – when there was no form of communication to summon help. Of this I would boast, magnifying the risks. Looking back, I recognise an element of arrogance in my island mania. I would be different from other undergraduates. I would be the man who owned uninhabited islands and marooned himself there alone.

He would, in other words, be The Man Who Loved Islands, as I have been and no doubt as Tom will be. It is not, I think, something to be ashamed of. The growing sense of your own capacity to survive and thrive in a difficult environment; to handle a boat in strange and disturbing seas; to look after yourself with no crutch to lean on: all of these experiences are wonderful for the kind of immature young men my family seems to produce. But one grows out of it and moves on to other things. Perhaps, I now think, the love of islands is a symptom of immaturity, a turning away from the complexities of the real world to a much simpler place, where choices are obvious and rewards straightforward. And perhaps that can be taken on another step: is the whole Romantic episode, from Rousseau to Lawrence, a vastly enlarged and egotistical adolescence? And one last question: is this why women tend not to like the Shiants? Because they are so much more adult than men?

At a loss of a hundred pounds to Colonel Macdonald, the Shiants were finally transferred to my father and he spent the month of August 1937 there on his own. He nearly drowned, when a collapsible canoe did indeed collapse halfway between Eilean Mhuire and Garbh Eilean but that wasn't the only catastrophe. His supplies had been sent up by train from Fortnum & Mason – it was a different world – in smart, waxed cardboard boxes. They were delivered to the quayside in Tarbert. From there they were loaded onto the fishing boat and on arrival at the Shiants offloaded on to the beach. My father waved goodbye to the fishermen, who said they would return in a month's time, carried the boxes to the house and began to open them. As he folded back the cardboard flaps, he found a neatly typed note from the Manager:

Dear Mr Nicolson,

Please find enclosed the supplies as requested. Unfortunately, due to Railway Regulations, we are not permitted to dispatch flammables by rail and therefore have not been able to include the safety matches you requested. Trusting this will not be of any serious inconvenience, we remain,
Yours etc. . . . .

Faced with the prospect of a month without a fire, my father dismantled his binoculars and with one of the lenses managed to focus a few rays of the watery Hebridean sun on to some dry bracken. Somehow a flame sprang up and he carried it between cupped hands to the fireplace in the house.

For the four weeks he would have to nurture the fire like a dying lamb, returning to it at least once every two hours to see that its heart still beat. All went well, until one day returning from a walk on the heights of Garbh Eilean, he was horrified to see from above that a yacht had anchored in the bay and a party from it was picnicking on the beach between him and the house. If he was to get back to the fire, whose thin grey thread of smoke he could just see trickling upwards from the chimney into the sky, he would have to pass the picnickers. That in itself would not have been so bad if he had been wearing any clothes. He wasn't. It was a 1930s habit to walk about in wild places undressed.

Unobserved from the beach, he waited crouched behind a rock for the picnickers to leave. They were having a marvellous time.

Sprinklings of laughter came drifting up to him. The young men and women in their yachting skirts and blue jerseys lay back on the warmth of the shingle. The hours went by. The trickle of smoke from the chimney had thinned to invisibility. There was nothing for it. Dressed only in what he describes as 'a apron of gossamer fern' my father strolled with as much dignity as he could, past the picnickers and on to the house where with flooding relief he could dress himself and restore his faltering fire to life.

The following year, he invited a friend from Oxford, Rohan Butler, to the Shiants and although Vita never came to the islands, his father and his brother Ben hired a ketch to visit them. Harold wrote in his diary that night:

> We cast anchor. We get into the dinghy, and hum along the placid waters, and all the puffins rise in fury. As we approach the beach, two figures run down to it. Nigel and Rohan. We walk round to his little shieling. Niggs is glad to have a day like this to show me his romance. It is like a Monet, all pink and green and shining. I have seldom in life felt so happy. After lunch, we go round the islands in the dinghy. The cliffs are terrible and romantic. We sing for the seals and they pop up anxious little heads. It is lovelier than can be imagined.

The Shiants have never quite been what others have imagined. 'Islands in Scotland', mentioned like that in London, the words tossed away at a party, as the cigarette ash is brushed from the sleeve, always sound too comfortable. You can see the illusion in your listeners' eyes, the warm air, the distant horizons, the polychrome sunsets; they are imagining a glass of old malt in a deep armchair, bannocks in the tin beside the bed, a blue tweedy atmosphere, perhaps a hint of Scottish baronial. Anyone who has persevered this far will know by now that the Shiants are not quite like that. And the rats don't help.

It seems at times my father may have suffered from this very delusion. It came to an abrupt end in the summer of 1946. He had decided to invite two of London's most glamorous girls to the Shiants. Both Lady Elizabeth Lambart and Margaret Elphinstone, the daughter of an Invernesshire grandee, were beautiful. Both were grand and both would be bridesmaids at the wedding of Princess Elizabeth the following year. Margaret Elphinstone was the niece of the Queen. What can have been in Nigel's mind?

He arrived a week before they did to tidy up. The weather was filthy. 'I found the house in quite a good state,' he wrote bravely in his diary, as the rain slashed around him. 'There are a lot of holes, some made by the rats and some by the weather. You can see right through the ceiling and roof in the other room and the door is off its hinges. The stove has rusted to bits and has been thrown outside.'

Day after day he washed, scrubbed and painted. The sound of

scurrying rats accompanied his 'scrubbage programme', skittering across the rafters, sliding down between Compton Mackenzie's panelling and the wall, stealing his cheese at night. The clean-up was not a success. 'Scrubbing is a beastly job,' he wrote in the diary. 'One makes circular sweeps with the brush, expecting to clear a path of cleanliness with the soap, but all it does is leave a soapy smear, and soon one's other cloth becomes so dirty that it simply re-dirties the floor. I clearly haven't got the technique right.' The rats were so disturbing that he decided to erect a tent in which the girls would be put to sleep at night. He turned for consolation to Harold J Laski on *Liberty in the Modern State*, reading about the coming disintegration of the capitalist system by the light of a guttering flame.

Malcolm MacSween had forgotten to put a tin opener in with the supplies. He tried opening the cans of soup with an axe, but it spoiled both axe and soup. Within three days, the fresh meat, bacon and eggs started to go bad. Nigel threw them away. That left him with 'potatoes, oat-meal and bread as my main diet. There is enough of all of this to last a fortnight.' No doubt the girls would love it. He started to poison the rats and within a day or two thought that the poison was working so well that the girls could sleep in the house itself. If they noticed the holes in the skirting board, he would tell them that once, many, many years before, there had been a plague of rats. But wasn't everything lovely now?

Doubts continued to haunt him. What if the grown-up rats had died, leaving their little babies behind who would spend all night squealing for their mothers? What if the grown-up rats had died but in the house? The girls would never have been exposed to such smells. Everything else, apart from the weather, seemed to be all right. He had washed all the pots and pans again, boiled the cloths, painted the windows and laid a small gravel terrace outside. At least at first sight, Number One, The Shiants would look welcoming. But behind this sweet facade lay the terrible anxiety. He should never have asked them.

The night before the girls were due, he thought he should sleep in the room he had prepared for them, if only to accustom the rats to the idea that this was not their playground but a place fit for human habitation. He woke up in the early hours, as the summer light was leaking in through the window. A rat was sitting on his bed looking at him. 'I shall simply have to warn the girls.'

They arrived. He toured them round the sights. He gave them some of his oatmeal, bread and potatoes. They went to bed at midnight. At half-past three in the morning, Nigel, on the camp-bed in the other room, heard them screeching with horror. A rat had got inside the chest of drawers he had installed for their change of clothes in the morning. It was running up and down the nearly empty drawers like a tap dancer in paradise. Nigel – social mores were different then – asked through the door whether he could do anything to help. 'No, no!' they shrieked. 'If you let it out, it'll run all over us.' They spent the rest of the night awake, shaking, hidden under their blankets.

The calamity wasn't yet over. The wind and tide had got up in the night. Nigel, in his anxiety, had forgotten to tie the dinghy to the mooring ring in the rock on the side of the beach. (It happens to us all: I have lost two boats like that; Hughie Mac-Sween lost one, which he watched floating away from the islands, only for it to be picked up by a fishing boat and delivered back to him at the end of the week.) No such luck for my poor father. The dinghy had been swept away and then smashed on the rocks of Eilean an Tighe.

When the fishing boat arrived to pick them up the next morning, there was no way of reaching the boat from the shore. Nigel entered the freezing waters of the Minch, swam out to the boat and returned to the beach with a rope. Elizabeth and

Margaret stood waiting in their floral prints. Nigel tied them on, one by one, and they swam out towards the herring drifter, speechless with cold, while their skirts spread like peonies around them.

Nobody knows when the rats arrived. In 1925, Malcolm MacSween told Compton Mackenzie that they 'came ashore from a Norwegian ship' twenty years before, but there was no wreck on the Shiants then. In January 1876, the Newcastle barque *Neda* had been wrecked on Eilean an Tighe and on 13 February 1847, the Norwegian schooner *Zarna*, of Christiansund, was wrecked here, perhaps on Damhag, en route to Norway from Liverpool with a cargo of salt. The crew somehow managed to get ashore, salvaging two sails, 'with which the Seamen contrived to make a tent for Shelter.' The rats may have come on either of those ships, or neither. They may have been here ever since ships began to ply these seas in any number in the eighteenth century. 'Since the great rat took possession of this part of the world,' Dr Johnson heard on Skye in 1773, 'scarce a ship can touch at any port, but some of his race are left behind. They have within these few years began to infest the isle of Col.'

Twentieth-century life on the Shiants has certainly been intimate with the rats. Bullet Cunningham, lobster fishing here before the war, was staying in one of the old bothies.

You saw the old thatched houses we were staying in? Some of the walls are up yet. The rats there, I was dead scared of them. My father and the others, a very regimental man he was, he went out one day to lift the creels and left me to do a bit of cooking. And I was going to cook potatoes and some herring for dinner for them coming home. I boiled the herring, the herring was ready and all things like that ... and I was just going to get the potatoes ready and I saw a rat coming through the holes in the walls – a rat like that

– and as soon as I saw that I got dead scared and I just ran out of the house and left the pot on the fire. My father came home and of course none of the dinner was cooked and my father came home and when he saw and I told him what had happened, do you know what he said? 'There's not a rat in the world quite as rat-like as yourself.'

The rats have a reputation. Tell anyone in Lewis or Harris that you are going out to the Shiants for a week and a distant, quizzical note enters the voice. 'Ah yes,' they say carefully, as if you had announced that your next holiday was to be in Broadmoor, 'and what are you thinking of doing about the little creatures?' Malcolm MacSween put some cats on here, but it is said in Harris that the rats ate them too.

The rats are certainly horrible things, mostly, I think, for their lack of fear. When the house has been full of shepherds, I have slept on the floor and woken up with one a yard from my face. It looked at me quite undauntedly, even when I jumped and shooed it. We have poisoned them consistently, year in, year out, but only around the house and that has had no effect on the wider population. They are on all three of the islands and are thought to number about three thousand. They can breed when they are three months old and produce four or five litters a year, each with between six and twenty-two babies. The reproductive potential is spectacular. With an unlimited food supply, the three thousand Shiant rats at the beginning of the year could, mathematically, have multiplied to something like 1.8 million by the early autumn. They don't because life here is a desperate struggle.

They are not the rats you find at home in the barn or the sewer. Those are brown rats, *Rattus norvegicus*, relatively large, relatively aggressive and relatively horrible. These are *Rattus rattus*, the ship, black or plague rat, originally from South-East Asia and now one of the rarest mammals in the United Kingdom. Because the brown rat is bigger and stronger, there are very few black rats left. Only on the Shiants and on Lundy do they exist in any number.

This is a glamorous status. The Shiant rat is now infinitely rarer than, say, the puffin, which may well be Britain's commonest sea bird. As a result, a string of rat investigations have been made in the last few years. Margarine-coated sticks have been stuck in the soil at intervals across the islands to see where the rats lived. (A nibbled stick meant a rat.) The unsurprising result was that every stick was nibbled. Rats have been caught to see what was in their stomachs. (A mixture of things from shoreline crustacea to moss and grass.) Most eccentrically of all, an English biologist received a grant to find out where the rats went on their nocturnal wanderings.

The interesting question, though, is how the rats and the birds manage to coexist. Why haven't the rats wiped out the birds? The answer is a vindication of the puffins' strategy. The birds are here only from early April to mid-August: four and a half months. While they are, the rats make hay. (Evidence from elsewhere has shown that a rat can kill an adult puffin.) But it seems as if the rats can't make sufficient impact on the bird population before they leave for the Atlantic. Come late August, the rats are suddenly proteinless and in all likelihood the population crashes. It is just then, incidentally, that the pressure of the rats on the house, which they seem to neglect for the summer, becomes most intense. Winter starves hundreds if not thousands of the black rats and so keeps their predation on the birds to a level at which a kind of equilibrium is reached. It has been different where the bigger brown rat has preyed on sea birds. On Ailsa Craig, and other brown rat-infested rocks, the rate of predation, which must be slightly higher, has sent the bird numbers irrevocably downwards. So the Shiants have a rat-puffin balance, if a fine one. We shall never rid the islands of the rats and the rats will never rid the islands of the puffins. It wouldn't take much to change this, though, and there is one thing everybody dreads: the arrival of a pregnant mink. It might kill the rats but it would also decimate the birds.

The one difference which the twentieth century made to the Shiants was the idea that they should be 'conserved'. The shoulders of what Hughie MacSween once described to me as 'our beloved Islands' now sag beneath a heavy load of modern conservation labels. They have been designated under a succession of governments as a Site of Special Scientific Interest, an Area of Outstanding Natural Beauty, a Special Protection Area, a Nature Conservation Review Site (Grade 2) and a Geological Conservation Review Site. Most recently, under the European Community's Birds Directive, they have become part of the Natura 2000 Network. It all reminds me of some ancient military personage: Admiral of the Fleet Lord Shiant of the Minches SSSI AONB SPA NCRSii GCRS EcN2000. He staggers under the honours he wears. Every February, I am obliged by law to tell the Land Management Administrator of Scottish Natural Heritage, the government's conservation agency, at their North-West Regional Headquarters Annex in Inverness, exactly what I have been doing with the place.

1. Information and expenditure [actual and planned]
2. Details of maintenance [completed and outstanding]
3. Information on any positive works undertaken to safeguard the interest of the site

and finally, the one that is more pleasure to answer than any other:

4. Details of access arrangements including for pedestrian access only.

There was one occasion when SNH wrote to me asking what kind of vehicular access there was to the site. As it is, the answer to all the questions is always the same: 'No change.'

At one moment in the early 1970s the conservation movement reached out its long acquisitive hand towards the islands. I have the letters on file and I read them now with an amazement at the arrogance they display. They begin with a letter from George Waterston, the Scottish Director of the Royal Society for the Protection of Birds, the RSPB, one of the most powerful and rich of all British conservation organisations. It is addressed not to my father but Colonel Sir Tufton Beamish, President of the RSPB.

23rd March 1970

Dear Tufton,

The Shiant Islands

This very interesting group of small islands lie some 12 miles north of Skye and about 5 or 6 miles east of Lewis.

The islands comprise a most important seabird breeding station; and when I landed there many years ago with James Fisher (from a National Trust for Scotland Cruise) we found vast numbers of Razorbills and Puffins nesting.

There is an attractive small bothy near the landing place at Mol Mor between Garbh Eilean and Eilean an Tigh. It seems to me that the group of islands would make a most attractive Bird reserve, and I wondered whether you could approach the proprietor, Mr Nigel Nicholson, MP?

My hackles rise even thirty years later. Why did George Waterston think that he could do things here any better than we could? Beamish, an old friend of my father's, sent the letter on with a fair wind.

27th March 1970

You could be confident that we would take sensible and active advantage of an opportunity to make a bird reserve on the Shiant Islands.

My father replied, asking what the RSPB would like to do with the Shiants. He had no answer for two and a half years. He then received a long letter from George Waterston's successor as the head of the RSPB in Scotland, Frank Hamilton, explaining what they had in mind. Nigel would have to agree not to alter or develop the Shiants without consulting the RSPB. He would also 'agree subject to consultation' to various improvements such as 'tree planting, provision of water flashes, erection of hides for public viewing etc. etc. These are not necessarily suggested for the Shiants, they are merely an illustration of the sort of things sometimes included in an agreement.' Mr Hamilton also suggested that the RSPB should be responsible for visitor control. That is what had happened on the island of Handa off the Scottish mainland, where a management agreement had been put in place and where the news of the RSPB's involvement had resulted in an increase in the number of visitors:

> Numbers have gone up to such an extent that a summer warden has become necessary to control and to mitigate damage both to the wildlife and the habitat. And the way we have done this in that particular case is to lay out a definite path to which we ask people to keep, thus ensuring that 'delicate' areas are protected. It is not uncommon for us to develop such a path as a nature trail giving visitors information about particular points of interest.

Finally, with some delicacy, Frank Hamilton brought up the slightly longer-term question:

> Legal ownership would in no way be affected, although you might, if you felt it worthwhile entering into such a management arrangement, consider the possibility of writing in a provision for the Society to be given the first option to purchase in the event of your deciding to sell.

Something in Mr Hamilton's description of the RSPB's vision for the Shiants produced a response from my father for which I shall be forever grateful. He told Mr Hamilton that he was a little puzzled by the RSPB's motives. What was the point of making somewhere a nature reserve which, thanks to 'its very isolation, inaccessibility and lack of human habitation', was already as protected from interference as any place could be? In fact, if the RSPB got involved with the Shiants, that might well be the most intrusive development the islands would ever have known: 'A sudden influx of visitors might lead to disturbance, the appointment of a Warden, rules and regulations, "nature trails" – in fact all the business of regulated access which presupposes and even encourages such access.' Nigel would have to consult the RSPB on all manner of details, such as the areas which could be grazed by my tenant's sheep, the erection of hides for public viewing, visitor control, permission for my friends to land and camp there, and so on and so on. And for what purpose?

Mr Hamilton replied with a new reason for the RSPB to get involved: the Shiants were threatened by oil rigs in the Minch. Only with the RSPB at the Shiants' side could they be protected from this new threat:

> If an agreement, or better still a lease, were entered into by the two parties this would ensure that, should a developer come along at some later date, we could show them that there was a legal document to indicate that the R.S.P.B. thought highly of this place, enough to make it a reserve.

My father saw this for what it was – an empire-building bogey – and rejected the argument. If there was oil discovered in the Minch, the Shiants would be spoiled anyway. The RSPB could do nothing about it. With an agreement, however, he would be landed with an obligation to refer to the RSPB in everything he did. The answer was 'no'. Mr Hamilton replied, hoping that my father would 'appreciate that our desire is to see the Shiants unspoiled for many generations to come.' There hasn't been a squeak out of them since. I told John Murdo Matheson this story once. He said, 'Promise me one thing, Adam. You will never, ever let one of those organisations get their hands on this place. It would be the end of it, the real death of it. It needs to belong to a person who loves it.'

'It does,' I said, 'and it will.'

Tangled in with these two modern Shiant strands, as a place for holidays and a place for nature conservation, is a third: the working environment for the shepherds. The categories are not quite watertight: the shepherding trips to the islands are a kind of hard-working holiday. But I have always felt that the shepherds' relationship to the islands, because of their repeated, deep familiarity with the contours of the place, decade after decade, and because of the sweat expended and the dangers undergone here, is much deeper and less trivial than all the passing summer visits of the proprietors, whether Leverhulme, Compton Mackenzie, my father or me. I believed the man who told Hughie MacSween in the Tarbert pub that he was the true owner of the place. However much we attend to the Shiants, however much Mackenzie's novel or this book are a tribute to them, there is no matching the intimacy that Malcolm MacSween, DB Macleod or Hughie achieved with them.

One can only sit back and listen to the stories: the day when Hughie lost his dinghy from the beach and thought he should try and float out to it on the lilo he had been using as a mattress in the house; or the day when trying to rescue some sheep stuck far down the cliff on Eilean Mhuire, dangling off a rope held by two of the boys up on the top, he slipped on the rain-slicked grass and hung there for a while, dependent on the strength of the men who were holding him. 'That was the only time I really frightened myself there,' he says, grinning and pulling on the lobe of his ear.

'Now I start to hear about it,' Joyce says as Hughie confesses to me the excitements of his life thirty years ago.

Hughie won't be stopped now. His stories rumble on, ever quieter. What about the day when his uncle Calum, it was during the war, decided he had to take the cattle off? They were on Eilean an Tighe. The first beast they took out in the dinghy but they were worried one of them would put its hoof through the planks. So the rest of them were swum out on a rope and then attached to the steam derrick on the deck of the Cunninghams' puffer. The men waited below in the dinghy as the poor beast was lifted by its horns high into the air, bellowing at the indignity and with fear. Just as the animal was high above the gunwale, the men in the dinghy guiding it in by the tail, the bullock emptied the entire contents of its four stomachs over the men below. That was the last time any cattle were seen on the Shiants.

> At one time when they were there, a cow had somehow got itself into the house and had shut the door behind it. Who knows how long it had been there. It was lying down and we managed to get it on its feet and took it outside. It had not eaten or drunk for days, weeks maybe, who knows? So we brought it out and gave it water and it drank so much of the water, it was the water that killed it.

A deep drag on the cigarette: 'Yes, yes. Aye, it was the water that killed it.'

Throughout his youth, Hughie had gone out to the Shiants with Donald Macleod, the butcher on Scalpay, known as 'D B' for 'Donald Butcher'. He was a marvellously friendly, charming, avuncular man, his grey hair standing in stiff toothbrush bristles on his scalp, always in a big tweed jacket with leather patches on the elbow, and a habit of calling me 'my dear', holding me without affectation or ceremony by the elbow or shoulder. He was still the tenant of the islands when my father first gave them to me and would sometimes come out for the day on the fishing boat when I was there, to see the islands, just to have another look. What I never knew was that he was a poet and songwriter, famous in Scalpay and beyond for his songs, some of them a little risqué. There is a well-known one about a magnificent cockerel for whom the hens become increasingly desperate – 'we couldn't hear ourselves for the laughter,' one Scalpay woman said to me when telling me about D B's songs. Others were more romantic, often about his love for Mary, his wife. His most famous song was about the *Scalpay Isle*, a Scalpay woman fishing boat belonging to Norman Morrison. You can still hear it on the Gaelic radio from time to time. Iain MacSween, Hughie's son, sometimes requested it to be played on a Sunday night when his father was out with the sheep on the Shiants, listening to the radio in the house there, and it is still sung at the Mod, the annual national Gaelic singing competition, where a prize called the Shiant Shield, endowed by Compton Mackenzie, is presented every year for the best example of traditional singing.

Something persists here in the world of the Shiants, a wholeness in the culture, despite the batterings it has received, which has disappeared from the rest of Britain. The idea of a butcher in southern England writing a song that brings together the wild romantic sea and landscape, his own love and fearfulness, his sense of the future and the persistence of his song after death – stock themes as these might be – is quite inconceivable. This is the enriched world to which the Shiants belong, to which D B belonged, to which Hughie and Donald MacSween belong and from which I am quite removed.

Another man with Scalpay connections, the great modern lyric poet Norman MacCaig who died in 1996 and whose mother was from Scalpay, asked, in the voice of 'A Man in Assynt', as the poem is called, the devastating question: 'Who possesses this landscape? / The man who bought it or / I who am possessed by it?'

It is a reframing of all Donald MacCallum's radical and passionate questions in the 1890s. Can one really buy a place like this with all its attendant associations? Do the conventional rights of property apply here as they might to a car or a flat in London or Glasgow? Can I say as the 'owner' of the Shiants that I 'own' them any more than any of those people who are heir to the sort of inheritance which so effortlessly shaped Donald Macleod's poem? His own words answered those questions by not even addressing them, by his assuming an unadulterated intimacy with this world. How can an outsider ever compete with that?

Of course they can't. In the late 1990s, with the coming of a Scottish parliament, these questions received a new burst of life. At its quietest, the land reform movement was insistent on at least a right of universal access to wild land. At its most radical, a view that did not in the end find much favour with the Scottish Executive, the idea of a private individual owning land was itself called into doubt. On a Scottish internet discussion group, alba@yahoogroups.com, the owner and convener of the group, Robert Stewart, a member of the SNP National Council, suggested early in 2001, just as I was finishing this book, that 'all Scottish mountains, and certain other uncultivated moorland [should] be brought into perpetual national common ownership.' I asked why and what benefits might accrue either to the place or to the local community from public ownership?

Stewart replied, in brief, that the land had traditionally belonged to the people and that it had been stolen from them by the Crown and its vassals: 'I, personally, believe that land "ownership" is arrogant and pretentious. I cannot see how humans can claim to "own" and buy and sell land any more than we can claim to own and buy and sell the air that we breathe or the rain that falls from the sky.'

The same was true of all claims to ownership of fish or game, but all Scots, he felt, should have a right to rent 'a portion of arable land sufficient for their needs.'

> In Adam's case, my objection would be to the concept of any person 'owning' three islands in the Minch. In my view, those islands should be taken into national common ownership to be managed and tenanted, but not sold, by the local community.
>
> He asks what benefits would accrue either to the place or to the local community from public ownership. My answer would be that the main benefit is that control of the land remains with the local community, thus seeking to reverse the past experience of communities throughout Scotland, many of which have suffered at the hands of unscrupulous landowners, both foreign and home-grown.

I am in a strange position here. If I didn't own the Shiants, I might easily say the sort of things that Robert Stewart says. Without some kind of institutional framework, there is no guarantee that a private owner, however beneficial, might not turn nasty and exclusive. Or at least that his heirs or successors might. But I am not in that position. I do own the Shiants. I love them and I have a duty to my son. I want Tom to be able to love them, and to love them without feeling an overpowering sense of illegitimacy in doing so. As the history in this book has shown, the idea that some moment existed in the past when the islands were held in communal bliss, which was then disrupted by greedy and rapacious landlords, does not match the facts. There were originally five family farms here, which at some time in the middle ages were agglomerated and held in common under a quasi-feudal system, owing rent in kind to the clan chief. That lasted until the deep disruptions of the eighteenth century, brought about by the coming of the market. There is nothing in this that can suggest the people of Lochs have any more right to the Shiants than I do.

Importantly, though, their right to them is no less than mine. It has been my purpose in this book to show how much the Shiants are part of the lives of everyone who lives on the opposite shore. They are not some naked place on which castaway fantasies can be played out, as if no one had ever lived there, but a richly human landscape. It is important to me that my ownership of the Shiants should reflect that and give the local community all the benefits which that community would receive if it owned them itself.

I would go further: private ownership of a place like this, if community-minded, can actually be more open and more flexible (responsive, for example, both to Scalpay and to Lochs, different communities with in some ways equal claims) than exclusive community ownership might be. Private ownership does not need to be hung about with the sort of regulations and notices by which public ownership is usually accompanied. No one who comes to the Shiants need ever know that they are welcome there. They can simply find it wild and beautiful. And anyone who wants to stay in the house, ratty or not, can get in touch with me on adam@shiantisles.net or, after 5 March 2005, with Tom on tom@shiantisles.net and they can have the key.

In the course of the debate in the discussion group, I quoted the words of Donald MacCallum and said that in many ways I agreed with them. It is historically true that all property is theft, reinforced with violence. Robert Stewart ended with this:

> In admitting that"What the Rev. MacCallum said is true', Adam Nicolson himself declares that no one has the sole right to 'own' the Shiant Isles and no one has the right to buy or sell them. He faces a dilemma. Should he maintain his claim of ownership of the Shiant Isles, which he admits is 'dependent on a succession of acts of violence, quite

literally of murder, rape and expulsion', or should he make
history as the landlord who reversed history and returned
the islands to common ownership?

There is a flat-faced appeal to vanity in that but, in response,
I can only say that I couldn't think of giving the islands away,
that it would not be fair to my own son and that the expression
of the dilemma is in the solution I propose: community-minded
private ownership, with a resolution to share this place as much
and as widely as we can.

The question remains, of course: what happens when you pass
them on? Does Tom believe in this? Will his son? And his? New
Scottish legislation produced in 2001 will mean that whenever
property of this kind is sold, the local community, funded by
Lottery money, will have the right to buy it at a market price.
That is fine by me: if for whatever reason we have to sell the
Shiants – and I hope it never comes – then community ownership
is as good an idea as any. But that legislation will not apply to
a transfer of land within the same family. Nor do I want to
hedge Tom's freedom about with covenants and restrictions on
what he can do with the islands. If he doesn't have any sense of
the social obligation which ownership of land entails, or of the
vitality of the tradition to which ownership of these islands
gives us access, then no restrictive covenant is going to teach
him. But I know him. He grasps as clearly as anyone the need
to be generous. The question is not, in the end, one of regulation
but of a culture of mutual respect and decent regard, not only
because the history in these islands is of eviction and dispossession, but because respect and decency are absolutely good in
themselves.

As the winter comes again, the gales return. The wind blows
pieces out of the big cairns on the top of Eilean an Tighe, and
the stones lie as lumpy grey hail around them on the grass. When

you get up in the morning, it is to a wind-combed world. The surface of the sea is woolly with the spray and there's a haze above it like the fine hairs on a cashmere jersey. In the house, the roof space roars as the wind sucks and tugs at it and outside, there's a fierce clarity, a denuded air, to the islands, as if they were on the butcher's slab and the wind was slicing the flesh away.

There are days when the strength of wind can scarcely be imagined. I was talking to Bullet Cunningham about *Freyja*. What did he think of the boat? Did it look well made? 'Oh yes, it looks like it's all right. You'll have to tie her down though. You'll have to put some weight in her. And tie her well. Or in a bad gale of wind the wind will lift her up.'

'But it weighs six hundred pounds,' I said.

'Oh yes, the wind will lift it, no bother. We had three boats on the Shiants once, on the beach there, tied together and we went over from the cottage where we were staying and the gale was bad and they were like that.' He put his hand vertically in the air like a blade. 'They were standing on their bows like that, the three of them upright. We had to pull them down and put more stones in them.'

The wind is inescapable here. Its relentlessness more than its strength is what can make you unhappy. I have been here with my wife Sarah at times when the rain and wind have slapped against us day after day. We were staying in a tent – the house felt too ratty – and we went to bed in the wind and woke up in the wind. Every voice was blurred by the wind, every minute besieged by it. It did not go well. She wanted to leave. She was unable to see the point in being out on a shelterless rock in a meaningless sea, under a muffled grey sky, where there are no loos and no baths, where there is not even a little copse or spinney in which one can sit down to read, where the house itself is little better than a shed, where the wind blows and blows and where your husband is for some reason obsessed with every fact and detail of this godforsaken nowhere.

So I took her, on one of these unhappy, disconnected days, to a place on the spit of rock through which the natural arch is driven, at the north-east corner of Garbh Eilean. It is quite a scramble to get there, down a crumbly half-cliff face, across some weed-slithered rocks at sea-level, and then up again over barnacle-encrusted boulders. But once there – and this only works in a long, old swell – you can find yourself suddenly in the presence of something marvellous. All is quiet; you are for a moment in the lee of the island and the air is able to mimic stillness. Then, from nowhere, it happens. I suppose it is some effect of air and water, the compression of one by the other, but it is not science you encounter. Quite casually, and with no fanfare, no advance warning, from between your feet the islands start to groan. A long, deep moaning emerges from the slits between the dolerite slabs. It begins slowly and builds, a deep and exhausted exhalation. It is like finding a room in which you thought you were alone suddenly occupied by another, a voice emerging from a long dead body.

Did that make things better? Not really. It was scarcely a Martini advertisement, nor perhaps the most appropriate way of convincing a disenchanted spouse that the Shiants were wonderful. Where were the sandy beaches? Where the machair, the sweet, shell-sand pastures, the fertility, the richness, the sense of life beyond the bone?

I was not finished. On the next quiet day, we went cave-visiting. One, just beyond the natural arch, is a huge fretted cavern, forty yards long, the water inside it invisibly deep and turquoise blue, gurgling and slopping against the pink, coralline-encrusted walls. You can reach it only by boat, and if you tethered a raft in there, you could hold a dance inside, candelabra suspended from the dripping roof, shags and black guillemots alert to the music.

But even that is not the greatest of the Shiants' sea displays. Out at the far north-western tip of Garbh Eilean, where the Stewarts attempted to kill their shepherd and where Mrs MacAulay fell to her death, where you can go only in a calm, is the most haunting sea cave of all. Its mouth is covered except at low tide. Even then, not much of it appears. A little jagged-arched orifice opens above the guano-thick green of the sea. The birds hawk and hiss, gab and gibber above you. The echo of their voices runs three times around the little amphitheatre in which the cave is set, rising to its own small crescendos and then dropping into silence. Down on the sea, the noise ricochets around you, the fishwives of Hell on a weekend outing. It is dark and cold in here. The sun never reaches this place.

We look at the mouth of the cave. Inside, as the swell slops back from the entrance, you see the pink and dangling innards, rock tonsils thickened with coralline reaching down to the tongue of the sea. It is the gullet of the monster. The opening is too small for a boat to enter – I have slipped the nose of a canoe in there, no more – and you must wait outside. And wait you must because this cave will in time, not with every swell, work its magic. It comes soon enough. The swell withdraws, and after it a barrel-deep, reverberant, bass-booming of the rock, followed, and this is the moment at which you abandon all critical distance, by a breath of foggy air, rolling and curling out of the mouth, expelled ten or twenty yards towards you, enveloping you, your boat and your wife in its salty, geological folds. Who needs a flowery meadow when islands can do that for you? Who thinks of legislation or designation or clan history or the politics of landscape when the wild can so easily step outside any frame designed to encompass or reduce it?

October is buffeting onwards. I am alone, writing in the house, with the light of the two paraffin lamps on the table beside me,

the dogs curled into doughnuts by the fire and the waves breaking on the shore outside, less than a stone's throw away. The places in which I swam between the anemones and the bladderwrack in the summer are chaos now. From time to time, a handful of the sea spray lands on the windows and rattles them. Sarah is at home with the girls and the wind shuffles through its endless conversations outside. A gannet is sailing above the storm, in close beside the beach so that I can watch it above the stirred and stained green-and-white surface of the sea. The day is dark and the gannet is lit like a crucifixion against it. I could never tire of this, never think of anything I would rather watch, nor of any place I would rather be than here, in front of the endless renewing of the sea bird's genius, again and again carving its path inside the wind, holding and playing with all the mobility that surrounds it like a magician with his silks, before the moment comes, it pauses and plunges for the kill, the sudden folded, twisted purpose, the immersion, disappearance and the detonation of the surf. The wind bellows in my ears as if in a shell. No one can own this, no individual, no community. This is beyond all owning, a persistence and an energy which exists despite the squabbling over names and titles, not because of it.

I had wanted to have my son Tom with me at this end of the year. I am here to see the geese returning from Greenland and I wanted him here with me, but he is at school and I couldn't take him away. Perhaps these moments are better alone, anyway. What would he have done as I sat for hours at this table writing about the islands which, I am sure, come for him with all the burden of my own expectations attached? I sometimes wonder if they are not too much of a parental landscape for him. Will my own presence not loom too much over them?

It didn't happen with me and my father. He made the gift a real one, allowing me freedom from the moment the deed was signed. A connection remained. I told him once that buying the Shiants was the best thing he had ever done and I could see that the words moved him, more I think because I had said them than because he believed it. The Shiants have been a conduit between us for years, a way of talking about something we both loved without ever having to say that we did. He wrote to me once at school about 'a cloud of midges hanging around your head on a still evening you-know-where' – and I can still remember the feeling that enveloped me then of an almost overwhelming sense of connectedness and significance, of this deep intimacy which a common affection for you-know-where could provide. Nothing else was quite so free or rich. That is the feeling which has fuelled the writing of this book and which I want to give Tom: not the islands but our shared attachment to them.

It may not happen, but that doesn't matter. I don't need Tom Nicolson to live with the intensity of Shiant-love that his father has known. All populations go through their cycles of dearth and wealth and there is no reason why my own closeness to the Shiants shouldn't diminish for a lifetime or two. It is for him to do what he will. Even in prospect, I love the idea of Tom being on the islands with his friends, discovering it all, feeling his way into its heart, making all the mistakes that I and my father made, slowly acquiring the odd, deep, distant attachment to a place of such unresponsive rock. But if that doesn't happen to him, I don't mind. His best and repeated joke to me is that When The Time Comes he is going to put a generator in and have a Sky satellite dish attached to the roof of the cottage. I will leave it ten years but in a funny way, I can't wait to be his guest here.

The time I have had on the Shiants is coming to an end. I know the islands now more than I have ever known them, more in a way than anyone has ever known them, and as I sit here in the house I have a feeling, for a moment, of completeness and gratitude. My love affair with these islands is reaching its full term. Yesterday, one of those early winter days opened, when the whole of the Hebrides lies cold and still around you, the hills in Skye washed purple, the mountains in the Uists a faded, sea-washed blue. A big, slow swell was travelling the length of the Minch, as though the muscles were moving under the skin of the sea. I went up to the far north cliff of Garbh Eilean and lay down there on the cold turf where the tips of the grasses are reddening with the acid in the soil. I put my head over the edge of the cliff and watched the sea pulling at the black seal reef five hundred feet below me. I had my mobile in my pocket. The reception is good up there and I rang Tom at his sixth form college in Chichester. 'Listen, Tom, listen,' I said and held the phone so that he could hear the sea.

'You're mad,' he said.

'I know.'

'Have you seen the geese yet?'

'No, nothing yet. But it's lovely here.'

'I know it is, Dad. I've gotta go. I've got History. Talk to you soon. Bye.'

I was left alone in the silence, with the pale sun on my face, and, as the dogs nosed for nothing in the grasses, I started to fall asleep there to the long, asthmatic rhythm of the surf. The islands embraced and enveloped me. Twenty yards to my left the Viking was asleep in his grave and the words of Auden's poem ran on in my mind:

> *Look, stranger, at this island now . . .*
> *Stand stable here*
> *And silent be,*
> *That through the channels of the ear*
> *May wander like a river*
> *The swaying sound of the sea.*

NOTE

Several Gibb and Henderson papers on the geology of the Shiants are to be found at www.shiantisles.net/geology.

Pat Foster's full report on the first season's survey of the Shiants is available at www.shiantisles.net/archaeology. The findings of later years' investigations will be put on to the website as they become available.

Pat Foster's report on the excavation is to be found at www.shiantisles.net/excavation.

If anyone knows of the whereabouts of the photographs taken by William Norrie of the Shiart Campbells please e-mail the author at adam@shiantisles.net.

ACKNOWLEDGEMENTS

I owe a great debt of thanks to many people in Lewis, Harris and Scalpay. They include: Bullet Cunningham; Neil Cunningham, who offered to shepherd me and *Freyja* out into the Minch in his launch on a threatening day out at sea; Rachel Cunningham; Cathy MacAulay; John MacAulay; Katie Mary Macdonald; Kenneth Angus 'Toby' McIver; Kennie Mackenzie, who has died since this book was written; Dan Macleod; Malcolm MacLeod, who brought many of the experts in this book out to the islands for me, in all sorts of weather, with unfailing courtesy and seamanship; Mary MacLeod; Sophie Macrae; Thomas Macrae; Angus MacSween; Aileen MacSween; Joan MacSween; Liza MacSween; D. R. Morrison; Donald Morrison; John Angus Morrison; Kenny Morrison; Margaret Morrison; Donald 'Nona' Smith; and all the children of Scalpay school who lay down on the hermit's stone for me one afternoon as if they did that every Tuesday.

Above all, I am deeply indebted to three families who have looked after me and the islands over many years: Hugh and Joyce MacSween; Donald and Rachel MacSween; and now John Murdo and his mother Mary Ann Matheson. In many ways, those three families are the Shiants for me.

In writing this book I have called on the expertise of many disciplines and I gratefully acknowledge all the people who have willingly and enthusiastically given me information, guidance and ideas. They include: John Barber, AOC Scotland; David Barker, The Potteries Museum, Stoke-on-Trent; Guy de la Bedoyere; Keith Branigan, University of Sheffield; Mike Brooke, University of Cambridge; Jonathan Bulmer; Hugh Cheape, National Museums of Scotland; Linda Čihaková; Thomas Owen Clancy, University of Glasgow; Trevor Cowie,

National Museums of Scotland; Ken Crocket, Scottish Mountaineering Council; David Daněček, Plzen University; Robert Dodgshon, University of Wales at Aberystwyth; Andy Douse, Scottish Natural Heritage; Gail Dundas, National Maritime Museum, Greenwich; Johanne Ferguson, Scottish Natural Heritage; Ian Fisher, Royal Commission for Ancient and Historic Monuments in Scotland; Judith Fisher; Patrick Foster, Czech Institute of Archaeology; David Fowler, Stornoway Library; Ian Fraser, School of Scottish Studies, University of Edinburgh; Simon Fraser; Bob Furness, University of Glasgow; Miranda Grant; Veronica Guiry, Natural Environment Research Council; Mary Harman, Scottish Natural Heritage; Mark Haworth-Booth, Victoria and Albert Museum; Gillian Hughes; Fergus Gibb, University of Sheffield; Mike Harris, Centre for Ecology and Hydrology; Susan Haysom, Scottish Natural Heritage; Michael Henderson, University of Manchester; Felicity Jones, University of Edinburgh; Bill Lawson, Co Leis Thu?; Commander John Lewis; Petr Limburský; Andro Linklater; Tim Lodge; David McCrone, University of Edinburgh; Maggie Macdonald, Clan Donald Library; Bob McGowan, National Museums of Scotland; Ian Mackenzie, School of Scottish Studies, University of Edinburgh; David Maclennan, Scottish Natural Heritage; D J MacLeod; Mary MacLeod, Western Isles Council; Morag MacLeod, School of Scottish Studies, University of Edinburgh; Andrew Martin, National Museums of Scotland; Donald Meek, University of Aberdeen; Ian Mitchell, Joint Nature Conservation Committee; Colin Moody; Stephen Moran, Inverness Musum; Donnie Morrison, Western Isles ICT Advisory Service; Luboš Novák, Plzen University; Nicholas Oppenheim; Steve Percival, Sunderland University; Rosemary Philip; Wanda Pryhouska, Prague Castle; John Randall, Registrar-General for Scotland; Alison Rothwell, RSPB; David Sanders; Angus Smith; Candy Sorrel, Natural Environment Research Council; Paul Stapp, University of York; Ian Stephen; Simon Stephens, National Maritime Museum, Greenwich; Robert Stewart, Scottish National Party; Jim Sutherland; Charles Thomas; Kate Thompson, Joint Nature Conservation Committee, Seabirds and Cetaceans Branch; Derick Thomson; Paul Tyler, Western Isles Council;

Robbie Watson; Patricia Weekes, Inverness Museum; Tara Wenger, University of Texas at Austin; Ruaraidh Wishart, National Archives of Scotland; John Wood, Highland Council; Jana Žeglitzová, Prague Castle.

The following people and institutions have kindly lent, given, drawn or made accessible the photographs, maps and illustrations in this book: Clare Arron (dedication page, p373); Robert Atkinson/School of Scottish Studies (pp12, 312); Charlie Boxer (p24); Linda Čhaková (p43); the shade of William Daniell (p79); Patrick Foster (pp127, 172, 189, 232, 248, 264); John Gilkes (pp36–7, 106–7, 237, 290); Aileen MacSween (p149); National Museums of Scotland (p95); Rex Nicholls (pp1, 14, 155, 177, 214–15); Royal Commission for Ancient and Historic Monuments in Scotland (title page); Olivia Sanders (pp7, 52, 182, 292, 295); Mischa Scorer (p337); Douglas Scott (pp46, 277); James Smith (p50); *Stornoway Gazette* (p19); Chris Tyler, *West Highland Free Press* (p5); Patrick Ward (pp64, 203, 374). Other photographs are by the author.

The author and publishers are grateful for permission to use quotations from the following works:

p60 '*Brown-haired Allan . . .*', from Margaret Fay Shaw, *Folksongs and Folklore of South Uist*, 3rd ed., Aberdeen UP, 1986, pp259–60

p101 '*Let's go much as that dog goes . . .*' from Denise Levertov, 'Overland to the Islands' in *Selected Poems of Denise Levertov*, Bloodaxe Books

p165–6 '*He brings northward to meet the Lord . . .*' from Thomas Owen Clancy and Gilbert Markus, *Iona: The Earliest Poetry of a Celtic Monastery*, Edinburgh UP, 1995, p147

p166 '*He left Ireland, entered a pact . . .*' from Thomas Owen Clancy and Gilbert Markus, *Iona: The Earliest Poetry of a Celtic Monastery*, Edinburgh UP, 1995, p139

pp230 '*That night/the scarecrow came . . .*' from Derick Thomson, 'Am Boxachròcais', 'The Scarecrow' in Black, RIM (ed.), *An Tuil: Anthology of 20th Century Scottish Gaelic Verse*, Edinburgh UP/Polygon, 1999, pp455–6

pp258–60 '*The house of the story-teller . . .*' from Alexander

Carmichael, *Carmina Gadelica*, Scottish Academic Press, 1983, ppxxviii–xxx

p272–3 '*The girl of my love . . .*' from Donald Macdonald, *Lewis: A History of the Island*, Gordon Wright Publishing, 1990, p71

p330 '*Brown John, catch me . . .*' from Margaret Fay Shaw, *Folksongs and Folklore of South Uist*, 3rd ed., Aberdeen, 1986, p121; and 'Did you see the modest maiden' from Margaret Fay Shaw, *Folksongs and Folklore of South Uist*, 3rd ed., Aberdeen, 1986, p225

p363 '*Who possesses this landscape? . . .*' from Norman MacCaig, 'A Man in Assynt', in *Collected Poems*, Chatto and Windus, 1990, pp224–31, used by permission of The Random House Group Limited

p373 '*Look, stranger, at this island now . . .*' from W H Auden, 'XXV', in Edward Mendelson, *The English Auden*, Faber, 1977, p157

My agent, Caroline Dawnay, continues to be the guide and inspiration to me that she has been for many years. At HarperCollins, Susan Watt has overseen this book with a masterly understanding of what it needed to be, for which I am deeply grateful. Vera Brice, who designed the book, gracefully tolerated an author who failed to make up his mind and both Antonia Loudon and Katie Espiner made life with HarperCollins a great pleasure.

I would like to thank the many friends and relations who have come to the Shiants with me over the years, especially Kate and Charlie Boxer, Pots and Ivan Samarine, Montagu and Sarah Don, Patrick Holden and Becky Hiscock; also Andrew Palmer and Will Anderson, who did their utmost to get there but were prevented by storms.

This book is a long thank-you to my father, without whose appetite in 1937 for 'remoteness, isolation, grandeur' it would not have been written. Unmentioned in these pages, but constant, is my deep debt, thanks and love to Sarah Raven.

BIBLIOGRAPHY

Estate papers, official
records etc.

In the National Archives of Scotland
Seaforth papers   GD 40; GD 427; GD
46
Stornoway Sheriff Court Records   SC
33
SSPCK papers   GD 95
Minutes of Skye and Lewis
Presbyteries   CH 2/273; CH 1/2
Customs Records   CE 86

*In the Library of the National Museums
of Scotland*
Harvie-Brown papers

In the National Library of Scotland
Sibbald Collections: Advocates' MSS
33.3.20

In the Public Record Office
Log of HMS Triton 1746   ADM 51/1005
HMS Triton Muster Book   ADM 36/
4366 Pt 1

In Stornoway Library
Ordnance Survey Name Book for Lewis
(microfilm)

At Museum nan Eilean, Stornoway
Sites and Monuments Record (digital
archive)

Official Publications

*Report of the Commissioners of Inquiry
into the condition of the Crofters and
Cottars in the Highlands and Islands of
Scotland*, 1884
*Report of the Royal Commission to
Inquire into the Possibility of Certain
Sporting or Grazing Subjects in the
Crofting Counties being occupied by
Crofters or Small Tenants*, 1895
*Report to the Secretary for Scotland by the
Crofters Commission on the Social
Condition of the People of Lewis in 1901
as compared with Twenty Years ago*, 1902

Books and Articles

Adomnan, *Life of St Columba*, trans. R
Sharpe, London, 1995
Anderson, James, *An Account of the
Present State of the Hebrides*, London,
1785
Angus, Stewart, *The Outer Hebrides*,
Strond, 1992
Angus, Stewart, and Hopkins, P G,
'Ship rat *Rattus rattus* confirmed on
the Shiant Islands', *Hebridean
Naturalist* 13 (1995), pp18–22
Armit, Ian, *The Archaeology of Skye and
the Western Isles*, Edinburgh, 1996
Atkinson, G C, *Expeditions to the
Hebrides*, ed. D A Quine, Lusta, 2001
Atkinson, Robert, *Island Going*, (1949),
Edinburgh, 1995
Auden, W H, *The Enchafed Flood: or the
Romantic Iconography of the Sea*,
London, 1951
Bitel, Lisa M, *Isle of the Saints: Monastic*

Settlement and Christian Community in Early Ireland, Cork, 1990

Black, R I M (ed.), *An Tuil: Anthology of 20th Century Scottish Gaelic Verse*, Edinburgh, 1999

Boyd, J M, and Boyd, I L, *The Hebrides* (3 vols), Edinburgh, 1996

Branigan, Keith and Foster, Patrick, *Barra: Archaeological Research on Ben Tangaval*, Sheffield, 1995

Brooke, M de L, 'The Puffin population of the Shiants', *Bird Study*, 19 (1972), pp1–6

Brooke, M de L, 'Birds of the Shiant Islands, Outer Hebrides', *Bird Study*, 20 (1973), pp197–206

Bryan, Amanda, *The Minch Review*, Stornoway, 1994

Buchanan, J L, *Travels in the Western Hebrides, from 1782 to 1790*, London, 1793

Burn, A R, 'Holy Men on Islands in pre-Christian Britain', *Glasgow Archaeological Journal*, 1 (1969), pp2–6

Burt, Edmund, *Burt's Letters from the North of Scotland* (1754), Edinburgh, 1998

Caird, J B, *Park: A Geographical Study of a Lewis Crofting District*, 1958

Campbell, J L, *Canna*, Oxford, 1984

Campbell, J L, *A Very Civil People: Hebridean Folk, History and Tradition*, Edinburgh, 2000

Campbell, Neil, 'Fishing Tragedy, 1885', *Boillsgeadh*, 1999, p32

Carmichael, Alexander, *Carmina Gadelica* (1900–71), Edinburgh, 1983

Cheape, Hugh, 'Crogans and Barvas Ware: Handmade Pottery in the Hebrides', *Scottish Studies* 31 (1992–3)

Cowie, Trevor, 'Bronze Age Gold Torc from the Minch', *Hebridean Naturalist*, 12 (1994), pp19–21

Cowie, Trevor, 'The Bronze Age', *Scotland: Environment and Archaeology, 8000BC–AD1000*, eds K J Edwards and I B M Ralston, London, 1997

Clancy, Thomas Owen, 'Annat in Scotland and the origins of the parish', *The Innes Review*, 46/2 (1995), pp91–115

Clancy, Thomas Owen, and Markus, Gilbert, *Iona: The Earliest Poetry of a Celtic Monastery*, Edinburgh, 1995

Cranston, Maurice, *The Solitary Self: Jean-Jacques Rousseau in Exile and Adversity*, London, 1997

Crawford, Iain A, 'War or peace: Viking colonisation in the Northern and Western Isles of Scotland reviewed', *Proceedings of the eighth Viking Congress*, 1977, pp259–99

Crick, H Q P and Ratcliffe, D A, 'The Peregrine *Falco peregrinus* breeding population of the United Kingdom in 1991', *Bird Study* 42 (1995), pp1–19

Cunningham, Alasdair, 'Am Bata Beag [The Wee Boat]', trans. Morag MacLeod, *Tocher*, 46 (Summer 1993), pp236–239

Daniel, Glyn, and Renfrew, Colin, *The Idea of Prehistory*, Edinburgh, 1988

Daniell, William, and Ayton, Richard, *A Voyage Round Great Britain*, London, 1813–22

Darling, Frank Fraser, *Natural History in the Highlands and Islands*, London, 1947

Dewar, Donald, 'Land Reform for the 21st Century', 5th John McEwen Memorial Lecture, 1998

Dodgshon, R A, 'West Highland and Hebridean settlement prior to crofting and the Clearances: a study in stability or change?' *Proceedings of the Society of Antiquaries of Scotland* 123 (1993), pp419–38

Dodgshon, R A, 'Farming practice in the western Highlands and Islands before crofting: a study in cultural inertia or opportunity costs', *Rural History 3* (1993), pp173–89

Dodgshon, R A, 'West Highland and Hebridean landscapes: have they a history without runrig?', *Journal of Historical Geography* 19 (1993), pp383–98

Dodgshon, R A, *From Chiefs to Landlords: Social and Economic Change in the Western Highlands and Islands, c. 1493–1820*, Edinburgh, 1998

Duncan, Angus, *Hebridean Island: Memories of Scarp*, Phantassie, 1995

Emeleus, C H, and Gyopari, M C, *British Tertiary Volcanic Province*, London, 1992

Fairfax, Denis, *The Basking Shark in Scotland*, Phantassie, 1998

Fenton, Alexander, and Palsson, Hermann, *The Northern and Western Isles in the Viking World*, Edinburgh, 1984

Fenton, Alexander, *The Island Blackhouse*, Edinburgh, 1995

Fisher, James, and Lockley, R M, *Seabirds: An Introduction to the Natural History of the Seabirds of the North Atlantic* (1954), London, 1989

Furness, Robert W, 'Does Harvesting a Million Metric Tons of Sand Lance per Year from the North Sea Threaten Seabird Populations?' *Ecosystem Approaches for Fisheries Management*, Alaska, 1999

Furness, Robert W, 'Seabird Fishery interactions: quantifying the sensitivity of seabirds to reductions in sandeel abundance', *Marine Ecology Progress Series* 202 (2000), pp253–264

Gaston, A J, and Jones, I L, *The Auks*, Oxford, 1998

Geddes, Arthur, 'Conjoint-tenants and Tacksmen in the Isle of Lewis 1715–26', *Economic History Review*, 2nd Series, 1 (1948), pp54–60

Geddes, Arthur, *The Isle of Lewis and Harris: A study in British Community*, Edinburgh, 1955

Gibb, F G F, and Gibson, S A, 'The Little Minch Sill Complex', *Scottish Journal of Geology*, 25 (1989), pp367–370

Gibb, F G F, and Henderson, C M B, 'The Structure of the Shiant Isles sill complex, Outer Hebrides', *Scottish Journal of Geology*, 20 (1984), pp21–29

Gibb, F G F, Henderson, C M B, and Foland K A, 'The Shiant Isles Main Sill: structure and mineral fractionation trends', *Mineralogical Magazine*, 60 (1996), pp67–97

Gilbertson, David, et al., *The Outer Hebrides: The Last 14,000 Years*, Sheffield, 1996

Goodenough, Kathryn, *The Shiant Isles Site of Special Scientific Interest*, Geological Conservation Review Report, SNH, 1999

Goodrich-Freer, A, *Outer Isles*, New York, 1902

Graham-Campbell, James (ed.), *Cultural Atlas of the Viking World*, New York, 1994

Graham-Campbell, James, and Batey, Colleen E *Vikings in Scotland*, Edinburgh, 1998

Grant, I F, *Highland Folk Ways*, London, 1961

Grant, J S, *Discovering Lewis and Harris*, Edinburgh, 1987

Harman, Mary, *An Isle Called Hirte: A History and Culture of St Kilda to 1930*, Lusta, 1997

Harris, M P, *The Puffin*, London, 1984

Harvie-Brown, J A, and Buckley, T E, *A Vertebrate Fauna of the Outer Hebrides*, Edinburgh, 1888

Henderson, C M B, Gibb, F G F, and Foland, K A, 'Mineral Fractionation and pre- and post-emplacement processes in the uppermost part of the Shiant Isles Main Sill, *Mineralogical Magazine* 64 (2000)

Heraughty, Patrick, *Inishmurray*, Dublin, 1982

Hogg, James, *A Tour of the Highlands in 1803* (1888), Edinburgh, 1986

Hunter, James, *The Making of the Crofting Community*, Edinburgh, 1976

Hunter, James, *On the Other Side of Sorrow: Nature and People in the Scottish Highlands*, Edinburgh, 1995

Johnson, Samuel, *A Journey to the*

Western Islands of Scotland (1775), London, 1984

Key, Gillian and Fielding, A H, 'Population characteristics of the ship rat *Rattus rattus* on the Shiant Islands, Hebrides, Scotland', report to SNH, 1997

Kissling, Werner, 'The character and purpose of the Hebridean Blackhouse', *Journal of the Royal Anthropological Institute*, 74 (1944), pp75–99

Lawrence, D H, 'The Man Who Loved Islands', *The Lovely Lady*, London, 1933

Lawrence, Martin, *The Yachtsman's Pilot to the West Coast of Scotland: Castle Bay to Cape Wrath*, Huntingdon, 1990

Lawson, Bill, *Harris Families and How to Trace Them*, Northton, 1990

Lethbridge, T C, *Herdsmen & Hermits: Celtic Seafarers in the Northern Seas*, Cambridge, 1950

Lethbridge, T C, *The Power of the Pendulum*, London, 1963

Linklater, Andro, *Compton Mackenzie: A Life*, London, 1987

Little, Colin, and Kitching, J A, *The Biology of Rocky Shores*, Oxford, 1996

Lloyd, Clare, et al., *The Status of Seabirds in Britain and Ireland*, London, 1991

Lockley, R M, *Puffins*, London, 1953

Love, J A, 'The Birds of the Shiant Islands', SNH, Stornoway, 1995

Madsen, Jesper, et al., *Goose Populations of the Western Palearctic*, Copenhagen, 1999

MacAulay, John, *Birlinn: Longships of the Hebrides*, Strond, 1996

MacCaig, Norman, *Collected Poems: A New Edition*, London, 1993

Macculloch, J, *A Description of the Western Islands of Scotland* (3 vols), London, 1819

Macculloch, J, *The Highlands and Western Isles of Scotland* (4 vols), London, 1824

Macdonald, A, '"Annat" in Scotland: A Provisional Review', *Scottish Studies* 17 (1973), pp135–46

MacDonald, A D S, 'Aspects of the Monastery and Monastic Life in Adomnan's *Life of Columba*', *Peritia* 3 (1984), pp271–302

Macdonald, Donald, *Tales and Traditions of the Lews*, Edinburgh, no date

Macdonald, Donald, *Lewis: A History of the Island*, Edinburgh, 1990

MacGillivray, William, *A Hebridean Naturalist's Journal 1817–1818*, ed. Robert Ralph, Stornoway, 1996

MacGregor, A A, *The Farthest Hebrides*, London, 1969

Mackenzie, Compton, *The North Wind of Love*, London, 1944–5

Mackenzie, Compton, *My Life and Times*, London, 1963–79

Mackenzie, Donald A, *Scottish Folk Lore and Folk Life*, Edinburgh, 1936

Mackenzie, Osgood, *A Hundred Years in the Highlands*, London, 1921

Mackenzie, William, *Old Skye Tales: Traditions, Reflections and Memories* (1930–4), Portree, 1995

Mackenzie, W C, *History of the Outer Hebrides*, Paisley, 1903

MacLellan, Angus, *The Furrow Behind Me*, trans. J L Campbell, Edinburgh, 1997

Maclennan, David, '*Rattus rattus* on the Shiant Islands: A Study of distribution and abundance', SNH, Stornoway, 1996

Maclennan, David, 'The Seabirds of the Shiant Isles', SNH, Stornoway, 1999

MacLeod, Dan, 'Tragedy at the Shiants', *Tional* (Dec 1992), p7

MacLeod, Donald, 'Oran an Scalpay Isle', *Isle of Scalpay Historical Magazine*, 1998, p52

Macleod, Morag, 'Christina Shaw and Peggy Morrison: Two Sisters from Harris', *Tocher* 41 (1987–8), p265

Macphail, Donald, 'Reminiscences', *Tional* (Dec 1993), pp4–5

Marine and Coastguard Agency, *Notes on Wreck Law*, Southampton, no date

Marsden, John, *Sea-Road of the Saints: Celtic Holy Men in the Hebrides*, Edinburgh, 1995

Martin, Martin, *A Description of the Western Islands of Scotland* (2nd ed., 1716), Edinburgh, 1981

Martine, Roddy, *Reminiscences of Eishken: A Hebridean Sporting Estate*, Eishken, 2000

Maxwell, Gavin, *Harpoon at a Venture* (1952), Colonsay, 1998

Mathieson, Robert, *The Survival of the Unfittest: The Highland Clearances and the End of Isolation*, Edinburgh, 2000

McCrone, David, 'Land, Democracy and Culture in Scotland', 4th John McEwen Memorial Lecture, 1997

McDonald, R A, *The Kingdom of the Isles: Scotland's Western Seaboard c. 1100–c. 1336*, Phantassie, 1997

McDonald, Robbie A, et al., 'The status of ship rats *Rattus rattus* on the Shiant Islands, Outer Hebrides, Scotland', *Biological Conservation* 82 (1997), pp113–117

McKay, M M (ed.), *Rev. Dr. John Walker's Report on the Hebrides of 1764 and 1771*, Edinburgh, 1980

McKee, Eric, *Working Boats of Britain: their shape and purpose*, London, 1983

Meek, Donald A, *Tuath Is Tighearna: Tenants and Landlords*, Edinburgh, 1995

Mitchell, Arthur, *The Past in the Present*, Edinburgh, 1880

Moisley, H A, 'The Deserted Hebrides', *Scottish Studies*, 10, I (1966), pp44–68

Muir, T S, *Ecclesiological Notes on Some of the Islands of Scotland*, Edinburgh, 1885

Munro, R W (ed.), *Monro's Western Isles of Scotland and the Genealogies of the Clans 1549*, Edinburgh, 1961

Nelson, Bryan, *Seabirds: their biology and ecology*, London, 1980

Nicolson, Alexander, *History of Skye* (1930), Portree, 1994

Nicolson, Nigel (ed.), *Diaries and Letters of Sir Harold Nicolson 1930–1962* (3 vols), London, 1966–8

Nicolson, Nigel, *Long Life: Memoirs*, London, 1997

North Lochs Historical Society, 'Murdo Macaulay', *Dusgadh* 5 (Dec. 1996), p7

Northover, J P, 'The Gold Torc from Saint-Helier, Jersey', *Société Jersiaise Annual Bulletin* (1989), pp112–137

O Maidin, Uinseann, *The Celtic Monk: Rules and Writings of Early Irish Monks*, Kalamazoo, 1996

Olsen, K M, and Larsson, H, *Skuas and Jaegers of the World*, Mountfield, 1997

Percival, S M, 'The population structure of Greenland Barnacle Geese *Branta leucopsis* on the wintering grounds on Islay', *IBIS* 133 (1991), pp357–364

Prebble, John, *Culloden*, Harmondsworth, 1967

Quammen, David, *The Flight of the Iguana: A Sidelong View of Science and Nature*, New York, 1998

Richey, J E, *The Tertiary Volcanic Districts of Scotland* (3rd ed.), Edinburgh, 1961

Rindorf, A, Wanless, S and Harris, M P, 'Effects of changes in sandeel availability on the reproductive output of seabirds', *Marine Ecology Progress Series* 202 (2000), pp241–252

Rixson, Denis, *The West Highland Galley*, Edinburgh, 1998

Robson, Michael, *Rona: The Distant Island*, Stornoway, 1991

Rykwert, Joseph, *On Adam's House in Paradise: The Idea of the Primitive Hut in Architectural History*, Cambridge, Mass., 1981

Scottish Executive, *Draft Code of Good Practice for Rural Landownership*, Edinburgh, 2000

Sellar, W D H, and Maclean, Alasdair, *The Highland Clan MacNeacail (MacNicol)*, Lusta, 1999

Shaw, M F, *Folksongs and Folklore of South Uist*, 3rd ed., Aberdeen, 1986

Skene, W F, *Celtic Scotland*, Edinburgh, 1880

Stapp, Paul 'Ship rats as predators of Shiant Islands seabirds', forthcoming

Statistical Account of Scotland (21 vols), Edinburgh, 1791–1799

Synge, J M, *The Aran Islands* (1907), Oxford, 1979

Teignmouth, Lord, *Sketches of the Coasts and Islands of Scotland and of the Isle of Man* (2 vols), London, 1836

Thomas, F L W, 'On the primitive dwellings and hypogea of the Outer Hebrides', *Proceedings of the Society of Antiquaries of Scotland*, 7 (1866–68), pp153–196

Waddell, Helen, *The Desert Fathers* (1936), New York, 1998

Walker, Bruce, and McGregor, Christopher, *The Hebridean Blackhouse*, Edinburgh, 1996

Walker, F, 'The geology of the Shiant Isles (Hebrides)', *Quarterly Journal of the Geological Society of London*, 86 (1930), pp355–398

Walker, J, *An Economical History of the Hebrides and the Highlands of Scotland* (2 vols), London, 1808

Wanless, S, Harris, M P, and Greenstreet, S P R, 'Summer sandeel consumption by seabirds breeding in the Firth of Forth, south-east Scotland', *ICES Journal of Marine Sciences*, 55 (1998), pp1141–1151

Watson, W J, *The History of the Celtic Place Names of Scotland*, Edinburgh, 1926

Whittow, J B, *Geology and Scenery in Scotland*, Harmondsworth, 1979

Wilson, James, *A Voyage around the Coasts of Scotland and the Isles*, Edinburgh, 1842

INDEX

116.70

Index of archaeological digs in ... & Virginia

Questions & methods:

p.223 - shell count as indicator of food supplies of people in famine years to 1680 on S [?] Islands

pp 228-230 on use of archaeology, plus historical records & documents to define turning points in the [?] development of culture [?] in the history of Scotland (and also of the development of English America through the spread of Scottish emigrants [?] to write to Virginia)